Psychology Series

Dynamic Personal Adjustment: An Introduction
H.L. Sachs, M.Ed.

In Quest of a New Psychology: Toward a Redefinition of Humanism
R. Johnson, Ph.D.

Language in Behavior
R. W. Howell, Ph.D. and J. Vetter, Ph.D.

LANGUAGE IN BEHAVIOR

Richard W. Howell, Ph.D.
University of Hawaii
Hilo, Hawaii

Harold J. Vetter, Ph.D.
University of South Florida
Tampa, Florida

HUMAN SCIENCES PRESS · New York

A division of Behavioral Publications, Inc.
72 Fifth Ave.
N.Y., N.Y. 10011

Library of Congress Catalog Number 74-8363
ISBN: 0-87705-157-7
Copyright © 1976 by Human Sciences Press, a division of Behavioral
Publications, Inc., 72 Fifth Avenue, New York, New York 10011

Printed in the United States of America
56789   987654321

Library of Congress Cataloging in Publication Data

Howell, Richard W
    Language in behavior.

    Bibliography: p.
    1. Language and languages. 2. Communication.
3. Linguistics. I. Vetter, Harold J., 1925–
joint author. II. Title. [DNLM: 1. Language.
2. Verbal behavior. BF455 H859L 1974]
P121.H73   301.2'1   74-8363

Contents

Acknowledgments

We should like to acknowledge our indebtedness to Dr. Harvey Tilker and his associates at CRM Books, a division of the Ziff-Davis Publishing Company, for graciously extending their permission to reprint material which appeared originally in *Anthropology Today*. Identification of these passages is made by specific footnote citation at appropriate places in the text. We also wish to express our appreciation to Mr. Thomas R. LaMarre and Mr. Ted Peacock, of F.E. Peacock Publishers, for their kindness in allowing us to reproduce material for which they hold the copyright.

In addition, our thanks are due to the following authors, editors, and publishers for granting the right to quote from or reproduce copyrighted material: *American Anthropologists; American Journal of Psychology;* Dr. John Atkins; Dr. Jean Berko; Dr. John B. Carroll; Dr. Joel Davitz; Harcourt Brace Jovanovich; Little, Brown and Company; Liveright Publishing Corporation; McGraw-Hill; Dr. Wilder Penfield; Philosophical Library; Prentice-Hall; Princeton University Press; *Speech Monographs;* Dr. Anthony F.C. Wallace; and *Word*.

Finally, we are especially grateful to our editor, Ms. Norma Fox, for her patience and counsel in helping to develop the manuscript for this book.

R.W.H.
H.J.V.

Preface

For most social scientists, it is not the study of language as such that is of special relevance, but rather the use of language as a means of getting at other kinds of information on social science. Thus the sociologist wants to know how language can help him to learn about social structure or interpersonal relationships; the psychologist looks at language as a key to some of the ways people learn, perceive, and interpret the world around them; and the ethnologist depends on language to reveal how culture categorizes and orders experience.

Inconvenient though it may be, however, language cannot be utilized naïvely with much profit. In order to investigate social science phenomena effectively through the clues provided by language, it is necessary to know something about the nature of language and of linguistic analysis. There is an obvious analogy between linguistics and statistics, in that both are legitimate disciplines in their own right and yet are widely used as tools by scholars whose primary interests are in other areas. There is also a second analogy: both are likely to be considered rather painful hurdles in the path of academic success for the graduate student.

Since we do not feel that the acquisition of a basic knowledge of linguistics need be painful, we hope on the one hand to present some fundamental linguistic concepts with sufficient clarity to instill confidence into the reader, and on the other hand to motivate him, through an exposition of the kinds of research that are possible, to acquire some of the skills of linguistic analysis.

Some understanding of linguistics is important, not only because the use of language is likely to be misguided without it, but also because the methods of linguistic analysis have been applied to essentially nonlinguistic events. Thus the use of the contrast within a frame was used by Conklin (1955) to analyze Hanunóo color categories, and by Frake (1961) to describe Subanun disease categories, while componential analysis has been widely used to deal with other semantic domains, including kinship systems (Lounsbury, 1956; Goodenough, 1956; Wallace and Atkins, 1960).

While basic techniques and concepts were being borrowed from structural linguistics to be used in the analysis and description of various semantic domains, a major shift in emphasis was taking place within the field of linguistics itself. To summarize this briefly (and no doubt too simply): before 1957, linguists had treated language as if it were a static semantic domain. A great deal of attention was devoted to the definition of relatively low-order events such as phonemes, which would be grouped into larger components such as morphemes, but virtually no attention was paid to the high-order sequencing of events that we call syntax. Today most linguists are primarily concerned to develop the rules that generate the possible utterances of a language. The older skills are still necessary, but they are no longer an end in themselves. Similarly, it is likely that an increasing number of anthropologists will try to apply

ideas of generative grammar to culturally patterned sequences of behavior. This has scarcely begun, but the techniques   are   promising   and   the   interest   is   there.
Goodenough (1971), for instance, has noted the relevance
of Eric Berne's *Games People Play* (1964), and has added his
own discussion of *recipes* for certain cultural patterns. The
older ethnographers did of course attempt to describe behavior patterns, but did not systematically attempt to render the descriptions in terms of what is significant for the
practitioners themselves. Now, on the other hand, we are
starting to see such formal studies as Colby's partial generative grammar of Eskimo folk narratives (1973).

Generative grammar involved a step away from the
Bloomfieldian abhorrence of meaning, at least in the
matter of linguistic analysis. The new respectability of
meaning, long a concern of many psychologists and
philosophers, has indeed led to an extension of generative
grammar to the loftier level of generative semantics. According to Werner (1972), at this point we can trace the
convergence of ethnoscience (or ethnolinguistics), computer simulation of semantic information-processing, the
ethnography of speaking, and generative semantics. It is
too early to judge how far the concern with meaning will
go before methodological difficulties will induce a backlash
and a return to problems that are operationally more grati-
fying.

As early as 1951, the psychologist Karl Lashley was
referring to "the syntax of action," and was discussing serial order with specific reference to language, but the real
development of psycholinguistics began at about the same
time, when a number of psychologists began to display
linguistic sophistication (Miller, 1951; Brown, 1958). By
the time Chomsky's *Syntactic Structures* appeared (1957), a
cadre of psychologists was ready to apply the new look in
linguistics to such problems as the acquisition of the first
and second language. Indeed, the importance of the gener-

ative-transformational approach to language was so great for psychology that Judith Greene's *Psycholinguistics* (1972) is really a detailed exposition of Chomsky's views as they pertain to psychology. This may be an extreme position, but it does suggest that linguistic theory is very important to our understanding of the psychology of language.

Sociolinguistics is the other main area in which linguistics has penetrated the social sciences. The field actually developed when linguists realized that they could not adequately describe speech varieties independently of their social contexts. The other side of this coin, the focus on contexts rather than speech varieties, has given rise within sociology to the closely related subdiscipline of ethnomethodology, in which problems of sequencing in conversations have already begun to draw serious attention (Schegloff, 1968, 1972; Schegloff and Sacks, 1969).

In summary, then, we are concerned with the linguistically oriented approaches to human behavior, including sociolinguistics, psycholinguistics, and ethnolinguistics. In addition, we are also interested in placing language within its behavioral and historical context. Thus we shall touch on the antecedents of language, including nonverbal communication and sound-symbolism, the biological basis of language, and derived systems such as the manual communication of the deaf, drum language, and secret languages. We cannot touch all bases, but we hope to range widely enough to suggest the myriad directions that language-based studies can take.

REFERENCES

Berne, E. 1964. *Games People Play.* New York: Grove Press, Inc.

Brown, R. 1958. *Words and Things.* New York: The Free Press.

Chomsky, N. 1957. *Syntactic Structures.* The Hague: Mouton & Co.

Colby, B. N. 1973. A partial grammar of Eskimo folktales. *Amer. Anthropol. 75:* 645–662.

Conklin, H. C. 1955. Hanunóo color categories. *Southwestern J. Anthropol. 11:* 339–344.

Frake, C. C. 1961. The diagnosis of disease among the Subanun of Mindanao. *Amer. Anthropol. 63:* 113–132.

Goodenough, W. H. 1956. Componential analysis and the study of meaning. *Language 32:* 195–216.

Goodenough, W. H. 1971. *Culture, Language, and Society.* Reading, Mass.: Addison-Wesley Publishing Co., Inc.

Greene, J. 1972. *Psycholinguistics.* Baltimore, Md.: Penguin Books, Inc.

Lashley, K. S. 1951. The problem of serial order in behavior. In L. A. Jeffress (Ed.), *Cerebral Mechanisms in Behavior,* pp. 112–136. New York: John Wiley & Sons, Inc.

Lounsbury, F. 1956. Semantic analysis of the Pawnee kinship usage. *Language 32:* 158–194.

Miller, G. A. 1951. *Language and Communication.* New York: McGraw-Hill Book Company.

Schegloff, E. A. 1968. Sequencing in conversational openings. *Amer. Anthropol. 70:* 1075–1095.

Schegloff, E. A. Notes on a conversational practice: Formulating place. In David Sudnow (Ed.), 1972. *Studies in Social Interaction.* New York: The Free Press, pp. 75–119.

Schegloff, E. A., & H. Sacks. 1969. Opening up closings. Paper delivered at annual meetings of the American Sociological Association, San Francisco, Cal., September 1969.

Werner, O. 1972. Ethnoscience 1972. In *Annual Review of Anthropology.* Vol. 1. Bernard J. Siegel (Ed.), pp. 271–308. Palo Alto, Cal., Annual Reviews, Inc.

1

Linguistics in Historical Perspective

It is probably not possible to trace in intimate detail the intricate network of interrelationships between our increasing linguistic sophistication and our broad social attitudes and programs, but a general connection is easily demonstrated. For example, when high-school and college students in Hilo, Hawaii, recently formed a group for the study and promotion of "Hawaiian pidgin," they had considerable moral support from the Hilo academic community. Yet there is a continuing tradition that regards the use of pidgin as a severe developmental handicap, if not an outright evil; and not too many years ago, there were schools on Hawaii where instruction was in Standard English for the elite minority, but in pidgin for the majority (who would presumably pass their lives as plantation workers). The student's present interest, then, comes after most of them have for much of their lives been powerfully encouraged to purge themselves of the local idiom in favor of the more respectable Standard English.

Obviously the student group is responding to a desire to strengthen or reestablish its local identity; and this is part of more general ethnic identity movements in Hawaii and on the mainland. It is doubtful, however, that pidgin would have been singled out for such serious attention without the dissemination of the contemporary linguistic attitude that all speech varieties are equally worthy of study and equally "legitimate." Of course the same influence is seen to an even greater extent among other groups, most notably perhaps among those who identify as Chicano or Black. In some cases the language selected for identification is not a serious part of the group's personal experience. Thus the recent interest in Swahili is a little arbitrary, because there are probably very few Black Americans who can reliably trace their genealogies back to Swahili-speaking ancestors. In Hawaii, many students who are enrolling in Hawaiian language courses have had little previous experience of the language beyond a few dozen floral, faunal, personal, and place-names. Third- and fourth-generation Japanese in Hawaii usually have an even more limited acquaintance with their ancestral tongue, yet they now swell Japanese classes.

In all these cases, the language symbolizes a group identity. The pidgin case is particularly instructive for two reasons: first, it is spoken by people of diverse origins, and thus is not directly related to ethnic origins (as in the case of Japanese, Hawaiian, or Spanish) or to racial origins (as in the case of Swahili); and second, it differs from the other languages in that it lacks even their mythical "purity," and thus their respectability.

LANGUAGE STUDY IN ANCIENT GREECE

While the idea of legitimizing a Creole language may seem socially dubious to some critics, even nonlinguists today accept the validity of such languages as Hawaiian, Spanish, Swahili, and Japanese—at least as suitable objects of study and as perfectly respectable media of communication. But until rather recently, students of language were quite narrow in their conceptions of academic respectability. According to Bloomfield (1933), the ancient Greeks "studied no language but their own; they took it for granted that the structure of their language embodied the universal forms of human thought or, perhaps, of the cosmic order [p. 5]." This lack of modesty no doubt restricted the kinds of statement that the philosophers could make about language, but they were the first European language theorists; their work began somewhere around the latter part of the sixth century B.C. They discovered the parts of speech for Greek, and also such syntactic constructions as that "of subject and predicate, and its chief inflectional categories: genders, numbers, cases, persons, tenses, and modes. They defined these not in terms of recognizable linguistic forms, but in abstract terms which were to tell the meaning of the linguistic class."

Hellenic interest in language was an outgrowth of philosophical pursuits. It was essentially in response to philosophical questions that Greek scholars speculated on the origin of language, the relationship between words and their meanings, and the application of principles of logic to grammar. Philosophical discussions were often directed toward linguistic problems. One of these discussions, as Ivić (1965) points out, is quite famous—the argument over whether the connection between the meanings of words and their sounds is logical and direct, or arbitrary and capricious. The "analogists" maintained that language is not dependent upon man-made conventions, but is a gift of nature. There was perfect correspondence between the sound of a word and its meaning, in their view; any imperfections that had arisen in this relationship in the course of time could be explained by etymological research, by systematic studies of words and their origins and derivations. The "anomalists," on the other hand, rejected the notion that there was perfect harmony between the sound and meaning of words. They drew on the existence of synonyms and homonyms, the demonstration of linguistic change over time, and the irregularity of grammar to show the imperfect nature of language.

LANGUAGE STUDY AMONG THE ROMANS

As in so many other spheres of activity, the Romans borrowed liberally from the Greeks in matters pertaining to language. Thus when a formal grammar was required with which to unify the Roman Empire and to compose a Latin literature (ca. 100 B.C.–200 A.D.), the model they chose was Greek. The most famous of the Latin grammars remained as textbooks through the Middle Ages, while spoken forms of Latin developed into what we recognize today as the Romance languages. The medium of written communication, however, remained classical Latin.

> The medieval scholar, accordingly, in both the Latin countries and others, studied only classical Latin. The scholastic philosophers discovered some features of Latin grammar, such as the distinction between nouns and adjectives and the differences between concord, government, and apposition. They contributed much less than the [Greek] ancients, who had, at any rate, a first-hand knowledge of the languages they studied. [Bloomfield, 1933, p. 6]

THE DEVELOPMENT OF NORMATIVE GRAMMARS

Somewhat later, the notion developed that general grammars could be written on the basis of universally valid canons of logic. Bloomfield attributes to this idea the subsequent development of normative grammars, in which authorities presume to dictate the way people *ought* to speak. This tradition is still very much with us, of course, in the form of concern over what is "correct" English.

Lamberts (1972) has recently documented some of the absurdities that the quest for correctness has added to our language. Chaucer, for example, probably pronounced "perfect" as /pǽrfit/ and spelled it *parfit*, but grammarians introduced the present spelling to make the word look Latin. Eventually the spelling dictated the pronunciation. *Comptroller* is a respelling of "controller"; and while the standard pronunciation for both is the same, the spelling pronunciation for the former (kâmptrówlər) is common, and may well replace /kəntrówler/. Cases in which the artificial pronunciation never caught on include "victuals" (from *vittles*), "debt" (from *det*), and "doubt" (from *doute*).

> Similarly, names like *Matthew, Thaddeus, Bartholomew, Dorothy, Martha, Katherine, Elizabeth,* and *Theodore* have the shortened forms *Matt, Tad, Bart, Dot, Marty, Kate, Bet,* and *Ted,* reflecting the time when the *th* spelling symbolized the stop /t/. The full forms were subjected to spelling pronunciation, presumably as being more dignified, but the nicknames have been left untouched. Thomas is an exception; so is the Thames in England and Canada. The Thames in Connecticut is gradually becoming /θéymz/. [Lamberts, 1972, p. 82]

The modern grammarians are the linguists, and it is hard to imagine that a contemporary professional linguist would abet the pedantic absurdity of such "improvements" on the basis of an alien model. This is part of the meaning of our earlier statement that all speech varieties are academically legitimate. This does not mean, of course, that all speech varieties are socially appropriate. What is socially appropriate constitutes "good" English. As Lamberts (1972) expresses it, " 'good' English in any given situation is the kind of English that certifies a person's competence to deal with the subject he is speaking or writing about. It is believable language [p. 23]." Professorial eloquence is about as inappropriate in an infantry barracks as extremely salty speech is in church.

CHOMSKY

While the development of the prescriptive attitude toward grammar, which is now viewed as reprehensible, has been widely attributed to the philosophical grammarians who were overly enchanted by their Latin model, the most influential contemporary linguist, Noam Chomsky, feels that the older scholars have been much maligned. He does not account for the normative attitude which has indisputably prevailed for some considerable time in our own schools, but he does note, with obvious justification, that the most famous of the treatises to grow out of the medieval tradition, the *Grammar* and *Logic* of Port-Royal (1660), were written in French, "the point being that they formed part of the movement to replace Latin by the vernacular [1968, p. 13]."

In an important sense, Chomsky traces his own academic heritage back to René Descartes (1596–1650), but this is almost certainly a belated recognition, since his views developed more immediately from modern structural linguistics. There was in effect an important discontinuity between the views of Descartes and his followers on the one hand, and the contemporary view of language on the other. However much Chomsky may care to read into Descartes, and however warm he may feel in recognizing a kindred spirit, it seems likely that Chomsky's brand of genius would have led him pretty much to his present theoretical position even if he had never heard of Descartes. In a similar sense one could see the origins of psycholinguistics in Descartes, or even in the Greek philosophers; but this is a dubious course if one selects as landmarks those discoveries that others have built on more or less directly.

Hindu Grammarians

Before continuing with European developments, we pause briefly for another glimpse into antiquity, this time in India. Roughly contemporaneously with the classical Greek philosophers, Hindu grammarians (traditional guardians of such sacred texts as the Rig-Veda, parts of which according to Bloomfield, date back at least to 1200 B.C.) began to turn their attention to the language of the upper caste. This language, Sanskrit, was subjected to minutely detailed analysis, probably for generations; the eventual result was the grammar of Pāṇini. Bloomfield (1933) describes it thus:

> This grammar, which dates from somewhere around 350 to 250 B.C., is one of the greatest monuments of human intelligence. It describes . . . every inflection, derivation, and composition, and every syntactic usage of its author's speech. No other language, to this day, has been so perfectly described. It may have been due, in part, to this excellent codification that Sanskrit became, in time, the official and literary language of all Brahmin India. Long after it had ceased to be spoken as anyone's native language, it remained (as classical Latin remained in Europe) the artificial medium for all writing on learned or religious topics. [p. 11]

In many respects, this ancient Hindu work may have been worth more than all other language studies combined until around the beginning of the nineteenth century. Thanks to the Greeks and the Latinists, Europe did have a linguistic tradition; but when Pāṇini grammar came to light, it presented Europeans with their first complete and accurate description of a language based on observation. Not only does it remain a model since unmatched, but it seems probable that it may never be matched—not because we lack those who have sufficient skill to accomplish the task, but rather because we do not have a group of scholars sufficiently motivated to produce a comparable *tour de force.* The task is something on the order of extending the value of π another dozen or so decimal places. Theory does not require such detail, and although it might be desirable for the development of good mechanical translation systems, it seems likely that the cost of achieving such detail would reach prohibitive levels long before perfection could be closely approximated. Also, while we are naturally interested in linguistic descriptions, they are not an end in themselves; they test theory and provide the material for theory, but the theory is not ultimately aimed at establishing more perfect descriptions. Chomsky's approach is exciting not because it will feed the computer better (although it may), but rather because it may bring us closer to an understanding of human mentality.

There are other, related reasons why we may not find it worth our while to emulate Pāṇini's magnificent achievement. We now understand what a tremendous variety of codes are described by a label such as "English." The codes are related, of course, but do we determine by a toss of the coin which variety to describe? We drive trucks, while the English drive lorries; we ascend in elevators, while the English avail themselves of the lift. It is often as difficult to account for such lexical differences as it is for grammatical differences, such as our need to go "to *the* hospital," while the English simply go "to hospital." Since we go "to school" and "to church," it might seem that such high frequency events lose the definite article, but it is not clear that the English spend more time in hospitals than we, and we go "to college" but "to the university," while the English also go "to university." This particular difference seems also to distinguish American and Canadian varieties, though the lexical differences are less. Other nationally identified varieties have similar differences; even in American English we have abundant regional and social variations, and English is but one general bundle of closely related codes. We could raise the same problems with other European languages, with Japanese, with Chinese, and probably with any other language. The point here is not to disparage the Hindu achievement, but simply to show that we have more urgent and more theoretically interesting tasks to occupy our attention and our efforts.

COMPARATIVE LANGUAGE STUDIES

Besides showing European scholars what a proper grammar looks like, the discovery of the Sanskrit work revealed the possibility of comparative studies. Of course, some obvious relationships had already been noticed; as Bloomfield (1933, p. 9) pointed out, the English *drink,* Dutch *drinken,* German *trinken,* Danish *drikke,* and Swedish *dricka* comprise one of the many sets that suggest there is a close relationship among the Germanic group of languages. There were also obvious similarities among the Romance group and among the Slavic group, but the discovery of the Sanskrit forms made the correspondences of these groups to the Greek forms more obvious. After the first great European Sanskrit scholar, Sir William Jones (1746–1794), had hypothesized that Sanskrit, Latin, Greek, and so forth, must have come from a common source, which might no longer exists, there followed a century of enthusiastic study that resulted in highly detailed comparative analyses. The excitement was not caused exclusively by the aesthetics of comparative or historical linguistics; it also arose because the newly discovered relationships implied the idea of tribal migrations, and raised the hope of deducing information on the origin of peoples and customs.

While the European and Hindu scholars provided the basis for our current linguistic researches, there were also other notable efforts, which have not, however, contributed directly to the discipline. Bloomfield (1933) noted that the Arabs worked out a grammar of the classical form of their language as it appears in the Koran; this provided a model for Jews in Mohammedan countries, who constructed a Hebrew grammar. In both these cases, the linguistic interest was related to religious concerns. In China, excellent lexical research was performed by the Han scholars (206 B.C.–220 A.D.), who were concerned to reconstruct the great classics after the enthusiastic bookburning of Shih Huang Ti in 213 B.C. The unifier of the Chinese Empire and founder of the Ch'in Dynasty had ordered the mass destruction largely because his literary opponents kept fighting him by means of allusions to the methods of government embodied in the classics (Karlgren, 1923).

In Japan, the great scholar Motoori Norinaga (1730–1801) was inspired to produce prodigious studies of Japanese by his extreme distaste for the high esteem enjoyed in his country by Chinese culture and Chinese language studies (Miller, 1967). Before the end of the eighteenth or by the early nineteenth century, then, virtually all serious language study was motivated by a desire to maintain the "purity" of a particular language, usually for religious or nationalist reasons. Gumperz (1965) credits the French with being the first to study dialects, which they did early in the nineteenth century; but their objective was to eliminate vulgar manifestations of the language, and even in modern India it is still inconceivable that anyone would want to know about the speech of illiterates.

The Nineteenth Century

To return to the point made at the beginning of this chapter, it should be clear by now that the current dictum that all speech varieties have equal legitimacy is a relatively new idea. Even aside from their social and academic legitimacy, there were effective restrictions on the kinds of speech varieties that were subjected to serious scrutiny. In the nineteenth century, the pursuit of comparative and historical problems almost necessarily centered on written forms of language, although this was not always done as a matter of principle.

Nevertheless, descriptive linguistics did develop increasingly during the nineteenth century. In particular, students of American Indian languages had no choice but to focus on spoken forms, because there was no pre-Columbian script to rely on. Since there were many dozens of apparently unrelated languages north of Mexico alone, which displayed the most varied types of structure, the challenge was enormous. There was no room for self-deception about the need for descriptive data; as Bloomfield (1933) expressed it, "In the stress of recording utterly strange forms of speech one soon learned that philosophical prepossessions were only a hindrance [p. 19]."

THE TWENTIETH CENTURY

In American linguistics, landmark publications include Edward Sapir's *Language* (1921), which is still available and is still of inestimable value as a general treatise on language; Bloomfield's *Language* (1933), which held the center of the stage for a quarter of a century; and Chomsky's *Syntactic Structures* (1957), which launched the current concern with generative grammar. His *Aspects of the Theory of Syntax* (1965) is yet another landmark, because it distinguishes deep and surface structures, and includes an explicit semantic component (inspired largely by the various works of Katz, Fodor, and Postal). While there is no single publication of comparable stature to mark the subsequent emergence of generative semantics, this new focus was perhaps predictable from the direction the linguistic field was taking under Chomsky's leadership (even though Chomsky himself takes issue with the generative semanticists).

There is at least a potential irony in this modern concern with meanings in linguistics. Studies on the psychology of verbal learning stem from the work of

Ebbinghaus (1885) on memory, and even today they depend to some extent on a thread of theory that can be traced back to the associationism of Locke (1632–1704). In that verbal learning theorists were almost totally lacking in linguistic sophistication, it might be said that they represented precisely what psycholinguistics was not. Psycholinguistics can be said to originate as far back in the history of philosophy as one cares to trace psychology, but the widespread use of the term and the development of psycholinguistics as a distinct discipline goes back only to the early 1950s, when George Miller (1951) and other psychologists introduced a knowledge of linguistics into the psychological study of language. This was long before the concept of meaning was given its new respectability in linguistics. Now, with the advent of generative semantics, it appears that there is a potential union of linguistics and verbal learning, with the latter's heavy involvement in word associations and "meaningfulness."

Ethnolinguistics, or ethnoscience, is essentially another development of the 1950s, but the immediate forebear of the science was a most remarkable fire-prevention inspector named Benjamin Lee Whorf. His essential idea, or at least the idea for which he is best known, is that patterns of thought and perception are molded by our language forms. In his work he had noted, for example, that men tend to be quite careless with matches and cigarettes around "empty" gasoline drums, even though they are probably more dangerous than full drums, around which great care is exercised. The label "empty" implies a lack of danger, and the men respond to the label as if there were indeed no danger around the "empty" drums (Carroll, 1956, p. 135). Eventually Whorf came under the influence of Edward Sapir, who held similar views on the way language influences perception and behavior. Sapir, in turn, seems to have been influenced by the earlier conceptions of Wilhelm von Humboldt (1767–1835), whom Bloomfield

(1933) credits with the first great book on general linguistics.

Sociolinguistics is more a development of the 1960s, an outgrowth of the problems encountered by linguists in describing dialect and other speech varieties, but the key point of departure is perhaps the distinction made in 1916 by the Swiss linguist Ferdinand de Saussure (Saussure, 1959). He distinguished *la langue,* the linguistic code of a group, from *la parole,* the actual speech performances of an individual. In English we usually refer simply to "language" versus "speech." Traditionally, we may say, linguists have been primarily concerned with language rather than speech, and they still are to the extent that they are concerned with what Chomsky calls linguistic competence (what an individual must know in order to engage appropriately in verbal interaction). Thus we must have rules by which to interpret what we hear, and we must have rules by which to produce utterances intelligible to the other party. Now, there is a gap between competence and *performance,* which is at least similar to the difference between language and speech; hence we may hear or produce "errors," without seriously interfering with the communication. For example, if we are told that "He can't make a—formulate that problem," the same rules that led the speaker to alter his sentence half-way through lead us to edit out the phrase "make a." The performance was faulty, but our linguistic competence permits us to endure such problems with minimal difficulty.

This rather sketchy review will be filled out a little more as we discuss specific problems and study specific areas, but for the moment we should try to bear in mind the idea that there is a great deal of overlapping interest in the fields of psycholinguistics, ethnolinguistics, sociolinguistics, and linguistics proper. Thus von Humboldt has a proper place in the history of linguistics, is often specifically mentioned as the ancestor of ethnolinguistics, and appears in some discussions of the history of psychology, at least in its more philosophical aspects. Similarly Whorf has been mentioned in connection with ethnolinguistics, but he is probably equally well known in psycholinguistics, and he was a solid descriptive linguist. Likewise, studies of bilingualism are often read equally easily as sociolinguistic or as psycholinguistic. The reason for the overlap is obvious: language is the key to most human thought, social behavior, and culture.

REFERENCES

Bloomfield, L. 1933. *Language.* New York: Henry Holt and Co.
Boring, E. G. 1950. *A History of Experimental Psychology.* New York: Appleton-Century-Crofts.
Carroll, J. B. 1956. *Language, Thought, and Reality. Selected Writings of Benjamin Lee Whorf.* New York: John Wiley & Sons, Inc.; Cambridge,: Mass. Technology Press.
Chomsky, N. 1957. *Syntactic Structures.* The Hague: Mouton & Co.
Chomsky, N. 1965. *Aspects of the Theory of Syntax.* Cambridge, Mass.: The M.I.T. Press.
Chomsky, N. 1968. *Language and Mind.* New York: Harcourt, Brace & World, Inc.
Ebbinghaus, H. 1885. *Über das Gedächtnis.* Leipzig: Duncker & Humblot.
Gumperz, J. H. 1965. Unpublished lecture of Anthropology 120, 24 September. University of California, Berkeley, California.
Ivić, M. 1965. *Trends in Linguistics.* The Hague: Mouton & Co.
Karlgren, B. 1923. *Sound and Symbol in Chinese.* London: Oxford University Press.
Lamberts, J. J. 1972. *A Short Introduction to English Usage.* New York: McGraw-Hill Book Company.
Miller, G. A. 1951. *Language and Communication.* New York: McGraw-Hill Book Company.
Miller, R. A. 1967. *The Japanese Language.* Chicago: University of Chicago Press.
Sapir, E. 1921. *Language.* New York: Harcourt, Brace & World, Inc.
Saussure, F. de. 1959. *Course in General Linguistics.* New York: Philosophical Library, Inc.

2

The
Origin and
Diversity
of
Languages

When Roger Brown produced his justifiably popular study *Words and Things,* (1958), he commented that theories on the origin of language had hardly changed since Plato's time. The speculations had rarely led to scientific inquiry, with the result that we are not offered theories so much as "a choice of myths [p. 135]." Fortunately, the picture has improved in the past 15 years. While we still lack a "satisfactory" origin myth, to use Brown's phrasing, we may at least take comfort in the knowledge that the question has led to scientific inquiry.

COMPARATIVE LINGUISTICS

When we examine the correspondences of sounds in groups of related languages, it is possible to reconstruct plausible protoforms. The protoforms of relatively closely related languages can then be compared to similar reconstructions of less closely related groups, to provide the basis on which to posit yet older forms. In this way it has been possible to describe proto-Indo-European, for example, and while not all languages have been placed in "families," groups of related languages have been identified all over the world.

Once the relationships have been established, there are various ways of placing the protolanguages in time and space. Thus, according to examples from Meinecke (1968), in the Polynesian languages the Hawaiian *k* corresponds to a *t* sound elsewhere. This suggests that the Hawaiian *k* is a development that took place after the local population had become physically separated from other Polynesian speakers. The idea is further supported by evidence from the sheltered speech community on the privately owned island of Niihau in the Hawaiian group, where the *k* sound alternates freely with the more conservative *t* sound. (If this sounds improbable to monolingual English readers, they should attend carefully to the way the *k* sound of "cool" is formed farther back in the mouth than the *k* sound of "keel" and "kill." Then, in succession, they should make a yet more forward *k* until "kill" becomes "till," perhaps passing through a stage in which the sequence will approximate "chill;" or they should begin with "till" and work back to "kill." In either case it is then easier to understand that the way the sounds are formed, the *k* and the *t* are not really so far apart.) Presumably the majority of Hawaiians at some time in the past customarily pronounced *t* sounds a little further back in the mouth than other Polynesians. The backing tendency, or "drift," to use Sapir's term (1921), continued until most Hawaiians were consistently pronouncing words that contained *t* with *k* sounds, and the *t* sounds dropped out altogether—except on Niihau.

To illustrate a little more broadly the way groups of

closely related languages can be compared in order to arrive at a protolanguage, we may note that Hawaiian *lani* "sky" corresponds to Tahitian *ra?i*. The vowels remain the same, but the Hawaiian -*n*- here corresponds to the Tahitian glottal stop, while the Hawaiian *l*- equates to the Tahitian *r*- (cf. *lima, rima* "five, hand"). A wider comparison among the Polynesian languages reveals that the *r* versus *l* problem is rather like the previously mentioned *k* versus *t* problem, in that the two sounds do not contrast in a way that results in different meanings. The question of - ? - versus -*n*- remains, but a wider comparison establishes that -*ŋ*- (as in "sing") is basic, and the presumed proto-Polynesian form of the word is *laŋi*. (The asterisk marks theoretical forms.) In the Melanesian group, Fijian *laŋi* is the same as the basic Polynesian form, but further west, Tagalog (in the Philippines), Javanese, and Indonesian all have the form *laŋit;* hence we should posit a proto-Austronesian form *laŋit;* and assume that the final -*t* disappeared in the course of the general eastward migration of the Polynesians and other Austronesian speakers.

Not all comparisons are absolutely tidy, but we see the same *n,* ? , *n* correspondences in words for "mouth, beak": Hawaiian *nuku,* Tahitian *?utu,* Tongan *ŋutu,* proto-Polynesian *ŋutu,* and Fijian *ŋusu.* The basic Polynesian - *t*- consistently corresponds to the Hawaiian -*k*-. But in the present case the Fijian form, which contains the -*s*-, departs from the Polynesian and is in accord with the -*s*- forms found among the western groups (Tagalog *ŋuso* "upper lip"; Javanese *nusu* "drink milk"; and Indonesian *susu* "milk").

Even this simple example quickly illustrates the complexity of comparative studies; but how far back does this sort of exercise push the origin of language? Comparative studies, especially if they are given quantitative treatment, can show the relative closeness of languages and permit the reconstruction of earlier forms, but they do not by themselves provide an absolute chronology. Glottochronology offers the hope of at least approximate dating, but as we have seen, it is not universally accepted as even moderately reliable. But if we give the fullest possible benefit of the doubt to George Grace's (1959) application of this technique to the separation of the relevant Melanesian languages and the Polynesian languages, we have a date of only 3,400 to 3,800 years ago for this separation, and comparative studies have nowhere provided a sound basis from which to derive dates of more than 6,000–8,000 years back (Trager, 1972, p. 175).

SYSTEMS APPROACHES

Since even the oldest reconstructed forms seem grammatically as complex as contemporary languages, we cannot through this avenue reconstruct from reconstructed forms far enough back even to provide a basis on which to speculate intelligently on the origin of language. In a work published posthumously, Swadesh (1971) did try to use many of the concepts and findings of comparative studies to define the most basic and universal features that presumably characterized an original language. At the present time we can only concede that the study provides food for thought; it may be years before the work can be properly evaluated.

A more exclusively "systems" approach to the origin of language has been provided by Charles Hockett (1960; Hockett & Ascher, 1964). By comparing the communication systems of many species of animal, it is possible to see which features are peculiar to language. Thus, for example, language is culturally transmitted, and we can communicate with reference not only to objects and events that are in the past and out of sight, but also to purely imaginary events. These are more the characteristics of man than of the system he employs, but important features of the system are arbitrariness, productivity, and duality.. The first, arbitrariness, refers to the fact that there is no necessary relationship between an event and its linguistic representation. The sound sequence in "cat" has nothing to do with the animal in question, and it has the meaning it does only because, in effect, we have decided to use that sequence to denote that category of animal. The same beast is represented in Japanese by a completely different sound sequence: *neko*. A nonarbitrary relationship would be *iconic*. We may impose iconic features on our speech by, for example, making loudness an expression of our emotional state. Thus we might softly caution a child who is about to bump into something if no danger were involved, but might shout the same warning if we were alarmed. The dances of the honeybee are arbitrary in that the movements are independent of the food substance (a waggle is not a picture of sugar), but to the extent that the movements are direct representations of the distance and direction of the food source, they are iconic.

Language is productive in that it can generate an infinite number of utterances, including messages that have never before been transmitted. It also features duality of patterning: this means that we have a set of sounds which we recognize as significant (it matters whether we use a *b* sound as against a *d* sound), but those sounds do not themselves have meaning; their meaning depends on the way they are combined into patterns. Thus the sounds that we represent as *o, d,* and *g* lack meaning by themselves, but they may be patterned in two meaningful ways: d-o-g or g-o-d.

Systems approaches help us to focus on what is truly distinctive about language, and to decide where in our evolutionary progression we developed the initial capacity for language. Thus, among our closest primate relatives (and many other animals) communication may be in part vocal, but the messages are in the form of calls, a limited inventory of closed signals that vary in intensity but not in form. According to Hockett and Ascher (1964), gibbons have one call for the discovery of food, another to indicate danger, another more social call for friendly interest, and one that seems simply to indicate the whereabouts of the signaller (a device that keeps the group from dispersing too much). The components of the calls cannot be, as it were, separated and recombined (as with t-i-p and p-i-t) to generate new meanings. Even if we make the maximum allowances for Swadesh's "ultimate reconstructions," there is still an appreciable gap between his original, basic language and the vocal systems of communication of other primates.

COMPARATIVE ANATOMY

Since language is so clearly a product of the brain, it is not surprising that there have been many attempts to see just where man's brain differs from the brains of other primates in a way that would give us additional understanding of the origin of language (for example, see Geschwind, 1964). Noam Chomsky has long argued that there is an innate and specific mechanism of language acquisition in the brain, and recently Lenneberg (1971) has suggested that such a capacity includes our mathematical abilities as well. Aside from comparing the brains of various species and deducing what we can from fossil materials, there is yet another brain-based approach that offers interesting possibilities.

Speech ability (and speech pathology) seems to be related to the question of cerebral dominance, and this in turn is related to the question of handedness. Lamar Roberts (1966) has noted that a number of animals show a preference for one hand (or paw) over the other, but claims that humans are the only predominantly right-handed animals. The point is far from established, but if there is evidence of handedness among groups of fossil men, then this at least suggests that the groups may possibly have had language. Responding to Roberts' paper in the same article, H. W. Magoun cited the claim of Davidson Black (Black, *et al.*, 1933) that the stone tools of Peking Man (*Homo erectus*) were more suited to right-handed than to left-handed use. This would push the origin of language back several hundred thousand years, a time depth that sounds reasonable enough to most students of the subject now. Magoun then notes that cave paintings of Cro-Magnon Man (some 25,000 to 50,000 years old) show silhouettes of hands, and 28 out of 35 silhouettes in one cave are of the left hand; this means that the actual outlining was done with the right hand (Roberts, 1966, p. 26). A related approach that may offer possibilities for comparative studies is that of Bever (1971), who has examined *auditory* cerebral dominance in relation to various language capabilities.

For half a century most of us have accepted the commonsense dictum of Edward Sapir (1921) that in scientific terms, there are "no organs of speech; there are only organs that are incidentally useful in the production of speech sounds. . . . Speech is not . . . carried on by one or more organs biologically adapted to the purpose [p. 9]." This position is currently threatened, however, by recent comparative studies of human and nonhuman primate communication and the development of our "speech organs." Jane Hill (1972), for example, suggests that limitations in the display systems of social primates may in the past have given a selective advantage to the vocal tract anatomy that accompanied the development of our upright posture. She suggests that human vocal tract anatomy may turn out to be at least as important as brain capacity to our understanding of the origins of language. Similarly, and more technically, Lieberman, Crelin, and Klatt (1972) have carried the argument farther. They claim that language ability depends on the ability to produce certain *specific* sounds, which are beyond the capacity of newborn humans, chimpanzees, and Neanderthal Man. The idea is mentioned here not so much because it is likely to be widely accepted, but more as an example of the lines of research that are currently being pursued and could perhaps throw light on the origin of language, even if this specific argument is never generally adopted. If it were adopted, it could bring the origin of language to a time far more recent than most present theories place it, conceivably to a mere forty or fifty thousand years ago.

Interesting as the studies on the development of the vocal tract may be, however, there are two good reasons for concentrating on the development of brain mechanisms. First, there are highly effective visual-manual language systems, as against our vocal-auditory language systems. Lieberman *et al.* (1972) stress the speed of communication with spoken language, which "allows modern man to communicate at least ten times faster than any other known method. . . . No non-speech acoustic alphabet has yet been contrived that can be made to work more than one-tenth as well as speech [p. 299]." But the visual-manual system employed by the deaf is exceedingly fast. Perhaps the use of fingerspelling alone would be slower than speaking, but a top-notch bilingual who uses fingerspelling in conjunction with the more global signs can translate a vocal presentation into a manual presentation more or less instantaneously. There may be some loss of precision in the translation, but it is fast, and more importantly, it is language. Further, the manual communication is effectively used by individuals who have been profoundly deaf from birth, which would surely signify that language ability is essentially a problem of the brain and is not absolutely dependent on specific speech organs. This does not rule out the possibility that a specifically vocal system conferred selective advantages on man, but there are potential advantages in a visual-manual system as well. It makes silent communication over a distance possible, for example, and this would be quite useful in cooperative hunting and fighting ventures.

The second line of argument that favors a concentration on the development of the brain is the recent success that Gardner and Gardner (1972) have enjoyed in teaching the chimpanzee Washoe to communicate by means of a visual-manual system based on the American Sign Language used by the deaf. Washoe is not likely to achieve an important academic chair, but she has certainly learned to construct and respond meaningfully to sentences communicated by signs. In other words, she shows a limited but very real language capacity, which, to speculate a little, may well have been exceeded by the precursors of *Australopithecus,* possibly more than five million years ago. This does *not* mean that any of the earlier prehominids had language, not even of the standard that Washoe has mastered. Chimpanzees left to their own resources do not show the language capacity that Washoe has developed under careful and enlightened tutoring. The point is that at least a limited language *potential* did probably exist among the ancestors of man, several million years ago.

THE DIVERSITY OF LANGUAGES

Whenever, wherever, and however language originated—whether it was a single development or whether it developed independently in more than one human population—we do know a considerable amount about the way languages can multiply. For a number of reasons (which we shall discuss shortly), it is not really possible to state how many languages are in use throughout the world today.

Trager's (1972) estimate of 2,500 to 5,000 is probably representative of most educated guesses.

The Origin of Diversity

To put it simply, languages are in a constant state of change, and when the speakers of a language disperse and form separate speech communities, the changes continue; but they will not be the same changes in each community. When the changes have become sufficiently noticeable, we refer to different dialects of the original language, and when the cumulative changes have become so great that the members of the two speech communities can no longer understand each other, then we say that the two speech varieties lack *mutual intelligibility* and now constitute different languages.

The criterion of mutual intelligibility sounds straightforward enough, but in practice it is often difficult to apply. Most Americans can understand most other Americans (though we may find that some local varieties take a bit of getting used to), and we understand most of the British English that we hear in the United States. If we were to nose around different localities in England, however, we would find speech varieties that would take considerable getting used to, but we would probably still agree that they are "English."

On the other hand, as Trager (1972) and many others have noted, in Scandinavia speakers of "Swedish," "Danish," and "Norwegian" talk to each other without difficulty. In this case, which is matched by dozens of others around the world, the names of the languages reflect political rather than linguistic facts. There are several major varieties of Chinese, some of which, according to Chao (1947), are as different from each other as are English and German, and yet we refer popularly to "Chinese." In brief, the specification of a particular language often depends on social and political considerations as well as on linguistic factors. Further, some peoples are more receptive than others to the comprehension of different speech varieties. So even the matter of mutual intelligibility is not all that simple.

As we mentioned earlier, there is a drift in language (Sapir, 1921) that accounts for some part of language change, and thus for diversity. In addition, languages in contact influence each other. Most obviously, words are borrowed and often become so well incorporated that the average speaker may not recognize them as having once been foreign. Much less obviously, languages influence each other structurally, as we shall see below.

Languages thus change in response to certain internal dynamics, such as the drift that accounts for the Hawaiian *k* where other Polynesian languages have *t*, and they also change as a result of contact. Further, changes occur in response to cultural developments. As our culture develops specializations, for example, we develop appropriately specialized vocabularies (chemical, geological, medical, electronic, and so forth). Whether the new terms become popular (television, astronaut, Vietnamization) or not, they represent increments to the language and constitute a source of change.

Language Types

The study of almost any foreign language involves features that may not be familiar to us. For the English speaker, the simplest kinds of grammatical difference may be the positioning of adjectives after rather than before the noun, as in Spanish *casa blanca* (house + white), where we say "white house," or having to indicate whether each noun is masculine or feminine (in Spanish, *el toro* "bull" is masculine, but *la mesa* "table" is feminine). More exotic differences for the English speaker might involve the learning of tones for each word. Many languages, most notably in Africa and Asia, are tonal, which lends them what we hear as a singsong quality. Some idea of the way tones distinguish words can be obtained from our own intonation patterns. If, for example, we say we are going somewhere and the listener asks "Where?" with a rising intonation, it implies that he did not quite understand (or believe) what we said. It is a request that we repeat the statement. If, on the other hand, the "Where?" has a falling intonation, it is a request for more detailed information. The only difference in the sound pattern is whether it rises or falls, and that makes a difference in the meaning. In Mandarin Chinese, syllables may have four tones and thus four meanings; in Cantonese there are six possibilities, three tones in each of two registers.

In developing language typologies, nearly any criterion can be used: whether or not a language is tonal, for example. In the nineteenth century languages were often classified as analytic or synthetic, depending on whether grammatical categories were expressed by single words or were incorporated within the words as inflections (Greenberg, 1968). The discovery of the grammatically complex word-units of some American-Indian languages then added a polysynthetic category. Sapir (1921) reviewed these and other typologies in some detail, noting that few languages, if any, would fall into any of these types cleanly and completely. He also offered his own more perfect typology, which would be more simply stated than explained; but typologies based on forms have at least temporarily passed out of vogue. Yet it may be instructive to note that Chinese is essentially analytic, in that most words can potentially serve as nouns, verbs, or adjectives. English is similar in that we have words such as "hit," which also serve those functions: Mac hit Jane; a hit play; the play is a hit. But English is synthetic in that it has such internal changes as sing-sang-sung, or man-men. A synthetic language can express grammatical differences by prefixing, infixing, suffixing, and other similar processes.

The Altaic languages and Japanese, among others, are agglutinating languages, in which grammatical particles are strung onto a root. To give the flavor of this, an extreme example of literary Japanese may be taken from Chamberlain (1924): *kirashimerarubekarazaredomo* "though (one) should not have been caused to cut," which is formed by stringing particles onto the root *kir-* "cut," in approximately the reverse order of the English gloss. That is, the English has the "though" first, which corresponds to the *-domo* of the Japanese, and so forth.

Nineteenth-century concern with typology was linked to evolutionary thought, but we have now accepted the notion that we cannot place known languages in any sort of evolutionary sequence. Formal typology still has some potential value for mechanical problems such as machine translation, and for the theoretical problem of deriving specific grammars from a universal grammar. Genetic classifications are of continuing interest, of course, since we would like to account for the historic relationships of all languages and of the people who speak them.

References

Bever, T. G. 1971. The nature of cerebral dominance in speech behaviour of the child and adult. In Renira Huxley & Elisabeth Ingram (Eds.), *Language Acquisition: Models and Methods*, pp. 231–261. New York and London: Academic Press Inc.

Black, D., C. C. Young, W. C. Pei, & T. De Chardin. 1933. Fossil man in China, *Mem. Geol. Surv. China*, Ser. A, No. 11.

Brown, R. 1958. *Words and Things*. New York: The Free Press.

Chamberlain, B. H. 1924. *A Simplified Grammar of the Japanese Language*. Chicago: University of Chicago Press.

Chao, Yuen Ren. 1947. *Cantonese Primer*. Cambridge, Mass.: Harvard University Press.

Gardner, B. T., & A. Gardner. 1972. Development of two-way communication with the chimpanzee, Washoe. Presented at the 71st Annual Meeting of the American Anthropological Association, Toronto, November 29–December 3, 1972.

Geschwind, N. 1964. The development of the brain and the evolution of language. In C.I.J.M. Stuart (Ed.), *Report of the 15th Annual Round Table Meeting on Linguistic and Language Studies.* Monograph Series on Languages and Linguistics No. 17. Washington, D.C.: Georgetown University Press.

Grace, G. 1959. The position of the Polynesian languages within the Austronesian (Malayo-Polynesian) language family. *International Journal of American Linguistics Memoire 16.*

Greenberg, J. J. 1968. *Anthropological Linguistics.* New York: Random House, Inc.

Hill, J. H. 1972. On the evolutionary foundations of language. *Amer. Anthropol. 74:* 308–317.

Hockett, C. F. 1960. The origin of speech. *Sci. Amer. 202:* 88–96.

Hockett, C. F., & R. Ascher. 1964. The human revolution. *Current Anthropol. 5:* 135–168.

Lenneberg, E. H. 1971. Of language, knowledge, apes, and brains. *J. Psycholinguistic Res. 1:* 1–29.

Lieberman, P., E. S. Crelin, & D. H. Klatt. 1972. Phonetic ability and related anatomy of the newborn and adult human, Neanderthal Man, and the chimpanzee. *Amer. Anthropol. 74:* 287–307.

Meinecke, F. K. 1968. Linguistic unity and diversity: Polynesian, a case study. Paper presented at the University of Indiana, March 29, 1968.

Roberts, L. 1966. Central brain mechanisms in speech. *Brain Function.* Vol. III. E. C. Carterette (Ed.), *Speech, Language, and Communication,* pp. 17–36. Berkeley and Los Angeles, Cal.: University of California Press.

Sapir, E. 1921. *Language.* New York: Harcourt, Brace & World, Inc.

Swadesh, M. 1971. *The Origin and Diversification of Language.* Chicago and New York: Aldine-Atherton.

Trager, G. L. 1972. *Language and Languages.* San Francisco, Cal.: Chandler Publishing Co.

3

Antecedents
of
Language

Communication in the broadest sense is the process whereby two or more entities are joined. Thus communication between cities may be accomplished by means of railroad lines, air routes, highways, river systems, and so forth. We may nudge a companion and, by means of a nod, direct his attention to an event in a specific location. A peeping Tom usually counts on one-way visual communication, while an exhibitionist seeks two-way communication. But *language* is the distinctively human form of communication, upon which not only civilization but culture itself depends. Language is the means by which we are able to accumulate knowledge, to build upon that knowledge, and to transmit it from one generation to the next. There are, as we shall see, nonhuman societies of considerable complexity which lack culture, and there are some rather elaborate systems of communication that are qualitatively different from language. In brief, the infrahuman societies and modes of communication are essentially the products of what we think of popularly as instincts, in contrast to language and culture, which are not instinctual, but rather are learned. This overly simple statement needs a wealth of qualifications, but these will be introduced in the course of the discussion. Our objective here is to examine some of the features of communication among infrahuman species, in order to gain a useful perspective from which we can view language.

COMMUNICATION AMONG INSECTS

Kroeber (1948, p. 34 ff.) has provided a useful discussion of the essential difference between insect and human societies. Many species of social insect live in communities that may number hundreds of thousands or even millions of individuals, and thus compare with our largest cities in population. In some respects such insects are more socialized than we are, since the individual tends to subordinate his own welfare more or less completely to the welfare of the group. Typically there is a thoroughly developed caste system; some species of ants and most termites have subdivided or added castes, especially a soldier caste.

> This professional army again may be differentiated into an aggressive corps with powerful jaws; a sort of flame-throwing or gas-throwing service that squirts a dangerous liquid; a defensive or shield-bearing division that blocks the gate with an enormous impermeable forehead. Workers, in turn, may come in two or even three sizes for indoor and outdoor labor. . . . Nor are the castes always inflexible. Certain ants use their large-jawed soldiers to crush for them hard-shelled seeds that the workers can bring in but cannot crack. When autumn comes on and the harvest of these seeds is over, when the community goes into winter retreat and ordinarily need fear no further insect enemies, these warrior-millers have become useless and would be a drain on the hoard of the hive. Like the drones among the honeybees, they are therefore killed by the workers . . . not only individuals but even classes are sacrificed for the good of the society. [Kroeber, 1948, p. 35]

Pheromones

When an insect society is examined in detail, the complexity of the behavior patterns that serve to sustain the group is awesome, and it may be difficult to realize that there is no conscious intelligence of the kind that is so important to the maintenance of our own societies. A great deal of the communication that governs insect behavior depends on secretions called *pheromones.* The fire ant, for example, makes a trail to a food supply or to a new nest site by releasing minute quantities of a particular pheromone through its sting, which intermittently touches the ground. When workers encounter the substance, which serves as an attractant, they move automatically up the gradient to the source of the emission. So long as the food supply holds out, the ants will secrete the pheromone. Thus the greater the supply of food, the more ants will follow and intensify the trail. But as the supply diminishes, the ants cease to emit the pheromone, and the number of individuals attracted to the trail quickly decreases. The pheromone itself is rather volatile, and the trail laid down by a single individual becomes too weak to attract after about two minutes. As Wilson (1963) points out, the effectively short life of the individual trail is useful as an index to the abundance of the supply, and it also means that trails do not linger beyond the time of their usefulness to confuse hunting workers later.

Pheromones have a wide range of functions in the insect world, perhaps about as many as there are activities that require some sort of communication (though there are, as we shall see, other ways of communicating). They enter into the formation of migratory locust swarms, for example, and are widely observed as sex attractants. The female gypsy moth has about 0.01 μg gyplure, which under optimum conditions would be potent enough to excite more than a billion males! The responses to the pheromones are not learned, however, but are automatically released. This is seen quite clearly when experimenters manipulate such situations artificially. An ant that has just died, for instance, will be groomed by other ants as if it were living, but after a day or two products of chemical decomposition accumulate, and this stimulates workers to bear the dead ant away from the nest, to the refuse heap. This sounds quite sensible to us of course, but the process continues thus (Wilson, 1963):

> When other objects, including living workers, are experimentally daubed with these substances, they are dutifully carried to the refuse pile. After being dumped on the refuse the 'living dead' scramble to their feet and promptly return to the nest, only to be carried out again. The hapless creatures are thrown back on the refuse pile time and again until most of the scent of death has been worn off their bodies by the ritual. [p. 8]

Pheromones are also important to honeybees, to regulate the reproductive cycle of the colony and to mark the target when a worker stings an intruder (this accounts for the tendency of angry swarms of workers to sting at the same spot). In addition, when a worker discovers a new food source, it may release a type of alcohol that attracts other workers and thus communicate some information about the food source. But the bees are much better known for another means of communicating this kind of information.

The "Dancing" Bees

The studies of the German naturalist von Frisch (1955) have shown that bees are able to convey the location and direction of food discoveries to others in the swarm by means of a series of maneuvers which are as stylized, in some respects, as the figures in classical ballet. Von Frisch constructed a hive with glass walls, which permitted him to observe the behavior of the bee tenants when they returned from a food-seeking flight. When the source of the nectar was close, say within 100 feet or less, the finder bee would perform a "dance" consisting of a circular movement. To indicate longer distances, the bee would run in a straight line while moving its abdomen rapidly from side to side, then would make a turn and repeat the maneuver. For distances in excess of 200 yards, the number of turns made by the bee decreased. A run followed by only two turns, for example, might indicate that the food source was several miles away.

After observing this behavior, the other bees were able to fly directly to the food. It was apparent that they received cues to the location of the food from the direction of the "run" made by the finder bee. An upward vertical run in the hive indicated that the food source would be found by flying into the sun, whereas a downward vertical run indicated that the food source was away from the sun. Von Frisch found that if they were restricted to a horizontal surface and deprived of sunlight, bees were unable to communicate the direction of their finds. We have already suggested that pheromones contribute to the dissemination of food information among the bees, but Wenner and Johnson (1967) have argued that the smell of food substance itself is important. That scent may be important is not denied by the proponents of the dance theory (Esch, 1967; von Frisch, 1967), but they point out that the dance conveys the relevant information when scent is experimentally removed as a variable. More detailed information on insect ways is contained in Niko Tinbergen's very readable *Curious Naturalists* (1968).

Human Pheromones?

While there is some reason to suspect that human pheromones may exist (Wilson, 1963), the question is complicated by cultural factors. Hall (1966), for example, contrasts U.S. and Arab olfactory systems:

> Bathing the other person in one's breath is a common practice in Arab countries. The American is taught not to breathe on people. He experiences difficulty when he is within olfactory range of another person with whom he is not on close terms, particularly in public settings. He finds the intensity and sensuality overwhelming and has trouble paying attention to what is being said and at the same time coping with his feelings. [p. 47]

We shall return later to nonverbal communication among humans, but for now we will note that in addition to olfactory and visual modes of communication, all of the other senses may be utilized for communication by one species or another. For example, Swadesh (1971, p. 168) describes the repertory of vocalizations that are exchanged between a hen and her chicks under various circumstances. Of more immediate interest, perhaps, are the means of communication employed by animals phylogenetically closer to ourselves.

THE DOLPHIN

The bottle-nosed dolphin, or porpoise, is not an embarrassingly close relative of ours, but it has received considerable attention in the past decade or so because it appears to have an aptitude for linguistic behavior. Equipped with a brain larger than ours, the dolphin shows some amazing capacities for complex learning. In addition, it possesses an elaborate and variegated set of sound-making capabilities. From the respiratory blowhole in its head, the dolphin produces both whistles and a sound that has been likened to a "raspberry," or Bronx cheer. It can also produce a series of clacks by gnashing its needle-pointed teeth. But its chief sound-making apparatus is a voice box that compares in complexity with the human vocal equipment. From this voice box it can emit a tremendously complicated range of barks, squawks, whistles, mewings, creakings, and other sounds that are more difficult to identify. They range from deep bass to a supersonic pitch far beyond the limits of human auditory perception.

John C. Lilly (1961, 1967), formerly of the Communications Research Institute of Miami, Florida, who is probably the best-known student of dolphin behavior, is convinced, after many years of research on the subject, that dolphins are capable not only of intelligent communication, but even of language. Dolphins appear to possess mimetic capacities, and by reducing the playback speed of tape-recorded dolphin vocalizations, Lilly felt that he could distinguish sounds that resembled a baby crying, the plucking of a banjo, human laughter, and other sounds that one normally associates with human beings. So far, however, Dr. Lilly has not succeeded in establishing the type of linguistic communication between himself and his aquatic subjects that would confirm even his more modest expectations of their vocal capacities. And other students of the dolphin seem less optimistic than Lilly. Caldwell and Caldwell (1968), for example, have found no evidence of a dolphin "language," but they have presented evidence of social responses to acoustic signals. While we may not yet be justified in celebrating the linguistic talents of the dolphin, the dramatic example of the chimpanzee should caution us not to lose hope of a possible breakthrough in the case of the dolphin.

THE CHIMPANZEE

The animal that is in all ways closest to man is the chimpanzee. We have probably all seen what a clever fellow the chimp is: he can be trained to ride a motorcycle, smoke cigars, and in general show us a picture of ourselves with remarkably little distortion. But until we learned of Jane Goodall's now famous observations of wild chimpanzees in Africa, we flattered ourselves that we were the only tool-making animal. It emerges, however, that not only do the chimps make rudimentary tools (sponges from crumbled leaves to soak up water, little fishing poles for catching termites, and so forth), but they also have some very familiar gestures. They embrace, kiss, tickle each other, and even condescend to accept a kiss on the hand from a new-comer who is trying to ingratiate herself with the group (Goodall, 1967, 1971). But there was nothing in the communication of chimps in the wild that really qualified as language. There were no gestures or vocalizations that were sequenced in the way we sequence words to form sentences—there was no evidence of an actual grammar, however elementary. And there was no evidence that they used sounds or gestures to refer to the past, the future, or events that occurred beyond sight or sound.

Viki

A prolonged attempt to teach a chimpanzee human language was reported by Hayes (1951). Keith and Kathy Hayes actually raised a chimp in their home, from the age of three days to about six-and-a-half years. The chimp, named Viki, was treated as nearly as possible like a human child in such matters as feeding, toilet training, discipline, and play. Viki not only learned to imitate much of the behavior of the adult humans with whom she lived; she also learned to respond to spoken commands. Nonetheless, to the end of the experiment, Viki never managed to mouth more than three (or possibly four) words: papa, mama, cup (and possibly "up"). The various attempts to teach human language to Viki and to other primate subjects were re-

viewed by Kellogg (1968), just as the remarkable breakthrough of two Nevada psychologists was beginning to
attract attention.

Washoe

In June, 1966, R. Allen Gardner and Beatrice T. Gardner of the University of Nevada undertook to teach a young
female chimpanzee the gesture language of the deaf. They
were not much concerned with language as such, and were
in fact rather naïve about the subject when they began.
They were interested in the theory of learning, and reasoned that in view of past failures and the natural behavior
of chimpanzees, an attempt to establish interspecies communication would be more likely to succeed if it were based
on gestures. To this end, they began an essentially operant
technique of rewarding the animal's own gestures when
these happened to resemble the gestures in the American
Sign Language.

The experiment began when Washoe (named after the
county in which the University of Nevada is located) was
between 8 and 14 months old, and after 22 months of
training and other interaction with the investigators and
their assistants, all of whom used only manual language in
the presence of the animal, Washoe had a repertory of
more than 30 signs. Most of the signs named objects and
pictures of objects. Once Washoe had eight or ten signs in
her repertory, she began to combine them.

> Among the signs that Washoe has recently acquired are the
> pronouns 'I-me' and 'you.' When these occur in combina-
> tions the result resembles a short sentence. In terms of the
> eventual level of communication that a chimpanzee might be
> able to attain, the most promising results have been sponta-
> neous naming, spontaneous transfer to new referents, and
> spontaneous combinations and recombinations of signs.
> [Gardner and Gardner, 1969, p. 672]

Combining signs in a patterned way constitutes a very primitive grammar, and the observation that a rather small list of signs are typically used in combination with signs from a longer list parallels the development of two- and three-word sentences in the process of language acquisition by human children. Washoe was approximately three years of age at this stage, and she was a year or so behind the human schedule for language acquisition, but the experiment is a considerable accomplishment for all parties concerned, human and ape. A year later Washoe's lexicon had increased to 85 or more signs, and the process of forming combinations had advanced slightly (Gardner and Gardner, 1971). If we think of the grammar in terms of the requirements of English, the subsequent development is rather modest, but this is not an appropriate comparison. The American Sign Language lacks many of the grammatical requirements of English (use of a copula, for example), and if we apply the usual criterion of evaluating a system in its own terms, Washoe's language should be compared with the system represented by the American Sign Language. (So far as we know, there has never been a rudimentary analysis of ASL grammar. But see Schlesinger, 1971, for some of the problems encountered in dealing with the grammar of Israeli Sign Language.)

The next step in the interspecific communications research has already been taken. Dr. Roger Fouts, who worked with the Gardners as a graduate student, has taken Washoe to the University of Oklahoma Institute for Primate Studies. At the Institute, which is under the direction of Dr. William B. Lemmon, Fouts has established that Washoe is not unique in her ability to learn American Sign Language. Several other chimps have been making good progress, and are using signs in communicating with one another (though it may be a while before they advance to the point where they will be able to "rap" with Washoe, because she has such a head start). Fortunately, Fouts is reporting frequently and in detail on his progress, and has provided summaries of related research (Fouts, 1972, 1973a, 1973b, 1973/1974).

A somewhat different approach to the language capacities of the chimpanzee has been taken by Premack and Premack (1972). The Premacks have taught their chimp (Sarah) to manipulate plastic pieces of various colors, sizes, and shapes; each of these pieces represents a different word. As of their 1972 report, Sarah had a vocabulary of some 130 terms, which she employed with a reliability of 75 to 80%, and she had learned to use and understand the negative article, the interrogative, and wh-questions, as well as such concepts as "name of," dimensional classes, prepositions, the conditional, and hierarchically organized sentences.

The most recent of the chimp language experiments seems to be that of the Yerkes Regional Primate Center, in Atlanta, Georgia. According to an article in *Newsweek* (January 7, 1974, pp. 75–76), a chimp named Lana has been taught to read and write simple sentences by using what is in effect a rather grotesque typewriter. On each plastic key of her computer console there is a hieroglyphic-type symbol that represents a word. The work was begun about two years ago; essentially the same kind of conditioning techniques have evidently been used as were employed in the other chimp experiments. After a year of mere "rote associations," Lana began to form her own sentences, with appropriate punctuation marks. Evidently she now has a vocabulary of some 50 words, but one of the psychologists involved, Duane M. Rumbaugh, has indicated that this will be increased to 100 words.

Next to the chimpanzee, the gorilla is generally considered to be the creature closest to man. Francine Patterson, at Stanford University, has begun to teach a young female gorilla the ASL. In a 1973 personal communication to Fouts (Fouts, 1973b), she reported that the 19-month old gorilla was using six signs and was combining the "more" sign with "food," "drink," and "out." And Fouts (1973b) reports that he was able in a brief study to teach an infant orangutan (again, somewhat more remotely related to man) several signs, and that the orangutan combined them into two-sign sequences.

While the work with apes has intrinsic interest, it also carries implications as to the origin of human language. Lieberman, Crelin, and Klatt (1972) have argued that language must be a recent development, because forms prior to modern man (*Homo sapiens sapiens*) lacked the necessary vocal apparatus. Whether or not Lieberman *et al.* succeed in convincing us with their argument about the human vocal apparatus, the demonstration that the great apes have at least rudimentary language capacity, and the existence of a highly developed system of manual communication among the deaf, suggest that human language may have begun as a gesture system rather than as a vocal-auditory system. This argument has been suggested most strongly by Hewes (1973) and Stokoe (1972).

LANGUAGE AND SYMBOLS

Even if language began as a gesture system, and even though the deaf can converse manually equally rapidly and over as wide a range of topics as those with hearing, it is customary to define language in terms of vocal symbols. By taking the vocal system as primary, we distinguish language from derived systems such as scripts. Even the manual system of the American deaf is derived, in the sense that the signs are supplemented by finger spelling, which is the equivalent of a script.

The most useful definition of language may still be that of Edward Sapir (1921): "Language is a purely human and non-instinctive method of communicating ideas, emotions, and desires by means of a system of voluntarily produced symbols [p. 8]." Washoe's accomplishments notwithstanding, language is still a distinctively human characteristic, but we may have to alter this definition if Washoe and her companions establish their manual communication as a characteristic of the Oklahoma chimp community over several generations. Even then, we may flatter our vanities with the supposition that such a system would remain primitive by comparison with strictly human systems.

Learning

The definition of language as noninstinctive precludes most of the forms of communication already discussed that are used by insects and other infrahumans. At least beyond the more elementary forms of animal life, communication patterns most commonly depend strongly on genetic considerations, but some modification is attributable to learning. The English chaffinch, for example, will develop a song of about normal length (two or three seconds) if it is raised out of hearing of other males; this can be said to represent the genetic component of the pattern. But the song of the isolated chaffinch lacks the phrasing and elaborate final flourish of the song produced by the normally reared chaffinch. And if a number of isolated chaffinches are placed together after babyhood, they will develop more complex songs; thus there is a strong social effect on the development of the pattern, but these songs still will not be the same as the song found in the wild population. According to Thorpe (1956), there is a critical period, around the eleventh month of life, during which the chaffinch develops the pattern that becomes its song for life. The question of genetic predisposition and the critical learning period will reappear in the discussion of the acquisition of language by children.

The Structure of Language

The systematic nature of language is reflected in its structure, which can be transposed in any number of ways without altering the way in which the components are related to each other. We can speak a sentence, for instance, and then write that sentence in such a way that each sound is represented by a graph. The sentence remains the same, even though the auditory channel is replaced by the visual channel. Similarly, instead of writing in the conventional way, we can convert the sentence to a visual one by finger-spelling it. Or, to complicate the picture even more, we can speak a sentence, write it, and then convert the written form into a series of electrical impulses (the dots and dashes of the Morse code, for example), which are converted back into conventional letters and are read aloud. Everywhere along the sequence of transpositions, the structure of the sentence remains intact. The Chinese telegraphic code employed for commercial purposes begins with a message in Chinese characters, each of which is represented by a four-digit number. The four-digit numbers are converted to dots and dashes for transmission; then the dots and dashes are converted back into numbers, which are looked up for their graphic value. The structure of the Chinese message is unaltered by the transmissions. Experienced persons can even read a message of four-digit numbers aloud in Chinese!

The Arbitrary Nature of Symbols

More importantly, perhaps, the term *system* refers to the rules whereby utterances are generated. These will be discussed in some detail in the next chapter, and more briefly below, when we examine duality in patterning. First, however, we should examine the significance of the term "symbol." The basic idea of a symbol is that just about anything can represent anything else; the association is essentially arbitrary. This becomes clear enough when we look at the different names that the same objects or events have in various languages. As we mentioned before, our "cat" is the Japanese *neko,* and neither sound sequence has any intrinsic connection with the animal itself. The names are strictly learned, not automatically elicited in the naïve human by the sight of the animal. Even in the case of onomatopoeia, where we are presumably duplicating real sounds with our voices (in which case the connection between our sound and the event being depicted is *not* arbitrary), there is considerable freedom in the way we make the representation. Thus our dogs go "bow-wow," while Japanese dogs go *wan-wan;* we "splash" water, while the same event is rendered by *pocha-pocha* in Japanese.

To go farther afield in demonstrating the essentially arbitrary nature of symbols, many psychoanalytically inclined individuals maintain the validity of the notion of "universal symbols," especially with regard to sexual matters. Of course we can see the similarity between a rod and a penis, or between a box and a vagina, but again, there is an almost infinite variety of objects that we can employ to represent the human genitalia. Alan Dundes (personal communication), for example, insists that the nursery rhyme about The Old Woman Who Lived in a Shoe owes its enduring quality to the fact that the shoe symbolizes the vagina—and perhaps it was a popular symbol at some time in the past. It seems doubtful, however, that the same symbolic value holds today. Parents do many things, including reading nursery rhymes to their children, for purely traditional reasons. Of course the shoe can represent the female genitalia, for that is the whole idea of the symbol; but whether a particular object absolutely *will* be used to represent something else is another, more arbitrary matter. In Japan, for instance, the female genitalia are often symbolized by the term *hamaguri* "clam" or by *mame* "dicotyledonous bean," while the male sexual member is a *matsutake* "mushroom."

A simple classroom demonstration that usually manages to show the arbitrary nature of symbols involves the use of various handy objects (eraser, chalk, pen, and so on) to illustrate a military campaign. Early in the demonstration an eraser is placed to show Pusan, in Korea, where American forces were penned up during the early part of the Korean war. Then Inch'ŏn is shown, and a description is begun of the famous landing at that port by forces under MacArthur. At about this time the instructor looks momentarily confused, picks up the eraser, and asks the class "What is this?" Almost invariably, a student will say "Pusan," whereupon the instructor will make his point by saying, "No, it's an eraser." The eraser has very effectively symbolized a Korean city, and the arbitrary nature of the representation could hardly be clearer.

DESIGN FEATURES OF LANGUAGE

Thus language is a system of symbols, but this sort of human communication can be more finely distinguished from infrahuman forms. In the previous chapter we mentioned some of the criterial features enumerated by Charles Hockett (Hockett, 1958, 1960; Hockett and Ascher, 1964). Some features of languages, such as displacement and cultural transmission, are better described as peculiarities of man than as peculiarities of the system. The features most distinctive of language, as we mentioned before, include arbitrariness, productivity, and duality of patterning.

The concept of arbitrariness has been elaborated above as a characteristic of symbols and probably needs no further clarification. Productivity will be illustrated in some detail when we deal with grammar in Chapter 8. Similarly the concept of duality will be implicit in our discussion of phonemes (Chapter 8), but we should add a further note here. Duality of patterning means that we have a set of sounds which we recognize as significant but which do not of themselves have meaning. The sounds that are significant for English may not be for other languages, just as other sounds may be important for other languages but not for English. The sounds themselves may be partly or completely shared by two quite different languages, but the ways they are arranged may be subject to rather different rules.

In Hawaiian, for example, consonants have to be separated by a vowel sound, and words have to end in vowels; thus, when a word such as "Christmas," which begins with a *kr-* sound, confronts a speaker of Hawaiian, a vowel sound has to be inserted between the two consonant sounds: *kali-* (for Chri-). We do not usually pronounce the *t* in Christmas, and there is no *s* sound in Hawaiian. So our *s* sound becomes another *k* in Hawaiian. But the *k* sound is immediately followed by an *m*, so another vowel is required (*-kima-*), giving *kalikima-* (for Christma-). And with another *k* for the final *-s* plus the required final vowel, our "Christmas" becomes *kalikimaka* in Hawaiian. Similarly, "Samuel" is *Kamuela,* formed by the same set of rules.

The fact that sounds that do not themselves have meaning can be used to form arrangements that do have meaning (dual patterning) means that a small number of components can be used to generate an infinite number of acceptable arrangements that have meaning. Some rules define the sounds that can come together to form words, which have meanings, and other rules define how the words are related to each other to convey greater units of meaning. This statement is an extreme simplification of a very complex problem that will be dealt with in greater detail in Chapter 8. In the meantime, however, we shall examine some very general considerations that underlie language as such.

REFERENCES

Caldwell, M. C., D. K. Caldwell. 1968. Vocalization of naive captive dolphins in small groups. *Science 159:* 1121–1123.

Esch, H. 1967. The evolution of bee language. *Sci. Amer.*, April, 1967, 216(4): 96–104. (Note also the exchange of letters between Wenner, Johnson, Wells, and Esch in *Sci. Amer.* 217(2): 6–7.)

Fouts, R. S. 1972. The use of guidance in teaching sign language to a chimpanzee (Pan Trolodytes). *J. Comp. Physiol. Psychol. 80:* 515–522.

Fouts, R. S. 1973a. Acquisition and testing of gestural signs in four young chimpanzees. *Science 180:* 978–980.

Fouts, R. S. 1973b. Capacities for language in great apes. Paper prepared for the IX International Congress of Anthropological and Ethnological Sciences, Chicago, September 1973.

Fouts, R. S. 1973/1974. Communication with chimpanzees. In E. Eibl-Eibesfeldt & G. Kurth (Eds.), *Hominisation und Verhalten.* Stuttgart: Gustav Fischer, Verlag.

Frisch, K. von. 1955. *The Dancing Bees.* New York: Harcourt, Brace & World, Inc.

Frisch, K. von. 1967. Honeybees: Do they use direction and distance information provided by their dancers? *Science 158:* 1072–1076.

Gardner, R. A., & B. T. Gardner. 1969. Teaching sign language to a chimpanzee. *Science 165:* 664–672.

Gardner, B. T., & R. A. Gardner. 1971. Two-way communication with an infant chimpanzee. In *Behavior of Non-human Primates.* Vol. 4, Ch. 3. A. Schrier & F. Strollnitz (Eds.). New York: Academic Press Inc.

Hall, E. T. 1965. *The Hidden Dimension.* Garden City, N.Y.: Doubleday & Company, Inc.

Hays, C. 1951. *The Ape in Our House.* New York: Harper & Row, Publishers.

Hewes, G. 1973. Primate communication and the gestural origin of language. *Current Anthropol. 14:* 5–24.

Hockett, C. R. 1958. *Course in Modern Linguistics.* New York: The Macmillan Company.

Hockett, C. R. 1960. The origin of speech. *Sci. Amer. 203:* 89–96.

Hockett, C. R., & R. Ascher. 1964. The human revolution. *Current Anthropol.* *5:* 135–168.

Kellogg, W. N. 1968. Communication and language in the home-raised chimpanzee. *Science 162:* 423–427.

Kroeber, A. L. 1948. *Anthropology.* New York: Harcourt, Brace & World, Inc.

Lawick-Goodall, Baroness J. van. 1967. *My Friends the Wild Chimpanzees.* Washington, D.C.: National Geographic Society.

Lawick-Goodall, Baroness J. van. 1971. *In the Shadow of Man.* Boston, Mass.: Houghton Mifflin Company.

Lieberman, P., E. S. Crelin, & D. H. Klatt. 1972. Phonetic ability and related anatomy of the newborn and adult human, Neanderthal Man, and the chimpanzee. *Amer. Anthropol. 74:* 287–307.

Lilly, J. C. 1961. *Man and Dolphin.* Garden City, New York: Doubleday & Company, Inc.

Lilly, J. C. 1967. *The Mind of the Dolphin.* Garden City, New York: Doubleday & Company, Inc.

Premack, A. J., & D. Premack. 1972. Teaching language to an ape. *Sci. Amer. 227:* 92–99.

Sapir, E. 1921. *Language.* New York: Harcourt, Brace & World, Inc.

Schlesinger, I. M. 1971. The grammar of sign language, and the problems of language universals. In J. Morton (Ed.), *Biological and Social Factors in Psycholinguistics,* pp. 98–120. London: Logos Press, Limited.

Stokoe, W. 1972. Motor signs as the first form of language. Paper presented at the 71st Annual Meeting of the American Anthropological Association, Toronto, December 1972.

Swadesh, M. 1971. *The Origin and Diversification of Language.* Chicago: Aldine-Atherton, Inc.

Thorpe, W. H. 1956. The language of birds. Reprinted from *Sci. Amer. 145* (October).

Tinbergen, N. 1968. *Curious Naturalists.* New York: Natural History Press.

Wenner, A. M., & D. I. Johnson. 1967. Honeybees: Do they use direction and distance information provided by their dancer? *Science 158:* 1076–1077.

Wilson, E. O. 1963. Pheromones. Reprinted from *Sci. Amer. 157* (May).

4

Nonverbal Communication

Communication between humans can take a multitude of forms, implicit as well as explicit, and frequently unconscious and unintended. When we nudge or nod, smile or scowl, fidget, flush, or yawn, we communicate nonverbally. When we interact socially, the very way we handle time and space serves to communicate, sometimes more tellingly than the verbal accompaniment. There are culturally defined conversational distances and durations, violations of which tell the other party that the relationship has been redefined, at least temporarily. A former companion who ignores our outstretched hand and cuts short our greeting tells us that he no longer considers the relationship to be close.

In a review of nonverbal communication, Mehrabian (1972) distinguishes the literal, nonverbal definition of the term from the more general meaning it is usually given in the literature. In the narrower definition the term refers to behavior such as facial expressions, hand and arm gestures, and postures. The broader treatment includes the acoustic, paralinguistic phenomena that accompany language, such as speech rhythms and other factors that communicate emotional states. (Some of these phenomena will be dealt with in the next chapter.)

CODIFICATION OF NONVERBAL BEHAVIOR

Ruesch (1966) postulates that there are three major categories of nonverbal codification: sign, action, and object language. Sign language:

> . . . includes those forms of codification in which words, numbers and punctuation signs have been supplanted by gestures; these vary from the 'monosyllabic' gesture of the hitchhiker, to such complete systems as the language of the deaf. [p. 209]

Action language comprises all movements that are not used exlusively as signals: walking and drinking, for example. Object language includes all "intentional and nonintentional display of material things," such as machines, art objects, and the human body. These three nonverbal means of communication differ with respect to the specific sensory modalities required for their transmission. Silent sign language is perceived exclusively by the eye, whereas action language may be perceived by both the eye and the ear, and may also be mediated by the senses of touch, temperature, and pain. Object language further includes the olfactory and gustatory senses.

The effectiveness of these three types of nonverbal language depends to some extent on the distance between the participants in the communication. Sign and action languages depend on immediacy, requiring the persons to be within visual range of one another. Object language, however, closely resembles written language in that the transmitter and the perceiver need not be visible to one another in order to complete communication successfully.

Closely related to action language are sign language and gestures. Over the centuries, every social group has developed systems of communication in which particular words, signs, and gestures have been assigned communicative significance. There are gestures that assume the auxiliary role of providing emphasis, timing, and direction. Because such denotation systems are not bound to phonetics, they enable persons who speak different languages to communicate with each other in ways analogous to the pictographic symbolizations that cut across verbal language barriers.

Certain social situations call for certain gestures. Where rapid motion is involved, gestures are mandatory, because limitations of time will prevent a verbally coded message from being understood. Thus the language of traffic is based almost entirely upon nonverbal signals, such as the hand signal used by drivers to indicate direction. In addition, gestures may be employed whenever verbally coded messages prove inadequate on other gounds. A good deal of humor depends for its effect on the notion that gestures are more universal than words, and so can convey ideas and moods when words fail. The dual nature of verbal and nonverbal communication makes it possible for the human being to create impressions based upon the differences between what he expresses in words and what he communicates through actions and gestures. Hence, a person who integrates both the nonverbal components of language (action and gestures) and the verbal message has an advantage over the person who selectively responds to only one, since the latter loses much information in the social situation. By doing this, he may misinterpret the message, due to a possible incongruity between the two components. A person who tends to solve incongruent relationships by disregarding part of the message is less capable of successful communication in society than a person who understands the whole message. Ruesch (1966) has noted that what we call mental illness is closely associated with disturbances in sign behavior, language, and communication. Aberrations in nonverbal sign behavior tend to accompany more severe and longer psychopathological conditions than do aberrations in verbal sign behavior. As Needles (1959) found in relation to mental functions, when an individual passes a certain emotional peak, speech breaks down and nonverbal communication (most commonly expressed through hand gesticulation) becomes important as a means of communication.

Gesture languages are found in many parts of the world, and sometimes exist as a separate system where, for some reason, oral language is not readily possible or desirable; examples of these are the systems of gestures used by the deaf, certain monastic orders, and some North American Indian tribes. These systems resemble one another so closely that they almost constitute a universal language.

Gestures such as waving and shaking hands in greeting all seem very natural to us as Americans, yet they do not seem so to people in some other countries. The gesture is only a significant means of communication when the person who initiates the gesture and the person who receives or perceives it attach the same meaning to it. The following mixtures of cross-cultural gestures that represent "greeting," quoted from Hiller (in Lindesmith and Strauss, 1951), serve to illustrate the shared and conventional character of human gestures:

> Among the Wanyika, people meet by grasping hands and pressing their thumbs together; dwellers in the region of the Niger join their right hands and separate them with a pull so that a snapping noise is made by thumb and fingers. The handshake of the Arab seems to be a scuffle in which each tries to raise to his lips the hand of the other. The Ainus draw their hands from the shoulders and down the arms to the fingertips of the person greeted, or they rub their hands together. . . . Polynesians stroke their own faces with the other person's hands. . . . The Fuegians in saluting friends

> hug 'like the grip of a bear.' Some peoples greet by placing one arm around the neck of the person saluted and chucking him under the chin, or encircling his neck with their arms. . . . Among the Polynesians, Malays, Burmese, Lapps, and others—a usual salute is that of smelling each other's cheeks. [p. 45]

These gestures constitute not only sign language, but also (and mainly) action language. Any observant traveler notes large and small variations in the gestures and other motor habits of different regions.

The expression of emotions and the circumstances that arouse particular emotions certainly vary culturally. A vivid example is presented by LaBarre (1947):

> The sticking out of the tongue among Europeans (often at the same time 'making a face') is an insulting, almost obscene act of provocative challenge and mocking contempt for the adversary, so undignified as to be used only by children. In Bengali statues of the dread black mother goddess, Kali, the tongue is protruded to signify great raging and anger and shock; but the Chinese of the Sung dynasty protruded the tongue playfully to pretend to mock terror, as to make 'fun of,' the ridiculous and unfeared anger of another person. Modern Chinese in South China at least, protrude the tongue for a monent and then retract it to express embarrassment at a faux pas.
>
> Kissing, as is well known, is in the Orient an act of private love-play and arouses only disgust when indulged in publicly.

In the language of the gesture, all over the world, there are varying mixtures of the physiologically based response and the purely cultural response, and it is frequently difficult to analyze out and segregate the two.

THE STUDY OF NONVERBAL COMMUNICATION

A large number of investigations have dealt with facial expressions, eye movements, gestures, postures, and body movements in the context of nonverbal communication. At the risk of some simplification, we might categorize these studies on the basis of fundamental differences in theoretical and methodological approaches to the analysis of nonverbal behavior. Among the proponents of a *traditionally oriented approach*, a prestudy decision is made concerning what elements of behavior (for example, facial expression or body movement) will be selected as objects of investigation, and then procedures are established whereby these behaviors can be counted and measured. Using such techniques as free association, and judgmental tasks in which raters determine by intuition the meaning of particular behaviors in an interaction, those studying these behaviors seek to derive meaning from the qualities of the events themselves. Thus, in situations subject to varying degrees of control, judges are asked to rate nonverbal cues on a particular dimension (or dimensions). Also, the behavior of the judges themselves, or of the body cues under investigation, may be correlated with other activities in an attempt to decipher the meaning of the nonverbal behavior. Behaviors are measured and counted, charts and statistics are presented, and the meaning of the interaction is abstracted from the statistical data on the judgmental task.

In contrast with this rigorously statistical, judgmental, task-oriented approach to the study of nonverbal behavior, investigators such as Birdwhistell (1970) and Scheflen (1964, 1965) employ the procedure of *contextual analysis.* Contextual analysis is rooted in general systems theory, according to which the organization of living systems is seen as a hierarchy of successively larger units. Scheflen (1965) examines the visually sensible elements of nonverbal behavior for "structural configurations as they appear in the stream of behavior [p. 246]." Posed behavior or experimentally controlled parts of interaction are not studied as they are in the traditionally oriented approach. The meaning of the behavior emerges from its function in the larger systems, not in the event itself. The experimenter does not ask what this gesture means, but rather how it fits into the interaction of the larger system (Scheflen, 1964). He does not measure and count behavioral events *per se*, but rather looks at the larger picture. Instead of charts and statistics, the results are simply descriptions and abstractions.

The two approaches, then, disclose a fundamental divergence in the way their respective proponents view behavior. The traditionalist watches behavioral events in restricted interactional processes, but the contextual analyst interprets the behavior only in its full structural context. This discrepancy between the theories leads to a second split in methodology. The traditionalist counts and quantifies behaviors in statistical presentations, whereas the contextual analyst gives behavioral *descriptions* (Scheflen, 1965).

TRADITIONALLY ORIENTED STUDIES OF NONVERBAL COMMUNICATION

Research directed toward the relationship between emotion and verbal expressive activity was reported by Sainsbury in 1955. Sainsbury measured the spontaneous gestural movements made by patients during psychiatric interviews in which topics judged to be disturbing or nondisturbing were discussed. His subjects included 16 depression and anxiety patients.

Recognizing that "spontaneous movements are closely dependent on emotional states," Sainsbury hypothesized that "gestural activity of patients will increase if they are affectively disturbed during the interview [p. 459]." An instrument called an electromyograph measured the action potential of the patient's gestural movements, and an integrator synchronized them with tape-recordings of the accompanying speech during the 30-minute interview. By concealing some of the recording equipment in an adjoining room, he hoped to reduce the patient's self-conscious inhibition of gestural activity. The interview was designed to begin and end with a discussion of topics thought to be undisturbing for the patient. During the intermediate stress periods, preselected problems of the patient were set forth for discussion.

A comparison of the number of body movements made during periods rated as disturbing and undisturbing revealed that movement was greater in the disturbing period, and that the differences were significant in 14 out of 16 interviews. The author also compared the proportion of body movements made during the discussion of each topic, and again found that the gestural movements increased significantly during the discussion of the disturbing topics in nearly every instance. In locating passages that evoked affective states and measuring the accompanying body movements, Sainsbury found that movements were consistently more numerous within periods marked by resentment and indignation; passages evocative of anxiety also ran up high movement scores. Finally, four patients were reinterviewed, and it was found that the topics accompanied by most gestures in the first interview were likewise accompanied by most gestures in the second interview.

Sainsbury concludes by observing that "the use of gesture increases with affective disturbance. Whether this is more the case with some effects than others did not clearly emerge from the results [p. 468]." Suggestions of this sort are only hinted at by such findings as that a large number of gestures consistently accompany emotional states such as resentment.

The relationship between body movements and moods in patients' interviews was studied by Dittman (1962). In developing his nonverbal variables for use in interaction research in psychotherapy, Dittman studied the frequency of body movement as it related to the stated mood or feeling. His procedure marked a technical advance over that of Sainsbury, in that he employed motion-picture recording techniques. He also differed from Sainsbury in his choice of postural-gestural cues for study. Whereas Sainsbury concentrated on movements of the hands, Dittman studied movement of three body areas (the hands, head, and legs) in relation to five stated moods of the patient. "Frequency of movements differentiated these moods reliably, and an interaction effect appeared between mood and body area [p. 480]." Dittman described this interaction by showing that patterns of body movement differ across body areas for different moods. The depressed mood, for instance, revealed few movements of head and hands, but many leg movements. These findings reveal that postural-gestural cues are informatively related to mood, in that certain bodily cues are instrumental in showing the state of feelings.

Thompson and Meltzer (1964) studied the communication of emotional intent by facial expression; whereas other authors studied the spontaneous, interactional flow of bodily movements in the expression of emotion, the interest of these investigators lay in ascertaining the extent to which "expressors" can convey to judges (students), by means of facial expressions alone, their emotional content. The ability to express emotion deliberately is emphasized. The experimenters focus on the variable of expressor behavior, rather than the behavior of judges. Differences in the ability of expressors to recognize and portray affect, and possible personality correlates to such ability, were of primary concern to the authors.

Choosing from a list of ten emotions (happiness, love, surprise, fear, determination, disgust, contempt, suffering, anger, and bewilderment), judges decided which emotions untrained expressors were portraying. There were two enactments of each emotion for four judges, and thus eight separate scores comprised the "enactment score" for each emotion. The results demonstrated that in over 60% of the trials, the expressors were successful in communicating the emotions; this figure varied from 38% success for contempt to 76% success for happiness. It was found that contempt was less adequately communicated than love, happiness, fear, determination, surprise, bewilderment, or anger. Thirdly, although the correlation was modest, the success of an expressor in enacting one emotion predicted his success in further portrayals. However, any expected personality correlate of these individual differences in ability to enact emotions failed to appear.

A final result involved the confusion between certain expressed emotions. Facial cues for certain affects were evidently more easily confused with other emotions. For instance, judges' ratings showed that contempt was easily mistaken for anger, and disgust for anger or contempt. Although the focus in this experiment is expressor behavior rather than judge behavior, it certainly reveals the informative ability of nonverbal behavior, particularly with respect to emotional communication.

Paul Ekman* has dealt extensively with nonverbal communication in a series of studies characterized by imaginativeness and originality (Ekman, 1964; 1965a, 1965b; Ekman, Friesen, and Tomkins, 1971; Ekman, Friesen, and Ellsworth, 1971). Although Ekman's original interest in this area was prompted by his concern for the significance of nonverbal behavior in psychotherapy, his subsequent research has been addressed to basic issues in the analysis of nonverbal communication.

*An informal and entertaining account of Dr. Ekman's work is provided in Chapter 7 (The Human Face) of Flora Davis' book *Inside Intuition: What We Know about Nonverbal Communication* (New York: McGraw-Hill Book Company, 1972). This volume is highly recommended as a nontechnical and readable introduction to the topic of nonverbal communication.

In one of his earlier studies, Ekman (1965a) examined spontaneous interactive nonverbal behavior in a standard stress interview that featured alternating ten-minute periods of stress and "catharsis." Ekman's study differed from prior investigations to the extent that he dealt with variations in nonverbal behavior as a "communicative stimulus," and studied the observer's response to this stimulus. Previous studies had tended to treat nonverbal body behavior as a response to some other factor, such as the structure of the interview or the patient's mood. Thus Sainsbury and Dittman report relationships between changes in nonverbal behavior and changes in the content and structure of the interview. They do not study the related question, What is communicated to the observer by a change in nonverbal behavior? Second, agreement between judges as to what is communicated, which is the principal concern of other studies, is rejected by Ekman; it is replaced by an emphasis on interjudge accuracy in understanding communication through kinesic activities. Thus, he asked judges to match photographs that showed nonverbal behavior and verbal speech excerpts from previously recorded and synchronized interviews. More specifically, judges were presented with one short written speech sample and a pair of photos, either one or both of which were from one of the two periods of stress or catharsis. They were asked to match one photo with the appropriate speech sample.

In a series of four experiments, in all of which he used a similar procedure, Ekman tested a number of hypotheses on the judges' ability to correlate these photographs and speech samples. He generally chose the nonverbal bodily cue given to the judges in the experiments from among three cues: the head, body, and whole person.

In the first experiment, Ekman tested the hypothesis that "untrained observers can discriminate from pairs of photos one taken during a given speech sample [p. 297]." The results confirmed the hypothesis. The second experiment tested whether "untrained observers can choose from pairs of photos one of which is taken during a given speech sample when responding to pictures as a whole." He found that judges could accurately match whole photos and speech; and in fact, it was later found that the level of accuracy was greater when they were matching the whole person with verbal behavior than when they were matching body cues and speech. The third study tested whether or not observers could match speech with body cues. This was also confirmed.

Because a different group of judges was used for each of the first three experiments, no information was obtained about their relative accuracy in matching speech and photos as a function of the specific nonverbal cue presented. This is the subject of the fourth experiment, which tested the hypothesis "that judges can choose from a pair of photos the one which is taken from a given speech sample when responding to either head or body position cues." A greater level of accuracy was obtained with the head cues than with body cues.

The study generally concludes that spontaneous body positioning and facial expression have a special communicative value in relation to verbal behavior, and are not just "noise." They especially mediate information about "momentary changes between stress and catharsis during an interaction consistent with concomitant verbal behavior [p. 726]." The amount of information does seem to vary with the type of kinesic activity presented, since Ekman found that accuracy in matching materials was related to the type of cue information provided (the head, body, or whole person).

After this first series of studies, Ekman conducted another series of ten experiments in which he dealt with the communicative value of body gestural behavior in providing information about the quality of an interpersonal relationship. Questions were raised as to whether nonverbal behavior can accurately communicate information about the quality of the relationship, and whether it is capable of reflecting changes in the relationship. Behavior in a standard stress situation was observed, as in the first series of studies. The issue to be judged differed somewhat; judges were not asked to match photos and speech. Rather, using photos, they were instructed to determine how the interviewer was reacting to the individual being interviewed.

In the first experiment, judges determined what phase of the interview was shown in the picture, from a photograph that contained both the interviewer and the subject. It was shown that judges can accurately distinguish between stress and final periods. Pictures in the second experiment contained only the subject; the elimination of the interviewer cues proved to decrease the judges' accuracy. In the third study, judges assessed several random photos of interviewers and subjects together, but were deprived of the information derived from a sequential ordering of nonverbal behavior. Their accuracy of judgment was significant beyond the level of chance. The fourth experiment was similar to the third, except that the photos contained the subject alone. Differences were found between the accuracy of judgment of the photos of interview A and of interview B; the accuracy was greater for interview A. Experiments five and six resulted in the finding that judges can accurately distinguish the interview period on the basis of nonverbal cues, but that the accuracy of the judge varied with the stimulus that the persons in the photos presented. The results suggest that accuracy is affected by: (1) whether the interviewer and subject or the subject alone is shown; (2) which particular stimulus is shown (interview A or B); and (3) the amount of information presented to the judges (a single photo or many photos).

Experiments seven through nine dealt with the possible contaminating effects of practice upon the judges' accuracy. First, it was shown that untrained judges can accurately determine whether randomly selected and ordered series of photographs were taken during periods of stress or catharsis. The stability of judgments of nonverbal behavior over time was tested thus: judges rated a random series of photos, then after a four-day interval they rated the same series, presented in a different random order. It was concluded that the assessment of the potential effects of practice on accuracy was contaminated by the individual differences in the judging behaviors of observers. And although a positive correlation was found in the ability of the judges across the stimulus persons, it cannot be concluded that an increase in accuracy over trials results from practice over trials. A final study in this group involved a measurement of the judges' accuracy when presented with a substantially increased and sequentially ordered sample of nonverbal behavior. No greater accuracy was obtained with sequential cues. Ekman concluded with a discussion of three kinds of information transmitted by nonverbal, postural-gestural cues: (1) information about subject affects; (2) knowledge of the interviewer's behavior; and (3) information about the quality of the interpersonal relationship between the interviewer and subjects. In fact, "the nonverbal behavior systematically changes as a function of gross modification in the quality of the relationship between the two people."

A third major study by Ekman (1965b) involved four experiments in which he showed that head and body nonverbal cues provide different affective information. Again, as in his earlier studies, he sampled nonverbal behavior in five standardized stress interviews as it occurred during the ongoing, verbally communicative, interpersonal relationship. Since previous studies gave evidence of the communicative potential of nonverbal behavior as a carrier of diverse messages, Ekman wished to begin to specify the "link between particular nonverbal cues and the inferences drawn by an observer [p. 726]." By showing two broad categories of nonverbal cues (those provided by the head and the body, taken from photographs of the same stimulus person) to a common group of observers, and by subsequently comparing the observers' ability to draw the same set of inferences about the affect from each of the two sources, he aimed in this experiment to specify something about the link between cue and inference. More precisely, the hypothesis tested was:

> Head cues carry information primarily about what particular affect is being experienced . . . but provide relatively little information about the intensity of the affect or the level of arousal; body cues reverse this pattern communicating information primarily about the level of arousal or degree of intensity of the affective experience, but provide relatively few cues about what particular affect is being experienced. [p. 727]

In each experiment, three separate groups of judges each received one version of the cue: the head, body, or whole person. Each judge was required to rate the emotion being experienced by the person in each photograph on three dimensions of affect: pleasantness, attention to or rejection of stimulation, and intensity (ranging from tension to sleep).

Differences between judgments of the head and body on each dimension proved to be insignificant, which provided additional support for the hypothesis. Because moderate differences were found between ratings of the head and whole on the sleep-tension parameter, it was necessary to qualify the hypothesis to admit that some information about sleep-tension is communicated by the head. Ekman also questioned whether known changes in interpersonal interaction could be inferred from head and body cues. A difference in pleasantness-unpleasantness ratings between stress and catharsis photographs was expected when head judgments were measured. Conversely, a difference in sleep-tension between the two types of photographic stimuli was expected when measuring body cues. Pleasantness scores did differ for the head, but not for the body. However, the predicted results did not occur on the sleep-tension dimension. A possible explanation is that "the two interview experiences [were] characterized by the same level of arousal [p. 732]." Thus the finding does not necessarily contradict the hypothesis. In conclusion, Ekman explains that only one class of information (namely, affect) has been considered in this study. Further studies of other information classes and further subdivision into more specific cues within each of these stimulus classes (the body and head) are needed (p. 735).

Dittman, Parloff, and Boomer (1965) undertook to determine whether observers "differentiate and respond to bodily cues as distinct from facial cues [p. 239]." Their method placed facial and bodily cues in conflict, so that an observer's response to facial cues might be influenced by an incongruent message from the body. The study emphasized the recognition of bodily cues rather than the recognition of any subtle inferences that might be drawn. For this reason, the discriminatory task set in the experiment remained quite simple. Two groups of judges (psychotherapists and professional dancers) assessed the states of feeling of subjects shown in short motion pictures, on a continuum from pleasantness to unpleasantness. It is interesting to note that, unlike previous studies in which still photographs were employed, the Dittman study made use of motion-picture segments of bodily motion. Three different series of these films, each with twenty segments, were developed. Fifteen segments were rated as crucial by the authors, and five others were inserted as buffers to reduce the judges' memory of specific segments. In five crucial segments, the subject's expression was pleasant for both face and body (P-P); in five, unpleasant affect was expressed in both (U-U); and in the final five, the subject's face expressed pleasant affect while the body expressed unpleasant affect (P-U; p. 240). Cues were presented to the judges in one of two ways: the whole person or the body. Three random orders of these twenty segments comprised the three series.

Results indicated that all of the judges were more influenced by the face than the body in their judgments. Although body expression yields information, the groups of judges differed considerably in their ability to respond to it. For example, the dancers tended to be more significantly influenced than the psychotherapists in their ratings of unpleasant affect on the basis of body cues. Uniformly, however, facial cues proved easier to assess than body cues for all of the raters.

Rosenberg and Langer (1965) investigated the communicative value of postural-gestural cues in expressing the meaning of an idea without using words. Using the Stick Figure Test (a series of 43 line-drawn stick figures depicting people in various postures), the authors sought to study gestures as a source of information independent of the situational context and of the human element. To examine the meanings conveyed by the various bodily positions of the figures, each stick figure was rated on six dimensions: a feeling dimension (postive-neutral-negative), a vertical dimension (up-down), a horizontal dimension (backward-forward), an achromatic dimension (black-gray-white), a chromatic dimension (red-green-yellow-blue), and a stability dimension (flighty-stable).

Results dealt with areas of interjudge agreement. The highest interjudge agreement occurred in the matching of stick figures with the vertical dimension, the achromatic dimension, and the feeling dimension of meaning. The lowest agreement occurred within the chromatic and horizontal dimensions. In addition, stick figures previously characterized as showing "intense inner dynamics" were precisely the stick figures that yielded the greatest interjudge agreement in the study. Similarly, less interjudge agreement was found on stick figures previously described as having "less emotionally intense inner dynamics [p. 596]." This finding is relevant to the communicative ability of postural-gestural cues in the area of affective information. The authors conclude that more study is needed of the configurational characteristics of postural-gestural activity that mediate modal verbal perceptions (p. 597).

A final study in this first group of investigations, characterized by their quantitative and detailed approach, is Rosenfield's (1966) study on the instrumental affiliative functions of facial and gestural expression. This nonverbal, bodily component of social behavior was viewed as behavior instrumental in satisfying and expressing affiliative motives.

Female undergraduate subjects were stimulated to win or to avoid the approval of another female student. Five postural-gestural cues were recorded in both approval-seeking and approval-avoiding conditions of interaction. Frequency of smiles, positive head nods (bidirectional movement on a vertical plane), negative head nods (bidirectional movement on a lateral plane), gesticulation (free movements of the arm, hand, or finger) self-manipulation (scratching, rubbing, etc), and postural shifts were recorded. Smiles were expected to characterize approval-seekers; gesticulations were expected to inform about involvement and attention; and postural shifts and self-manipulation were expected to indicate discomfort and avoidance. Results showed a positive correlation between the number of smiles and positive nods, but a negative correlation between these two behaviors and third (self-manipulation). The correlation between the number of negative head nods and postural shifts recorded was not significant, and these behavior measures had to be eliminated from the analysis of data.

Generally, the study revealed that overall gestural activity was greater for subjects in the approval-seeking condition, who especially showed a greater number of smiles and gesticulations. A second experiment, to determine the stability of gestural behavior measurement over time, revealed that the gestures were fairly stable (that is, there were low positive correlations), with the exception of self-manipulation. Also, behaviors were correlated with the need for approval. Smiles were found to have a positive correlation with the need for approval. Initially, the remaining gestures correlated negatively with this need; but with repeated interaction, they correlated positively with the need for achievement. Fear of rejection was related to postural shifts.

These findings indicate the instrumental function of certain gestures and their capacity to induce similar responses from others. They are not only signs of approval; they are also instrumental approval-seeking devices. Rosenfield made some additional comments on the possibility that smiles are informative about the nature of the affective state, whereas gesticulations inform about the intensity of the affect. He felt that this was supported by the greater activity observed in the approval-seeking condition, which he characterized as having a higher intensity of emotion. The study concludes with the assertion that the smile, although it has additional functions, is a nonverbal concomitant of approval-seeking behavior, and thus serves an instrumental affiliative function.

CONTEXTUAL ANALYSIS OF NONVERBAL COMMUNICATION

The studies we shall examine in this section as examples of contextual analysis incorporate the concepts and methods of *kinesics,* a term introduced by Birdwhistell (1955) to refer to the "systematic study of how one communicates through body movements and gestures [p. 10]." It emphasizes the patterned and learned aspects of body motion and their "independent" communicative value. This last point only serves to underline the obvious fact that body motion functions in a larger capacity than as a subsidiary to verbal communication. Rather than merely enhancing verbal communication, body motion is equally important to the understanding of the communication process. The basic assumptions that underlie the study of kinesics have been outlined by Birdwhistell (1963):

1. Like other events in nature, no body movement or expression is without meaning in the context in which it appears.
2. Like other aspects of human behavior, body posture, movement and facial expression are patterned and, thus, subject to systematic analysis.
3. While recognizing the possible limitations imposed by particular biological substrata, until otherwise demonstrated, the systematic body motion of the members of a community is considered a function of the social system to which the group belongs.
4. Visible body activity like audible acoustic activity systematically influences the behavior of other members of any particular group.
5. Until otherwise demonstrated such behavior will be considered to have an investigable communicational function.
6. The meanings derived therefrom are functions both of the behavior and of the operations by which it is investigated.
7. The particular biological system and the special life experiences of any individual will contribute idiosyncratic elements to his kinesic system, but the individual or symptomatic quality of these elements can only be assessed following the analysis of the larger system of which his is a part. [p. 158]

Birdwhistell (1962) characterizes communication as a system of interaction with structures independent of a lexical and nonverbal behavior of the individual participant. It is a "continuous process [composed of] isolatable discontinuous units both lexical and behavioral [p. 192]." But the behavioral elements must not be considered subsidiary to the lexical units, with the latter performing the cognitive function and the former mediating the affective function. Birdwhistell recognizes, as do the authors of the studies we reviewed in the previous section, the importance of individual behavior in communicating new information. However, Birdwhistell carries the argument beyond the "oversimplified" function of providing new information to the integrative aspects of the function. Serving this function, the "communicative units operate throughout the sequence of activity" to "relate the communicants to each other and to the content of the interaction [1955, p. 11]." The integrative function keeps the system in operation, gives continuity and predictability to the social system, regulates the interactional process, and cross-references messages, which leads to comprehensibility in the content (1962, p. 196).

Birdwhistell does not seek to examine the individual behavioral units apart from their contexts. Rather the full communicative function of the unit lies in its relationship to the whole, or the larger system. For this reason Birdwhistell does not look at singular kinesic behaviors apart from their interactional system. He does not ask of the individual behavioral units: What does this behavior mean? A list of the meanings of an independent unit of behavior is not valued. Just as "dictionaries of words may stand in the way of language in action so dictionaries of gestures stand in the way of kinesics—the human body in communicative action [1955, p. 13]."

Birdwhistell's early studies revealed that kinesic activity was patterned within the hierarchical structure of the communication system and its parts. As acoustic phoneticians achieved more precise descriptions of language, changes in pitch over the units of the sentence were shown to have a functional relationship with these syntactic elements. The units of the sentence were marked by terminal changes in pitch. A rise in pitch denotes a question, a fall in pitch denotes completion, and constant pitch denotes that the speaker is continuing. Birdwhistell found that movements of the head, eyes, and hands accompanied these changes of pitch throughout the syntactic unit. For instance, the eyelids as markers lowered at the completion of a syntactic unit, widened at the question, and remained half-open at points of continuation. More specifically, raising the eyelids at the end of the statement showed that an answer was expected: it was a postural cue, intended to elicit an answer. Similarly, upward and downward movements corresponding to the pitch changes characterized hand and head movements. Thus, Scheflen (1964) states that in establishing "postural-kinesic markers of the American syntactic structure," Birdwhistell has "effectively searched and found meaning of systematic kinesic activity within the structure of the communication system [p. 321]."

Scheflen (1964) directly continued Birdwhistell's work with postural-kinesic markers. In studying eighteen psychotherapeutic sessions by means of the contextual analysis approach, Scheflen noticed a striking structural similarity among the therapy sessions, regardless of the differences between the schools of psychotherapy and the individual therapists. Generally, he noted that kinesic activity is a reliable indicator of at least three aspects of the communication situation. According to the level of behavior, units of kinesic activity:

1. demarcate the beginnings and endings of structural units of the communication system
2. denote how individual communicants are related to each other
3. mark steps in the program of the interaction (p. 316).

In dealing with the ways in which postural cues mark structural units of the communication, Scheflen further conceptualized successively larger units in the hierarchy of the lexical communication system. Just as the syntactic sentence is preceded by the phoneme and morpheme, it is succeeded by the structural units of the point, the position, and finally the presentation in the therapy session. Scheflen found that posture and postural shifts mark the duration and termination of these structural units. Successively larger units of body posture and postural shifts mark the duration and termination of successively larger structural units in the interactive communication system. After the syntactic sentence, the next level of communication is the *point* (described as the making of a point in a discussion). Head and eye shifts mark the termination of one point and the transition to another. Shifts in the head posture such as turning the head left or right, tilting it, and flexing or extending the neck mark the end of a point in the lexical interchange. These behaviors were found to be quite stereotyped and repetitive throughout therapy. Often themes could be associated with a particular head position. For instance, one head position could be consistently associated with explanation, and another with interruptions. The *position* (a sequence of several points, forming a point of view) constitutes the next structural level in the communication. These periods, and transitions from one to another were marked by gross postural shifts that involved half the body. Especially noticeable was the body shift made from leaning back to leaning forward when a subject was changing from the role of listener to that of speaker in the therapy situation. The largest structural level studied by Scheflen is the *presentation* (the totality of one's positions in a given interaction). Postural markers involve a complete change in location. Thus Scheflen has shown that one function of the individual's bodily activity in communication is to mark units at multiple levels of the structure of a communicative system.

Secondly, he considered postural indicators of the quality of the interpersonal relationship, of how the individuals relate to each other. Three simultaneously occurring dimensions of postural activity were found to give information about the social relationship among the members. The inclusiveness or noninclusiveness of posture defines the space for activities and delimits access to and within the group. Vis-à-vis versus parallel body orientation gives evidence about the types of social activity. Thirdly, congruence and noncongruence of the stance and the positioning of the extremities indicate the association, nonassociation, or dissociation of the group members. An example of how the inclusiveness of a posture delimits the space of activities appears when three individuals sit side by side on the sofa. The outside two cross their legs inward across the space between them, thereby "boxing in" the center person. Vis-à-vis positioning occurs in situations of reciprocal exchange of information and feeling between two persons. Watching television, persons assume parallel positions in relation to each other. This positioning can indicate that only one person is needed to complete the task. Finally, congruence of the posture of body extremities can reveal information such as the similarity or dissimilarity in the roles and views of the group members.

Scheflen concludes his article on the significance of postures in communication with remarks about postural indicators of the progressive steps in the therapy program. On the part of the therapist, there are relationships between his therapeutic maneuvers and his body positions; this makes his postural cues a good source of information about the stage of the therapy session. The therapist's maneuvers are equated with the structural level of points, and are marked by head and eye positions. His tactics are equated with the level of positions, and are marked by gross bodily shifts in posture. In conclusion, Scheflen supported the significance of posture in communication by outlining it as an indicator of structural levels in the communication system, of ways in which the communicants relate, and of steps in the therapy program.

A second article by Scheflen (1965) deals with quasi-courtship behavior in psychotherapy. Again, by using the contextual analysis technique to study the communication system, Scheflen discovered that behaviors similar to those found in American courtship appeared in psychotherapy. In fact, these quasi-courtship elements in kinesic behavior appeared not only in psychotherapy, but also in business meetings and conferences (p. 247).

Scheflen outlined three common activities of early courtship in America: courtship readiness, positioning for courtship, and actions of appeal or invitations. In readiness for courtship, certain organismic changes are combined with token behaviors such as the tie preen in men. Positioning for courtship involves vis-à-vis configuration in a two-party group, or a parallel configuration in a three-party group, in which the two courters form a closed circle by each crossing his legs inward over the space between them. Actions of appeal are such characteristic body motions as swinging the hips in women and gaze-holding or head-cocking in both sexes. Qualifiers of courtship behavior include what Watzlawick, Beavin, and Jackson (1967) call metacommunications (communications about communications, or signals which indicate that, although two sets of behaviors seem to be courtship, they are not). The metacommunication allows a person who knows the rules to distinguish between the two sets of seemingly identical behaviors. Reference to the inappropriate context, such as the comment that "other people are present," is one qualifier of courtship. "Incomplete postural-kinesic involvement," exemplified when two commmunicants sit opposite each other and one person's eyes roam about the room, qualifies the relationship. The omission of important courting behaviors, such as the verbalizing of love while leaning away from your partner, is a qualifier of courtship. Finally, "lexical disclaimers" and "bizarreness of the performance of the courtship elements" serve to qualify the relationship.

In discussing the quasi-courtship complex as an entity, Scheflen notes that a few elemental courting behaviors when put together form a complex courtship pattern. "These same elements, arranged in a different way and combined with qualifiers, make up integrations that resemble courtship but have a quite different significance in an interaction [p. 250]." This set of behaviors is quasi-courtship; it is distinguished from actual courtship by its integration of courtship and qualifier behaviors, its appearance in inappropriate situations, and its thwarted progression, which never concludes in sexual consummation.

Having established the identity of quasi-courtship, Scheflen demonstrated its appearance in psychotherapy. In the psychoanalytic and more conventional psychotherapeutic interview, quasi-courting is covertly postural and kinesic. To bring the patient's conflict to the surface, some psychotherapists employ more overt quasi-courting in a verbal as well as a nonverbal manner. The following example, from a British family therapy session, exemplifies the quasi-courtship behavior typical of psychotherapy:

> Whenever . . . the therapist is in a conversation with either the daughter or the grandmother, the mother moves into courtship readiness and begins coquettish expressions and movements. Both of the other women immediately place a leg across the space between the mother and the therapist, 'boxing in' the mother who then decourts. [p. 252]

In addition to helping to bring forth patients' conflicts, the quasi-courting serves as a device to maintain the system. It helps to maintain communication by balancing the group between too much and too little integration of the members. Quasi-courting occurs in two contexts of disintegration: when one participant withdraws or is excluded, and when there is gender confusion. By soliciting the return of the member and by heightening gender identification, this behavior sustains the group's integration. Also, where the situation calls for it, quasi-courting allows for smooth decourting. When gender confusion persists, when courtship status-ambiguity continues, when quasi-courting by one member is too intense, when the group's state of tension is beyond toleration of further quasi-courtship, and when group members interfere actively with the behavior, then decourting is necessary, and it is facilitated by the presence of the quasi-courtship complex. Thus quasi-courting not only integrates the group, but it also helps to maintain a favorable "range of relatedness" among the members. Scheflen notes that in serving this dual function, quasi-courtship behavior becomes important to psycho-therapy not only as a covert technique, but also as a poten-tial deliberate technique.

CONCLUDING OBSERVATIONS

Consideration of the preceding studies in the light of their results leads us back to our earlier suggestion that we should categorize them according to the different kinds of information they report: affective communication, inter-personal relations, role behavior, and nonverbal behavior as an instrumental affiliative act. Beyond this simple group-ing, overall coordination of the results seems difficult, not because the studies contradict one another, but because they vary so in what specifically they tell about the commu-nicative value of nonverbal behavior. Some studies are more precise than others in delineating which body cues communicate which types of information. This difference is especially evident within the group of studies concerned with the function of postural-gestural cues in affective com-munication.

In addition, the findings can be differentiated in terms of their comprehensiveness, or scope. Thus the findings of Rosenberg and Langer (that postural-gestural cues func-tion as a mediator of verbalized modal perceptions) and those of Rosenfield (that bodily cues function as an instrumental affiliative act) are simple and direct. In contrast, Scheflen's findings on the functions of bodily cues are broader, and are derived from a substantially larger social context. Instead of denoting one particular function of kinesic cues, he outlines several. Just one of his studies shows that they are indicators of the structural levels in the communication system, of the quality of the interpersonal relationship, and of the steps in the therapy program.

Not only is it hard to group the studies according to their results without oversimplification, but the task of clearly dividing the studies on the basis of their methodology is quite difficult. At first the "traditional" and the contextual analysis approaches seemed straightforward and appropriate. A closer examination of the literature reveals a more ambiguous picture, however, with some members of the two groups overlapping in some methodological concerns. While it is true that one group is more quantitative in its approach and the other more descriptive, their respective orientations toward related issues are far less distinct in matters such as interjudge agreement versus interjudge accuracy. It was noted that interjudge agreement was the concern of the first group, while the second group addressed itself to the judges' accuracy. However, Ekman, a member of the "traditional" group with a definite statistical approach, specifically rejected this interest in interjudge agreement, replacing it with a concern for interjudge accuracy. His judgmental task involved the matching of photos with speech samples of previous interviews, ignoring the specific affect depicted. In this respect, then, Ekman is more akin to the contextual analysts.

Secondly, some "traditional" studies are closely aligned with the second group in their strong emphasis on the study of spontaneous interactive bodily motion. The contextual analysts are precisely concerned to study bodily motion or action, as opposed to a body movement or a static act. Further, they emphasize the examination of these patterned bodily motions in the context of communication. The "traditionalists" study posed behavior or spontaneous interactive behavior in a still photograph. Dittman and associates, although members of group one by virtue of their quantitative orientation, break away from that approach in using segments of motion-picture films of body motion as photographic stimuli.

Finally, although the contextual analysis approach seems more interesting for its novelty and comprehensiveness, one cannot conclude that it is decisively more valuable to the extent of back-seating the "traditional" approach. Rather both approaches are informative in the study of nonverbal behavior, and especially so when elements of the two approaches are combined.

REFERENCES

Austin G. 1966. *Chironomia or a Treatise on Rhetorical Delivery.* Carbondale, Ill.: Southern Illinois University Press.

Berelson, B., & M. Janowitz (Eds.). 1953. *Public Opinion and Communication.* New York: The Free Press.

Birdwhistell, R. L. 1955. Background to kinesics. *ETC Review of General Semantics 13:* 10–15.

Birdwhistell, R. L. 1962. An approach to communication. *Family Process 1:* 192–201.

Birdwhistell, R. L. 1963. Kinesic level of the investigation of emotions. In P. Knapp (Ed.), *Expression of the Emotions of Man.* New York: International Universities Press, Inc.

Birdwhistell, R. L. 1970. *Kinesics and Content.* Philadelphia, Pa.: University of Pennsylvania Press.

Bryson, L. (Ed.). 1948. *The Communication of Ideas.* New York: Harper and Brothers.

Dittman, A. T. 1962. Relationship between body movements and moods in interviews. *J. Consulting Psychol. 26:* 480.

Dittman, A. T., M. B. Parloff, & D. S. Boomer. 1965. Facial and bodily expression: A study of receptivity of emotional cues. *Psychiatry 28:* 239–244.

Efron, D. 1972. *Gesture and Environment.* The Hague: Mouton & Co.

Eisenson, J., J. J. Auer, & J. V. Irwin. 1963. *The Psychology of Communication.* New York: Appleton-Century-Crofts.

Ekman, P. 1964. Body positions, facial expression and verbal behavior during interviews. *J. Abnormal and Social Psychol. 68:* 295–301.

Ekman, P. 1965a. Communication through nonverbal behavior: Source of information about the interpersonal relationship. In Silvan S. Tompkins & C. C. Izard (Eds.), *Affect, Cognition, and Personality.* New York: Springer Publishing Co., Inc.

Ekman P. 1965b. Differential communication of affect by head and body cues. *J. Personality and Social Psychol. 2:* 726–735.

Ekman, P., W. Friesen, & P. Ellsworth. 1971. *Emotion in the Human Face.* New York: Pergamon Press, Inc.

Hall, E. T. 1959. *The Silent Language.* Garden City, New York: Doubleday & Company, Inc.

Hall, E. T. 1966. *The Hidden Dimension.* Garden City, New York: Doubleday & Company, Inc.

Holloway, J. 1951. *Language and Intelligence.* London: MacMillan & Co., Ltd.

La Barre, W. 1947. The cultural basis of emotions and gestures. *J. Personality 16:* 49–68.

Lindesmith, H. R., & A. L. Strauss. 1951. *Social Psychology.* New York: The Dryden Press.

Lindzey, G. (Ed.). 1954. *Handbook of Social Psychology.* Reading, Mass.: Addison-Wesley Publishing Co., Inc.

Meerloo, J. A. 1958. *Conversation and Communication.* New York: International Universities Press., Inc.

Mehrabian, A. S. 1972. *Nonverbal Communication.* Chicago: Aldine-Atherton.

Needles, W. 1959. Gesticulation and speech. *Internat. J. Psycho-Analysis 40:* 291–294.

Rosenberg, G., & J. A. Langer. 1965. A study of postural-gestural communication. *J. Personality and Social Psychol. 2:* 593–597.

Rosenfield, H. M. 1966. Instrumental affiliative functions of facial and gestural expressions. *J. Personality and Social Psychol. 4:* 65–72.

Ruesch, J. 1966. Nonverbal language and therapy. In Alfred G. Smith (Ed.), *Communication and Culture: Readings in the Codes of Human Interaction.* New York: Holt, Rinehart & Winston, Inc.

Ruesch, J., & W. Kees. 1964. *Nonverbal Communication.* Berkeley, Cal.: University of California Press.

Sainsbury, P. 1955. Gestural movement during psychiatric interview. *Psychosomatic Med. 17:* 458–469.

Scheflen, A. E. 1964. The significance of posture in communication systems. *Psychiatry 27:* 316–331.

Scheflen, A. E. 1965. Quasi-courtship behavior in psychotherapy. *Psychiatry 28:* 245–257.

Sebeok, T. A., A. S. Hayes, & M. C. Bateson (Eds.). 1964. *Approaches to Semiotic.* The Hague: Mouton & Co.

Thompson, D. F. 1964. Communication of emotional intent by facial expression. *J. Abnormal and Social Psychol. 68:* 129–135.

Watzlawick, P., J. M. Beavin, & D. D. Jackson. 1967. *Pragmatics of Human Communication.* New York: Norton.

5

Expressive Uses of Language

Investigations of the expression of emotion have generally taken two forms: (1) the study of manifest verbal content, and (2) studies of vocal but nonverbal content. Carl Rogers is a well-known pioneer of the former approach; Snyder (1947), Auld and Murray (1955), and Pool (1959) have also centered their efforts on content analysis. Many investigators, however, find that the most useful indicators of emotional meaning are to be sought in the nonlexical area. That is, the important question for affective communication is more *how* something is said than *what* is said. Thus, Ostwald (1963) states that vocal communication carries "information about the soundmaker's emotions, no matter how carefully he tries to hide them behind the acoustic symbols he emits." Normal human speech, then, consists of two simultaneous sets of cues: the articulated sound patterns that convey semantically meaningful material (words, phrases, sentences), and the discriminable qualitative features of the voice itself. Soskin and Kauffman (1961) call the latter set of cues the *carrier* on which articulated sounds are superimposed. Within this carrier may be the major cues to the speaker's emotional disposition.

THEORIES OF EMOTION

Without becoming enmeshed in the diverse arguments over what constitutes emotion, we may note briefly that theories of emotion can be divided roughly into three approaches. First are those that emphasize purely physiological processes; second are those that stress physiological factors plus the organism's awareness of change; and third are those that try to interrelate physiological and cognitive factors. Most investigators have considered emotion from one or the other of these two viewpoints: either that the situation produces some physiological change, which is then interpreted as an emotion, or that the situation precipitates an emotional response, which in turn produces a physiological change within the organism.

Our concern is not with theories of emotion, of course, but most experimental investigations are informed by theory, so it is important at least to realize that there are a welter of conflicting viewpoints. One major attempt at a theoretical synthesis is that of Schachter and Singer (1962), who emphasize the interaction of cognitive and physiological factors in defining emotional states. They note that although various emotional states differ with regard to the organism's overall level of physiological arousal or activation, there are subjective differences in emotional response patterns that nevertheless have the same level of activation. Thus, subjectively different emotional states may be associated with similar physiological reactions. Happiness and anger may produce relatively similar levels of activation, yet they are subjectively different. The differences in these emotional states are explained in terms of the individual's cognitive interpretation of the situation in which he experiences the state of activation. Hence, emotions are determined partly as a function of how a situation is viewed perceptually by the subject; and consideration of the activity level, as well as of cognitive variables, is necessary to determine the specific emotional response.

PARALANGUAGE

Whatever the arguments may be about the nature of emotions, we all respond emotionally to some extent, and we "read" the emotional states of others, sometimes accurately and sometimes not. Psychiatrists and clinical psychologists have to become intuitively responsive to their patients' feelings and emotions (Davitz, 1964). But nonintuitive means must be found to communicate about emotions and the indicators of states of affect. Special vocabularies have been developed by different groups who deal with acoustic phenomena. Musicians speak of intonation, timbre, and tempo; acousticians talk of noise, decibels, and frequencies; linguists speak of pitch, stress, and intonation; and voice therapists describe hoarseness, registers, and melody (Barbara, 1958). Trager (1965) described the acoustic phenomena that accompany language as *paralanguage*. Paralanguage is divided into *voice set* as background for, and *voice qualities* and *vocalizations* as accompaniments of, language proper.

Voice set involves the physiological and physical peculiarities which result in the patterns that identify individuals as members of a societal group, persons of a certain age, sex, state of health, body build, and so forth. Whether we whisper or shout, sound infirm or vigorous, and use a high-pitched or a low-pitched voice are matters of voice set, and have communicative significance. Voice quality can be analyzed into variations in pitch range and control, vocal lip control, control of the glottis, and control of rhythm, articulation, resonance, and tempo, but more simply it is what enables a grown woman to sound like a little girl and a grown man to whine (Trager, 1972). Vocalizations are activities such as laughing and crying, clearing the throat, and in general all of the non-talking noises we make in our social interaction.

According to Trager, different languages are accompanied by different paralanguage systems. Paralanguage, like language, is a cultural system, and is therefore learned and arbitrarily symbolic. Trager suggests that paralanguage is more simply structured than language, but is careful to point out that we should not conjecture that it existed prior to language. As a learned, cultural system, Trager maintains, paralanguage came into being with the invention of language. At the same time, some paralanguage phenomena may have been converted into language. Thus if one goes "Sh!" this is paralanguage, but if that becomes "hush," it has been converted into an item of language.

Dittman and Wynne (1961), exploring Trager's original statement on the paralanguage system (Trager, 1958), analyzed excerpts of psychotherapeutic interviews of varying emotional tone and excerpts from an unrehearsed conversation in a radio broadcast. The authors found the linguistic phenomena to be highly reliable, but concluded that Trager's paralanguage system lacked reliability. Further, the vocal characterizers and vocal segregates occurred too infrequently within the sample to permit a reliability check.

ACOUSTIC ANALYSIS

Part of the difficulty in dealing with the paralanguage concomitants of emotional states, Dittman and Wynne felt, is that language is composed of discrete elements, while emotional communication in speech is composed of continuous phenomena. The idea that the emotional factors in speech are best described as continua is seconded by Osser (1964), Piddington (1963), and others. The notion of continua appears also in the qualitative attributes distinguished by Ostwald (1963), along with the concepts of visualization of sound and acoustic measurement.

Qualitative attributes represent a combination of sensory and interpretative reactions toward a particular sound on the part of the listener. Qualitative attributes are subdivided into seven categories, each of which constitutes a gradient or continuum: (1) *rhythmicity* (from rhythmic to irregular); (2) *intensity* (from loud to soft); (3) *pitch* (from high to low); (4) *tone* (from tonal to noisy); (5) *speed* (from fast to slow); (6) *shape* (from impulsive to reverberant); and (7) *orderliness* (from compact to expanded). Most of these are more or less apparent, but the last two may need a bit of clarification. Shape pertains to the onset, growth, steadiness, duration, decay, and termination of an individual sound. A pistol shot, for example, has a sudden beginning, a rapid rise to peak intensity, and a quick decay to silence. The subjective experience is that of an abrupt, crashing sound. Orderliness is a gradient from order along the continuum toward the expanded pole, where the effect is chaotic, monotonous, dissonant, perhaps the way a foreign language sounds the first time it is heard.

Visualization and acoustic measurement refer simply to the transposition of sounds to other media. Scripts, for example, permit visualization. The International Phonetic Alphabet includes graphic symbols that permit rather fine representations of speech sounds. Acoustic measurements include even finer possibilities. Through the use of acoustic filters (analogous in their function to chemical filters), it is possible to separate sounds into their frequency components. Filters of varying fineness permit the study of different bands of the spectrum of sound in terms of their energy levels (Scott, 1957). Band-pass filters are of two kinds: fixed and adjustable. Fixed band-pass filters divide the sound spectrum into bands of equal sizes (octaves, half-octaves, and so on) from 20 cycles per second to 20,000 cycles per second. Adjustable band-pass filters permit the measurement of sound energy levels at points anywhere across the frequency spectrum. The amount of energy passed by each filter can be measured by a meter, or depicted visually by means of the sound spectrograph.

SPEECH AND EMOTION

Ostwald (1963) divides speech into two classes: denotative and emotive. Denotative speech is defined as that portion of verbal behavior which can be understood by reference to vocabulary, grammar, and other formal rules of language. Emotive speech starts with transcendental words and phrases capable of rapid fluctuations in meaning, and goes on to the borderland of linguistics.

Diversification of content characterizes the verbal utterances of persons in a state of heightened affect. The verbal flow of such speakers contains more words, and a greater variety of words, than do the utterances of persons with lowered affect, such as the mildly and more severely depressed; their speech contains few words and tends to include verbal repetition. These observations are consistent with the findings of Zipf in his studies on the relationship between emotional states and articulateness of meaning (Zipf, 1965). Whatmough (1956) also agrees: "A relationship between frequencies and affectivity is demonstrable. Low frequency goes with high affectivity [p. 212]."

Newman and Mather (1938), in their study of persons with affective disorders, found that patients in heightened affective states spoke with high diversification of content, while patients in low affective states spoke with low diversification of content. Other characteristics of the utterances of persons with affective disorders are summarized in Table 5–1.

Davitz (1964) classified speech as conveying information in vocal and verbal modes, the vocal mode being the acoustic attributes of speech, and the verbal mode the content of the speech. The meaning of a sample of speech, including its emotional meaning, is a function of what is said and how it is said, that is, the interaction of the verbal and vocal aspects of the total message. Davitz ties in these two modes with Schachter's theory of emotion; and although the evidence is not clear-cut, he suggests that perhaps the verbal aspect of speech primarily reflects the cognitive determinants of emotional states, while the vocal aspects are a function of the speaker's state of activation.

Some indirect support for this view is provided by the results of Davitz's research (which we shall discuss in detail later) on the vocal correlates of emotional expressions. Briefly, these findings indicate that subjectively active feel-

Table 5–1

ANALYSIS OF SPEECH CHARACTERISTICS OF 40 PATIENTS WITH AFFECTIVE DISORDERS*

	Depression	Mania
Articulatory movements	lax	vigorous
Pitch range	narrow	wide
Pitch changes	stepwise; infrequent	gliding; frequent
Emphatic accents	absent or rare	frequent
Pauses	hesitating	accented
Resonance	nasal	oral
Level of style	colloquial	elevated
Syntactic elaboration	meager	rich
Syntactic techniques	limited	diversified
Initiation of response	slow	quick
Length of response	short	long

*After Newman and Mather (1938).

ings tend to be communicated by a loud voice, with a relatively high pitch, flaring timbre, and fast rate of speech. In contrast, subjectively passive feelings are communicated by a softer voice, with a relatively lower pitch, more resonant timbre, and slower rate of speech. Therefore, if we assume that subjective emotional activity parallels physiological activation, the vocal aspects of speech may well reflect the level of activation associated with particular emotional states.

It would be unreasonable to assume that there is a one-to-one relation between physiological activation and subjective activity. The social situation must be considered, and so must the various social conventions that influence patterns of communication. Nevertheless, other things being equal, a person in a highly activated state probably tends to behave in ways that involve a relatively high expenditure of energy. Thus the activation dimension of emotional states is reflected to some extent in the forms of behavior that communicate emotional meanings.

Emotional Meaning and Vocal Expression

In order to investigate more effectively the communication of emotional meaning through vocal expression, three major techniques have been used to eliminate or control the verbal information conveyed by speech. In some studies, speakers attempt to express feelings by merely reciting the alphabet or by counting; this is based on the assumption that neither letters nor numerals carry meaning relevant to emotional communication (Davitz and Davitz, 1959a; Dusenberry and Knower, 1939). Other researchers have utilized standard verbal content that is presumably emotionally neutral; speakers recite the same few sentences while trying to express different feelings, so that whatever emotional meaning is communicated depends upon vocal rather than verbal cues (Pronovost and Fairbanks, 1939; Pollack, Rubenstein, and Horowitz, 1960). Still other researchers have capitalized on electronic filtering techniques that substantially decrease the verbal content of tape-recorded utterances without destroying the simultaneous emotional communication carried by certain vocal characteristics of speech (Soskin and Kauffman, 1961; Starkweather, 1956).

Ruckmick (1936) reviewed some earlier studies on the relationship of vocal expressions to emotions. In these studies changes in the pitch and intensity of voice, in its vibrato and in its general pattern, were visualized and analyzed through photographic recordings. The recordings were of dramatic and conversational performances, made by competent speech performers. The results generally indicated that heightened feelings definitely tended to find vocal expression at the higher end of the performer's pitch range, and neutral and depressed states to be expressed at the lower end of the pitch range.

In a series of studies by Pronovost and Fairbanks (1939), the relationship of pitch to simulated emotion was reported, and an analysis was made of the pitch characteristics of key affective states. The results are shown in Table 5–2.

Table 5–2

PITCH CHARACTERISTICS OF KEY AFFECTIVE STATES*

Simulated Emotion	Median Pitch Level	Total Pitch Range	Inflectional Range	Pitch Change
Contempt	low	wide	moderate	moderate
Anger	high	wide	widest	most rapid
Fear	highest	widest	moderate	moderate
Grief	low	narrow	narrowest	slowest
Indifference	lowest	narrowest	moderate	moderate

*After Pronovost and Fairbanks (1939).

Both Ruckmick's survey and the Pronovost and Fairbanks studies uphold the common observation that happy and angry persons who give voice to their feelings do so at higher pitch levels than sad or "indifferent" persons. Skinner (1935), on the other hand, believed that force was a more reliable index than pitch in the differentiation of the vocal reactions of happiness and sadness. He found that in happy states, vocal expressions are characterized by an increase in the use of force, while in sad states they are characterized by a reduction.

In a study by Davitz and Davitz (1959a), the investigators instructed each of 8 speakers to express 10 different feelings by reciting parts of the alphabet. These vocal expressions were tape-recorded and the recordings were played to 30 judges, who were given a list of 10 feelings and asked to identify the emotional meaning conveyed by each expression. Like all other researchers in this area, Davitz and Davitz found that on the average, feelings were communicated far beyond chance expectation. The accuracy with which the vocal expressions of the different speakers were recognized varied markedly, however; one speaker's expressions were identified correctly in only 23% of the cases, while another speaker communicated accurately well over 50% of the time. Listeners, too, showed a wide range of accuracy, varying from 20% correct to almost 50% correct. And finally, as most other studies have reported, the accuracy with which different feelings were communicated clearly differed; anger, for example, was communicated accurately over 63% of the time, while pride was identified correctly in only 20% of the cases.

Differences in the accuracy with which various feelings are communicated have been reported in several studies. Pfaff (1953) found that out of nine categories of feeling that he investigated, joy and hate were most accurately communicated, while shame and love were the most difficult to recognize. These kinds of difference are consistently mentioned in the literature, but only one relatively minor study has focused specifically on an attempt to account for this phenomenon. Beginning with the observation that the identification of an expression of emotion is essentially a problem in discrimination, Davitz and Davitz (1959b) reasoned that the subjective similarity of the feelings portrayed should be inversely related to the ease of discriminating between expressions of these feelings. For example, it would seem reasonable to expect greater difficulty in discriminating between anger and impatience than between anger and sadness. The results of their research generally support this position, though the data demonstrate that subjective similarity among feelings accounts for only a small part of the variation in accuracy of communication. Davitz and Davitz also report that given expressions of two similar feelings, such as anger and impatience, the subjectively stronger of the two feelings is communicated more accurately. Beyond these preliminary findings, the literature provides no answer to the question of why various feelings are communicated with different levels of accuracy.

The research has not been especially productive in defining the vocal cues that convey specific emotional meanings. Undoubtedly this is partly a function of the complex technical difficulties involved in the measurement of vocal characteristics (Scott, 1958; Dittman and Wynne, 1961).

The results of an early study by Dusenberry and Knower (1939) suggest that the sequential pattern of speech provides important cues for the recognition of emotional meaning. Testing this hypothesis in a later, more carefully designed study, Knower (1941) compared recordings of vocal expressions played backwards with those played in normal sequence. He found that the reversed expressions were recognized beyond chance expectation, but that the accuracy of the judgments was greatly impaired. He therefore concluded that the sequential pattern of speech was a significant aspect of emotional expression; but subsequent research has by and large failed to follow this lead in defining the particular sequences of vocal cues that are associated with the communication of various meanings.

If the sequence of cues is an important component of speech that carries emotional meaning, the next step in research would seem to be specification of the vocal characteristics that are involved in this sequential pattern. Two studies suggest that the rate, pitch, and timing of pauses in a vocal utterance are consistently related to the meanings expressed. Fairbanks and Hoaglin (1941) reported that the expression of feelings such as anger, grief, and contempt may be differentiated in terms of rate, ratio of pause time to phonation time, and aspects of pitch such as range and the rate of range. For example, anger tends to be expressed at a relatively fast rate; grief at a high ratio of pause time to phonation time; and fear at a relatively high pitch.

These findings notwithstanding, feelings can apparently be communicated accurately even when the range and specificity of the vocal stimulus is markedly reduced. Knower (1941), for example, found that even when speakers whispered (which eliminates the fundamental frequency of the normal voice), the accuracy of listeners in identifying emotions was four times that to be expected by chance. Pollack *et al.* (1960) also reported that the emotional meanings expressed by samples of whispered speech, played under increasing ratios of noise to signal, were identified at above chance levels of accuracy. Perhaps even more striking, they found that speech samples as short as 60 milliseconds could communicate emotion.

Thus, regardless of the technique used, all studies so far reported agree that adults can communicate emotional meaning accurately by vocal expression. The research to date also offers a few limited clues about the vocal characteristics of emotional expression, but these clues have not been consistently helpful in identifying the speech correlates of particular emotional states.

Dimitrovsky (1962) centered her study on the development of sensitivity to the vocal communication of emotion during childhood. Her subjects were children aged from five to twelve. They were asked to identify vocal expressions of four categories of emotion: love, happiness, sadness, and anger. The subjects heard tapes and were then asked to point to one of four stick-figure drawings which represented the above four categories. The subjects were, in addition, given a test of verbal intelligence. Dimitrovsky found that the children's ability to identify correctly the emotional meaning of vocal expression increased with age, as was to be expected. Yet there was no marked, consistent difference in the pattern of correct and incorrect responses made by the subjects at the various age levels from five to twelve. In addition, she found that "children at all age levels favored the emotions with negative valence, giving the responses 'sad' and 'angry' more than the responses 'happy' and 'loving'." From this she concluded that "the tendency to respond in terms of negative emotional meaning appears to be peculiarly characteristic of children."

One might question the above conclusions on the grounds that negative emotions are perhaps simply easier to identify, given the experimenter's statement that "expressions of sadness were most frequently identified." This was followed in frequency by the identification of expressions of anger. It seems, then, that rather than favoring emotions with negative content, the children perhaps only found them easier to identify. One wishes that Dimitrovsky had followed this study by a similar experiment with adults, to determine whether they, too, identified the negative emotions more frequently. Data of this kind would permit some evaluation of her statement that the tendency to respond in terms of negative emotional meaning is peculiarly characteristic of children.

A number of studies have used electronic filtering techniques that decrease the verbal content of the utterances without destroying the emotional communication provided by the vocal characteristics of speech. Among these studies is one by Kramer (1963). Paragraphs were read and taped by American actors, who tried to portray five different emotions. Japanese actors also tried to portray the same emotions in Japanese. Listeners made judgments of the emotions presented in normal recordings of the test passage in English, recordings in filtered English, and recordings in Japanese. Kramer concludes that:

> . . . the over-all percentage of correct matches was approximately the same for normal filtered recordings of portrayals by the American actors. The previous literature has assumed that the only difference in judgment between normal and filtered speech was due to the absence of words in the latter. Present study shows that this is not true; knowledge of how a person judges normal speech permits no prediction of how he will judge filtered speech.

Kramer also found that the judges were able to match emotions correctly with those that were portrayed in Japanese, though not all emotions were as easy for Americans to recognize in Japanese. This study not only shows the type of thing that can be done with electronic equipment, it also indicates the interest that has been shown in cross-cultural studies in this area.

Adams (1964), for example, made a cross-cultural study of expressive communication in an Egyptian village. In this village, friendliness, hostility, and other emotional attitudes were conveyed by subtle qualities of tone, pitch, and melody. Content had little to do with expressive communication, since content was often rote. In addition, Adams discovered that the "presentational meanings" in one culture differ greatly in another. For example, the speech melody and rhythm that connote "sincerity" in Egypt usually seem to an American to sound "cross" or "belligerent."

SENSITIVITY TO VOCAL EXPRESSIONS OF EMOTION

Research focused on the factors that determine the accuracy of recognition of vocal expressions of emotion is rather limited. There are, nonetheless, a few studies that suggest some possible correlates of sensitivity to vocal expression.

Gates (1927) noted that the age and intelligence of children were both positively correlated with their accuracy in identifying the emotional expression of one speaker. Dimitrovsky (1962) found that girls were more accurate than boys in judging vocal expression of feeling. This raises the question of whether there are differences between the sexes in the ability to perceive and express emotional meaning. Levy (1962) found no significant differences between the sexes in either ability. Her original hypothesis was that women show greater accuracy in these judgments than men, yet this contention was not supported by the experimental evidence. Dusenberry and Knower (1939) found that the women in their sample were superior to the men in the accuracy of their judgments, but the difference was not statistically significant. Pfaff (1954) reported a statistically significant difference in college women, who showed greater accuracy than an equivalent sample of men. Fay and Middleton (1940), on the other hand, failed to find reliable differences in sensitivity between men and women. Thus the studies concerned with differences between the sexes in the ability to recognize vocal expressions of emotion present, on the whole, a confusing and contradictory picture.

Beldoch (1961) conducted research on the possible interrelations between various modes of emotional communication. He raised the question of whether there is a general factor of sensitivity to emotional expression, or whether people may be sensitive to one mode of emotional expression without being especially sensitive to other modes. Although he reported finding significant correlations between the abilities to identify the expression of emotion in three different media (music, abstract art, and tape-recorded recitations), he concluded that the abilities are independent of each other in many ways.

Levitt (1962) also discounted the possibility that the identification of emotional meaning in various expressive modes could be explained in terms of some general factor. In his examination of the comparative communicative efficiency of vocal, facial, and combined vocal-facial modes, he determined that feelings were communicated more effectively by the facial than by the vocal mode.

RESEARCH BY DAVITZ

In a study by Davitz (1964), an attempt was made to identify the perceptual and cognitive processes likely to be involved in recognition of the emotional meaning of a vocal expression.

To begin with the vocal expression itself: it seems obvious that emotional meaning must be conveyed by auditory cues in vocal expressions. Therefore, it was assumed that in order to understand the meanings expressed, the listener must first be able to discriminate the auditory cues that carry these meanings.

Hearing the vocal cues of expression might be necessary for understanding, but it did not seem a sufficient basis on which to identify the meanings expressed. In one pattern or another, the nonverbal characteristics of speech, tone, timbre, inflection, and so on combine to represent symbolically a specific emotional meaning, and though the exact patterns of cues associated with various meanings cannot be defined with great precision, it is obvious that these patterns of interrelated vocal characteristics are complex symbolic stimuli. Therefore, to respond appropriately to these stimuli, to "understand" and identify the meanings expressed by these complex, nonverbal symbols, a listener must presumably have the cognitive ability to deal with abstract symbols, to perceive and meaningfully organize the numerous subtle, nonverbal characteristics that comprise a vocal symbol with emotional meaning.

Having perceived and somehow organized the vocal stimulus in his mind; a listener is required to interpret its emotional meaning. Although there is no explicit, standardized dictionary that defines emotions in terms of their vocal cues, reliable communication would seem unlikely without at least some implicit knowledge, on the listener's part, of the more or less conventional vocal cues of emotional meaning.

Since the subjects of these tests were required to name or label the feeling expressed, and to name it involved some sort of verbal ability, it was reasoned that verbal ability would probably be associated with the ability to identify emotional meanings.

The subjects were 61 graduate students, and the following variables were measured for each subject: (1) ability to make auditory discriminations, (2) abstract symbolic ability, (3) knowledge of the vocal characteristics of emotional expression, (4) verbal intelligence, and (5) ability to identify vocal expressions of emotional meaning. Under auditory discrimination, the following four dimensions were tested: (1) pitch, (2) loudness, (3) time, and (4) timbre.

The subjects' ability to identify vocal expressions of emotional meaning was measured by means of a 45-item tape-recording, which contained expressions of 8 different emotional meanings plus 5 unemotional or neutral items. Using a standard-content technique, speakers expressed each of the following emotional meanings: affection, anger, boredom, cheerfulness, impatience, joy, sadness, and satisfaction (see Table 5–3).

The study of perceptual and cognitive correlates yielded positive results. Each of the four variables (pitch, loudness, time, and timbre) was found to be positively related to a measure of ability to identify vocal expressions of emotional meaning, and a multiple correlation of 0.60 was obtained between a combination of all four variables and the measure of emotional sensibility. The results of this study support the view that emotional sensitivity can be conceptualized in terms of complex stimuli, intervening perceptual and symbolic processes, and subsequent verbal responses.

In another study, Davitz (1964) investigated some of the auditory cues associated with vocal expressions of emotional meaning. To explore this problem, two sets of variables were selected: one was concerned with dimensions of emotional meaning, the other with auditory characteristics of speech. The variables involved in emotional meaning were based on the research of Osgood, Suci, and Tannenbaum (1957), which yielded three aspects of emotional meaning: valence, strength, and activity. The speech variables used included loudness, pitch, timbre, and speed. The study considered the relation between each of the three variables of emotional meaning and each of the four speech variables.

Four female and three male speakers each expressed 14 different feelings in standard-content speech. In terms of content, the same 2 sentences were embedded in 14 different paragraphs, each paragraph designed to express one of the 14 emotions. The speakers read each paragraph designed to express a particular feeling, plus an unemotional paragraph. These readings were tape-recorded and

Table 5-3

CHARACTERISTICS OF VOCAL EXPRESSIONS CONTAINED IN THE TEST OF EMOTIONAL SENSITIVITY*

Feeling	Loudness	Pitch	Timbre	Rate	Inflection	Rhythm	Enunciation
Affection	soft	low	resonant	slow	steady & slight upward	regular	slurred
Anger	loud	high	blaring	fast	irregular up & down	irregular	clipped
Boredom	moderate to low	moderate to low	moderate resonant	moderate slow	monotone or gradient falling	—	somewhat slurred
Cheerfulness	moderate high	moderate high	moderate blaring	moderate fast	up & down	regular	
Impatience	normal	normal moderate high	moderate blaring	moderate fast	slight upward	—	somewhat clipped
Joy	loud	high	moderate blaring	fast	upward	regular	—
Sadness	soft	low	resonant	slow	downward	irregular pauses	slurred
Satisfaction	normal	normal	somewhat resonant	normal	slight upward	regular	somewhat slurred

*After Davitz (1964).

the two standard sentences embedded in each paragraph were spliced, so as to provide a recording of different emotional expressions with standard content.

The 14 feelings expressed were: admiration, affection, amusement, anger, boredom, cheerfulness, despair, disgust, dislike, fear, impatience, joy, satisfaction, and surprise. The recordings of all 7 speakers were judged by 20 persons, who were given the list of 14 feelings and asked to identify the feeling expressed, using the unemotional reading of each speaker as a base.

A final tape, which consisted of the reading of those feelings identified most frequently for male speakers and for female speakers, plus the unemotional reading by each of these speakers, was played to a second set of 20 judges, who were asked to rate each expression on four 7-point scales: (1) loudness (loud to soft); (2) pitch (high to low); (3) timbre (blaring to resonant); (4) rate of speech (fast to slow). In these ratings, the unemotional recordings of the speakers were also used as a base line. The recordings were rated on 9 scales of the Semantic Differential by a third set of 20 judges. Each of the three dimensions was represented by three scales: *valence* by (1) good to bad; (2) pleasant to unpleasant; (3) beautiful to ugly; *strength* by (1) strong to weak; (2) large to small; (3) heavy to light; and *activity* by (1) fast to slow; (2) active to passive; (3) sharp to dull.

The data were analyzed by correlating each of the dimensions of emotional meaning with each of the vocal characteristics of speech. The correlation of activity with each auditory variable was statistically significant.

These data, plus those collected in another study by Davitz (on erroneous judgments of vocal expressions of feeling), support the generalization that loudness, pitch, timbre, and rate of speech are a function of the subjective rating of the activity level of the emotion communicated. Valence and strength are presumably communicated by other, perhaps more subtle and complex, auditory cues.

Concluding Observations

In the studies we have reviewed, the form and content of emotional expressions have been treated separately. That is, either the studies have involved vocal expressions with standardized content, and hence have controlled the information conveyed by the verbal aspects of the message, or the content has been analyzed only with regard to the relative amount of diversification. But since in normal conversation meanings are communicated both vocally and verbally, an important problem for further research is the interaction of these components of speech in the determination of meaning.

References

Adams, J. B. 1965. On expressive communication in an Egyptian village. In Dell Hymes (Ed.), *Language in Culture and Society.* New York: Harper & Row, Publishers.

Auld, F., & E. J. Murray. 1955. Content-analysis studies of psychotherapy. *Psychological Bulletin 52:* 377–395.

Beranek, L. 1954. *Acoustics.* New York: McGraw-Hill Book Company.

Barbara, D. A. (Ed.). 1958. *Your Speech Reveals Your Personality.* Springfield, Ill.: Charles C. Thomas, Publisher.

Bekesy, G. von. 1960. *Experiments in Hearing.* New York: McGraw-Hill Book Company.

Beldoch, M. 1961. The ability to identify expressions of feeling in vocal, graphic, and musical communication. *Dissertation Abstracts 22:* 1246.

Carroll, R. P. 1937. *Emotion.* Washington, D.C.: Daylion Company.

Davitz, J. R. 1964. *The Communication of Emotional Meaning.* New York: McGraw-Hill Book Company.

Davitz, J. R., & L. Davitz. 1959a. The communication of feelings by content-free speech. *J. Communication 9:* 6–13.

Davitz, J. R., & L. Davitz. 1959b. Correlates of accuracy in the communication of feelings. *J. Communication 9:* 110–117.

De Rivera, J. H. 1962. A decision theory of the emotions. *Dissertation Abstracts 23:* 296–297.

Dimitrovsky, L. S. 1962. The ability to identify the emotional meaning of vocal expression at successive age levels. *Dissertation Abstracts 24:* 2983.

Dittman, A. T., & C. Wynne. 1961. Linguistic techniques and the analysis of emotionality in interviews. *J. Abnormal and Social Psychol. 63:* 201–204.

Dusenberry, D., & F. H. Knower. 1938. Experimental studies of the symbolism of action and voice. I. A study of the specificity of meaning in facial expression. *Quarterly J. Speech 24:* 424–435.

Dusenberry, D., & F. H. Knomer. 1939. Experimental studies of the symbolism of action and voice. II. A study of the specificity of meaning in abstract tonal symbols. *Quarterly J. Speech 25:* 67–75.

Eisenson, J., J. Auer, & J. V. Irwin. 1963. *The Psychology of Communication.* New York: McGraw-Hill Book Company.

Fairbanks, G., & L. W. Hoaglin. 1941. An experimental study of the durational characteristics of the voice during expressions of emotion. *Speech Monographs 8:* 85–90.

Fay, P. J., & W. C. Middleton. 1940. The ability to judge the rested or tired condition of a speaker from his voice as transmitted over a public address system. *J. Applied Psychol. 24:* 645–650.

Gates, G. S. 1927. The role of the auditory element in the interpretation of emotions. *Psychol. Bulletin 24:* 175 (Abstr.).

Knapp, P. H. (Ed.). 1963. *Expressions of Emotion in Man.* New York: International Universities Press, Inc.

Knower, F. H. 1941. Analysis of some experimental variations of simulated vocal expressions of the emotions. *J. Social Psychol. 14:* 369–372.

Knower, F. H. 1945. Studies in the symbolism of voice and action. V. The use of behavioral and tonal symbols as tests of speaking achievement. *J. Applied Psychol. 29:* 229–235.

Kramer, E. R. 1963. Judgment of portrayed emotion from normal English, filtered English, and Japanese speech. *Dissertation Abstracts 24:* 1699–1700.

Kramer, E. R. 1964. Elimination of verbal cues in judgments of emotion from voice. *J. Abnormal and Social Psychol. 68:* 390–396.

Krech, D., & R. S. Crutchfield. 1958. *Elements of Psychology.* New York: Alfred A. Knopf, Inc.

Levitt, E. A. 1962. The relationship between vocal and facial emotion communicative abilities. *Dissertation Abstracts 23:* 1783.

Levy, P. K. 1962. The relationship between the ability to express and to perceive vocal communication of feeling. *Dissertation Abstracts 22: 4082–4083.*

Licklider, J. C. R. 1951. Basic correlates of the auditory stimulus. In S. S. Stevens (Ed.), *Handbook of Experimental Psychology.* New York: John Wiley & Sons, Inc.

Newman, S., & V. G. Mather. 1938. Analysis of spoken language of patients with affective disorders. *Amer. J. Psychol. 94:* 913–942.

Osgood, C. E., G. J. Suci, & P. H. Tannenbaum. 1957. *The Measurement of Meaning.* Urbana, Ill.: University of Illinois Press.

Osser, H. A. 1964. A distinctive feature analysis of the vocal communication of emotion. *Dissertation Abstracts 25:* 3708.

Ostwald, P. F. 1963. *Soundmaking.* Springfield, Ill.: Charles C. Thomas, Publisher.

Pfaff, P. L. 1954. An experimental study of the communication of feeling without contextual material. *Speech Monographs 21:* 155–156.

Piddington, R. 1963. *The Psychology of Laughter.* New York: Gamut Press.

Pollock, I., H. Rubenstein, & A. Horowitz. 1960. Communication of verbal modes of expression. *Language and Speech 3:* 121–130.

Pool, I. S. 1963. Content analysis. In P. H. Knapp (Ed.), *Expressions of Emotion in Man.* New York: International Universities Press, Inc.

Pronovost, W., & G. Fairbanks. 1939. An experimental study of the pitch characteristics of the voice during the expression of emotion. *Speech Monographs 6:* 87–104.

Ruckmick, C. A. 1936. *The Psychology of Feeling and Emotion.* New York: McGraw-Hill Book Company.

Schachter, S., & J. Singer. 1962. Cognitive, social, and psychological determinants of emotional states. *Psychol. Rev. 69:* 379–399.

Scott, H. H. 1957. Noise measuring techniques. In C. Harris (Ed.), *Handbook of Noise Control.* New York: McGraw-Hill Book Company.

Scott, W. C. M. 1958. Noise, speech, and technique. *Internat. J. Psycho-Analysis 39:* 108–111.

Skinner, E. R. 1935. A calibrated recording and analysis of the pitch, force, and quality of vocal tones expressing happiness and sadness; and a determination of the pitch and force of the subject. Concepts of ordinary soft and loud tones. *Speech Monographs 2:* 81–137.

Smith, W. W. 1922. *The Measurement of Emotion.* New York: Harcourt, Brace & World, Inc.

Snyder, W. U. 1947. The present status of psychotherapeutic counseling. *Psychol. Bull. 44:* 297.

Soskin, W. F., & P. E. Kauffman. 1961. Judgment of emotion in word-free voice samples. *J. Communication 11:* 73–80.

Starkweather, J. A. 1956. The communication value of content-free speech. *Amer. J. Psychol. 69:* 121–123.

Trager, G. L. 1965. Paralanguage: A first approximation. In Dell Hymes (Ed.), *Language in Culture and Society.* New York: Harper & Row, Publishers.

Trager, G. L. 1972. *Language and Languages.* San Francisco: Chandler Publishing Co.

Whatmough, J. 1956. *Language.* New York: St. Martin's Press, Inc.

Zipf, G. R. 1965. *The Psycho-Biology of Language.* Cambridge, Mass.: The M.I.T. Press.

6

Sound
Symbolism
in
Language

Wolfgang Köhler (1947) credits the German poet Morgenstern with the observation that "All seagulls look as though their names were Emma" *(Die Möwen sehen alle aus, als ob sie Emma hiessen)*. The name flows as smoothly as the bird, but we *hear* the name and *see* the bird. Evidently we are somehow able to enjoy some part of the same subjective experience through different sensory modalities. The point can be made even more clearly if we ask subjects to match Köhler's (1947) nonsense words *maluma* and *takete* to the shapes given in Figure 6.1 (Köhler, 1947, p. 225). Again, nearly everyone reveals in his match a feeling that the smoothly convoluted figure best fits the sound series that is uninterrupted by stoppages in the flow of breath.

In speaking of language, the term "symbolism" ordinarily refers to the arbitrary relationship that obtains between a sound sequence or word and its referent. That is, the object that this word describes may be represented by

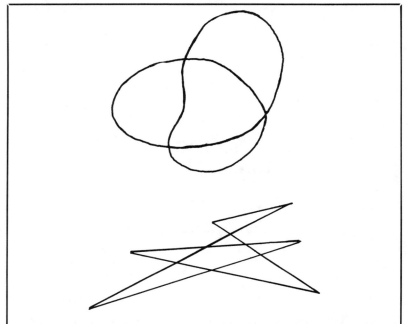

Figure 6.1. STIMULUS FIGURES TO ACCOMPANY TAKETE AND MALUMA. (Reprinted by permission from W. Köhler, *Gestalt Psychology*, New York: Liveright, 1947, p. 225.)

virtually any sound sequence, so long as the parties in communication understand that the connection exists. We say "book," but the Japanese say *hon*, the French *livre*, and so on. The type of symbolism we are discussing now is what Sapir (1929) called "a more fundamental, a psychologically primary sort of symbolism;" this he defined as expressive symbolism. This kind of symbolism certainly operates within specific languages, and possibly even universally.

Giving an English example of this phenomenon in which the affective component of meaning exceeds the referential component, Markel (1961) argued that there is a common affective connotation in many /gl-/ words: glad, glance, glass, gleam, glimpse, glitter, globe, glove, and glow. In the same vein, but somewhat earlier, Bolinger (1950) analyzed both the initial sounds and the residues in the following two series: glitter, glow, glare, and flitter, flow, flare. Thus the /gl/ indicates phenomena of light, /fl/ phenomena of movement, /itr/ intermittent, /ow/ steady, and /r/ intense. Similar examples are to be found in German, where initial /gr-/ seems to indicate the connotation "sinister, eerie": *grasslich, grauen, grausig, Greuel, greulich, gruselig.*

Needless to say, phonetic, or sound, symbolism is not peculiar to Indo-European languages. Samuel Martin (1964) suggests that Korean may be the champion, since it has more than a thousand lexemes that do not occur simply as isolated items: each is a whole set of words, with systematic variations in shape that correspond to subtle but structured differences in connotation. And Arabic has extensive, complex networks of connotative relationships, connected by means of the sound symbolism implicit in root radicals. To take but a single illustration, many words that contain *gh*ayn (no close English approximation of this letter is possible) as the first radical connote "concealment, darkness, obscurity." Thus we have *ghaaba* (to set, as the sun), *ghaara* (to seep into the ground), *ghabasa* (to become dark), *ghabana* (to hoodwink, gyp), *ghataa* (to cover, conceal), *ghatasa* (to immerse, submerge), *ghamma* (to cloud over), *ghilaaf* (covering, book jacket), and so on, for many more words. The early nineteenth-century French grammarian Antoine Fabre d'Olivet made a similar study of Hebrew, another Semitic language (Whorf, 1956).

The hazards of this line of inquiry are clear: semantic continuity may be governed only by the imagination of the investigator. Benjamin Lee Whorf, for example, saw "dispersal" in a set of words with Maya roots that included "sand," "white," "weave cloth," "much," and "dislocate." This was a bit much, even for the generally sympathetic Sapir (Carroll, 1956, p. 24). Whorf (1956) was on intuitively stronger ground when he suggested that the reason we will pronounce hypothetical new words such as "thog," "thag," "thig," and "thuzzle" with the *th* value found in "thin" and "threw" is that the voiced value of th occurs initially only in the cryptotype of demonstrative particles such as the, this, that, than, those, and so forth.

In order to place intuition under a tighter rein and provide systematic guidance to the study of phonetic symbolism, two kinds of empirical study have been made. They were classed according to their methodologies by Taylor (1963): one class is analytical, the other is word-matching. The analytical methodologies vary considerably, but the subject is generally asked to judge sounds of nonsense words along one or more dimensions of connotative meaning (size, roundness, movement, and so on). In the word-matching methodologies the subject is presented with pairs of words (usually antonymic) from two languages, at least one of which is unknown to him. He is then asked to match the corresponding members of the pairs in the two languages; significantly correct guessing is assumed to indicate that some type of phonetic symbolism is in operation. In a variation of the analytic methodology, subjects are asked to pair words in an artificial language with English stimulus words (for example, see Johnson, Suzuki, and Olds, 1964). As in the case of experiments that use stimulus materials drawn from natural languages, substantial agreement is interpreted as evidence for the presence of sound symbolism.

ANALYTIC STUDIES

The first published study of empirical phonetic symbolism was that of Edward Sapir (1929), who felt that some phonetic symbolism must be universal rather than language-specific. He had noted, for example, that "teeny" is smaller than "tiny;" this corresponds to the different sizes of the oral cavity when the vowels of each are pronounced. Sapir's analytical experiments tested the symbolic magnitude of different consonants and vowels. In his first experiment, he presented the subjects with pairs of consonant-vowel-consonant (CVC) nonsense syllables that differed by a single character, and asked them to rate the syllables on a scale of relative magnitude. For example, subjects were told that "mal" and "mil" both meant "table," and were asked which word designated the larger table. More than 75% of the subjects consistently selected "mal" as larger than "mil," which again parallels the difference in the size of the oral cavity.

In a second experiment, Sapir (1929) presented 500 subjects with 100 word pairs, each representing a different phonetic contrast. Again he found that "symbolic discriminations run encouragingly parallel to the objective ones based upon phonetic considerations [p. 233]." In his final experiment, he presented the subjects with a nonsense word that had an arbitrary meaning, which was used as a starting point. The word was then systematically varied by a single feature at a time, and the subject was asked to describe the change in meaning that accompanied the change in form. The procedure was too open-ended to yield quantitative results, but sample responses suggested that many subjects consistently responded to the phonetic cues in the presentations.

Basing his work on Sapir's data, Newman (1933) found that grammatical category had no effect on the scaling of eight vowels, and that younger subjects (aged 9–13) showed essentially the same subjective patterns as older subjects (aged 16 and up), but that they discriminated less well and less consistently. He found that the symbolic magnitude judgments were due to three mechanical factors: (1) the kinesthetic factor of the articulatory position of the tongue (front-back), (2) the acoustic factor of the characteristic frequency (high-low), and (3) the kinesthetic factor of the oral cavity size (small-large). In a second, similar experiment, Newman found similarities between a large-small and a dark-bright scale, but whereas the large-small scale was patterned on the three factors used in the first experiment plus vowel quantity, the brightness scale was patterned exclusively on the basis of articulation and frequency.

More recently, Davis (1961) has made a cross-cultural study in which jagged and curved drawings were matched with the nonsense words *uloomu* and *takete,* all modified from Köhler (1947; cf. Figure 6.1). Both African children who spoke only a Bantu language (Kitongwe) and monolingual English-speaking children matched *takete* to the angular drawing and *uloomu* to the curved drawing with significantly more than chance frequency. Davis therefore concluded that universal phonetic symbolism provided the proper cues for "correct" matching in both groups.

Not all investigators have reached the same conclusions. Bentley and Varon (1933), for example, conducted a highly complex set of experiments to test the findings of Sapir and Newman further, and they did not feel that their results supported the notion of phonetic symbolism. More formidable, perhaps, was a series of cross-cultural experiments by Taylor and Taylor (1962), the results of which supported the theory of phonetic symbolism within a single language, but cast a considerable shadow over the theory of universal phonetic symbolism. The experimenters first formed CVC nonsense syllables of six consonants and three vowels, to test the effects of the phonetic environment upon the phenomenon of phonetic symbolism. No significant effects were found. In the second experiment four consonants and vowels were used to form CVC patterns, to test the effects of syllable length, the number of syllables, and the stress position in two-syllable strings. The longer strings were perceived as larger, but stress posi-

tion was not found to have any significant effect on phonetic symbolism.

In their final experiment, Taylor and Taylor presented
nearly monolingual subjects, each speaking one of four
different languages (English, Korean, Japanese, and
Tamil), with the same CVC combinations as were used in
the second experiment, and asked the subjects to rate the
strings on five-point scales along four dimensions (size,
movement, warmth, and pleasantness). The experimenters
found that phonetic symbolism had significant effects in all
languages, but the symbolism was not the same for the
different languages. For example, initial *t* and *p* were regarded as very small in English but very big in Korean, and
initial *d* was regarded as very big in Japanese but very small
in Tamil. The investigators thus concluded that the phenomenon of phonetic symbolism does exist in natural languages, but specific examples are not universally understood in the same way. Interpreting these data in a later
article, Taylor (1963) hypothesized that a major variable of
phonetic symbolism must be the language habits of the
speakers of a given language. These habits force them to
associate a specific sound or sound sequence with a generalized meaning. For example, English speakers habitually
associate an initial *g* with bigness, simply because many
words that connote bigness in English begin with *g*. For the
same reason, Taylor argued, an initial *d* is associated with
bigness in Japanese (from *debu* "fat," *dekkai* "huge," *daikibo*
"on a grand scale," and so forth). Taylor claimed that this
hypothesis explained not only why speakers associate certain sounds with certain meanings, but also why the associations differ for speakers of different languages.

In a vigorous attack on Taylor's arguments, Weiss
(1964a) maintained that Taylor's criticisms of earlier research in phonetic symbolism were the result of bias and
selective reporting. Further, he stated that the language-
habits theory begs the question of why certain unrelated

words that share a connotation in a given language also share structural components, and it fails to explain why only initial consonants are associated with meanings. As for the Taylors' application of the theory, he claimed that only those words that supported the theory were given, while those that failed to support it were selectively ignored. Weiss therefore suggested that a theory of phonetic symbolism ought perhaps to rely on sound and semantic hierarchies, rather than using isomorphic relations between single sounds and single meanings. Such a theory, of course, happens to have been proposed by Weiss (1963, 1964a, 1964b, 1966).

Weiss developed the theory in part from his investigation of the effects of meaningful versus nonmeaningful referent categories on the phonetic symbolism response. Using a variation of the picture-matching methodology of Davis (1961), Weiss (1964b) worked with the dimensions of magnitude, brightness, and angularity by asking groups of 22 subjects to respond respectively to (1) the match of meaningless nonsense-word pairs to nonsense-picture pairs that represented the three dimensions; (2) the match of the same nonsense-word pairs with meaningful referent objects, presented verbally; (3) the match of nonsense-word pairs of "high meaningfulness" (established by pretesting) with the picture pairs; and (4) the match of nonsense words of "high meaningfulness" with the referent objects. All of the nonsense words were in the canonical form CVCV; thus the same phonetic contrasts were employed in each experimental condition. All four groups matched words to pictures or objects at significantly higher than chance frequencies. Moreover, the use of referent objects raised the scores of both high- and low-meaningfulness nonsense words, but it affected the three dimensions differentially. Weiss concluded that the results generally supported his hypothesis that referent meaningfulness aids the matching response. That is, intersubject agreement is higher when meaningful referents are provided, because they reduce the possible number of bases for judgment.

Finally, Vetter and Tennant (1967) examined the effects of oral-gesture cues on the phonetic symbolism response. In a sense they came full circle with the analytical methodology. They subvocally presented 60 subjects with the stimulus words "oho" and "iti," and asked the subjects to identify the larger referent. The subjects guessed in the expected direction at better than chance frequency. In a second experiment, 40 subjects were presented with pairs of nonsense syllables such as the ones used by Sapir (1929). Two experimental conditions, vocal and nonvocal, were used. Again, under both conditions the subjects correctly ranked the /a/ and /i/ elements at highly significant levels. Vetter and Tennant interpreted these results as suggesting that cues derived from the perception of mouth articulations produce responses similar to those produced by cues of phonetic symbolism. Future experiments in phonetic symbolism must therefore impose stricter controls upon the stimuli used, in order to eliminate extraneous variables.

WORD-MATCHING STUDIES

The word-matching methodology was given its classic form for phonetic symbolism experiments by Tsuru and Fries (1933), who presented 36 pairs of Japanese words to 57 subjects, then asked them to match the words to those of equivalent English pairs. No levels of significance were ascribed to correct guessing, but 69% of the guesses were reported to be correct. In another study in which the word-matching methodology was used, Brown, Black, and Horowitz (1955) presented 21 pairs of antonyms of sensory continua to 86 subjects. The pairs were presented audiovisually in three languages (Hindi, Czech, and Chinese), and the subjects were asked to match an English meaning

to each stimulus word. The experimenters found significantly better than chance guessing for all three languages,
but reported that guessing of words was no better for the
Indo-European languages than for Chinese. In order to
explain this correct guessing, the experimenters accepted
the theory of a "physiognomic language," composed of
universal, unlearned intersensory connections—a sort of
universal synesthesia. They postulated that the origin of
speech could have been in the arbitrary association of
sounds and meanings, but that it then progressed toward
phonetic symbolism, so that a given speech form survived
only if it were "representational." Brown *et al.* (1955) concluded, perhaps whimsically, that in the evolution of languages, "speech forms have been selected for symbolism
and that we are moving toward a golden millennium of
physiognomic speech [p. 393]."

Using a methodology similar to that of Brown and his
associates, Maltzmann, Morisett, and Brooks (1956) found
that English-Japanese and English-Croatian pairs were
matched well above chance levels, but that Japanese-Croa-
tian pairs were not. For phonetic symbolism to take effect,
apparently English words had to be involved, so Maltzmann *et al.* felt that the ability to match foreign words must
be based on a complex sort of learning process, which
probably involved mediated generalization. Brackbill and
Little (1957) tried to define the problem more carefully by
conducting similar experiments that involved three methods of presentation (auditory only, visual only, and both
auditory and visual) and two forms of presentation (one
English word in each pair, and both words foreign). They
found significantly higher than chance matching of En-
glish-Hebrew, Japanese-Chinese, and Japanese-Hebrew
pairs; Chinese-Hebrew pairs were matched well below
chance levels, however. Visual presentation improved
guesses for the English-foreign pairs, but not for the for-
eign-foreign pairs. Obviously universal phonetic symbol-

ism cannot apply to all words of all languages, but the positive findings suggest that there may be interesting possibilities for further research in connection with language typologies.

Maltzmann *et al.* (1956), on the basis of a *post-hoc* inspection of their data, suggested that various stimulus characteristics of the word pairs (length, spacing, place of articulation, and so forth) might have influenced intersubject agreement, and two tests yielded a "potency ranking" of the characteristics, in this order: connotation, vowels, length, spacing, and consonants. Brown and Nuttall (1959) reviewed the procedural differences in the preceding experiments (by Brown *et al.*, 1955, Maltzmann *et al.*, 1956, and Brackbill and Little, 1957) and tried to evaluate the effects of the differences in procedure by varying the audiovisual presentation of word pairs in English, Chinese, and Hindi. In all conditions, the number of correct guesses was significantly above the chance level, but the English-foreign language matches were best. Brown and Nuttall concluded that universal phonetic symbolism is sensitive to the form of presentation, because only the English-foreign condition allows subjects to determine the appropriate semantic contrast. Brown and Nuttall (1959) then reformulated Brown's original phonetic symbolism theory into one that requires a referent continuum:

> Antonyms naming opposite ends of sensible referent continua (in languages with which the subject is unfamiliar) contrast with one another on appropriate phonetic dimensions often enough to make possible better than chance matches with the equivalent terms in the subject's native language. This condition, if it exists, need not be explained by a myth about the origin of speech in physiognomic representation. It is possible that in the history of languages, antonyms evolve toward phonetic contrasts appropriate to this semantic contrast and that pairs so contrasting sound "right" to native speakers and so have a superior prospect for survival. [p. 445]

In a direct test of the Brown-Nuttall hypothesis, Weiss (1963) asked whether only antonym pairs would work in the English-foreign condition, or whether nonantonym pairs would also work. He presented 394 subjects with English-Hindi and English-Chinese word pairs, some of which were antonyms and some of which were on different semantic dimensions. Weiss reported highly significant levels of correct quessing for all pairs, but found no differences between the experimental conditions; thus the use of antonym pairs did not increase correct guessing. Moreover, the subjects reported that they had approximately the same degree of difficulty in guessing under both conditions, whereas Brown and Nuttall (1959) had predicted that the subjects should have more difficulty in guessing nonantonymic pairs (pairs without marked relation of meaning). On the basis of these data, Weiss concluded that the meaning dimension described by Brown and Nuttall (1959) is unnecessary for accurate guessing, but that a meaningful context (represented by the English words) provides a necessary orientation for the subject, directing his attention to the appropriate phonetic elements. That is, the presence of an English word in a test pair provides a category of experiences which the subject must use to find the appropriate meaning of a sound sequence. Weiss concluded that "to the extent that sound-sense relations congruent with the subject's experiences have found their way into all natural languages, correct guessing is likely to occur [p. 106]." Weiss (1966) elaborated upon this statement, on the basis of another experiment in which 318 subjects matched the Japanese equivalent of one of a pair of English stimulus words in 28 word sets. Again, the words were nonantonymic but sensation-related. From his results, which showed significantly correct guessing, Weiss concluded that his previous theory had been supported. He therefore postulated that the following sequence of events is an appropriate process of phonetic symbolism: (1) experiences are assimilated as categories, some of which are bipolar ("large-small") and others of which are not ("hoarse, vibrating"); (2) many experiences are accompanied by more or less characteristic sets of sounds; (3) consistent pairings of the sounds and experiences are learned, and are associated with the above categories; (4) conversely, the experiences and categories are hierarchically associated with the sounds; (5) when the subject is presented with an unmeaningful sound sequence, he attributes these learned associations to it; (6) the sounds associated with categories of meaning are incorporated into words that denote those categories; (7) some categories of meaning are shared by different language groups; and (8) some sounds associated with those categories are associated universally. Step 6 explains the phenomenon of phonetic symbolism, while steps 7 and 8 explain universal phonetic symbolism.

CONCLUSION

It is evident that the varied, often conflicting results obtained in studies of sound symbolism are attributable at least in part to differences in experimental design and procedure. Barik (1969) has pointed out that one major source of the differences in the findings of word-matching studies is the mode of stimulus presentation (auditory or visual). He questions the validity of the assumption that the spelling of a foreign word with which the subject is unfamiliar constitutes an adequate basis on which to judge the sound of the word, as in the case of Croatian words such as *crn* and *tvrd* (Maltzmann *et al.*, 1956). If stimuli are to be presented visually, some method such as the projecting of items on a screen, trial by trial, should be employed. This would prevent the subject from making cross-item comparisons, which is a consistent risk in studies where materials are presented in list or booklet form.

The phenomenon of universal phonetic symbolism has been seriously challenged by the cross-cultural study of Taylor and Taylor (1962), although other such studies are needed to substantiate this claim. The existence of language-specific phonetic symbolisms, however, has received wide empirical support. In view of these conclusions, the next step in the study of phonetic symbolism is the systematic examination of the patterns of connotative meaning of the sounds in a large sample of natural languages.

REFERENCES

Barik, H. C. 1969. Some critical comments on visual presentation in word matching studies of phonetic symbolism. *Language and Speech 12:* 175–179.

Bentley, M., & E. J. Varon. 1933. An accessory study of "phonetic symbolism." *Amer. J. Psychol. 45:* 76–86.

Bolinger, D. L. 1950. Rime, assonance, and morpheme analysis. *Word 6:* 117–136.

Brackbill, Y., & K. B. Little. 1957. Factors determining the guessing of meanings of foreign words. *J. Abnormal and Social Psychol. 54:* 312–318.

Brown, R., A. H. Black, & A. E. Horowitz. 1955. Phonetic symbolism in natural languages. *J. Abnormal and Social Psychol. 50:* 388–393.

Brown, R., & R. Nuttall. 1959. Method in phonetic symbolism experiments. *J. Abnormal and Social Psychol. 59:* 441–445.

Carroll, J. B. (Ed.). 1956. *Language, Thought, and Reality: Selected Writings of Benjamin Lee Whorf.* (Introduction.) Cambridge, Mass.: The M.I.T. Press.

Davis, R. 1961. The fitness of names to drawings: A cross-cultural study in Tanganyika. *British J. Psychol. 52:* 259–268.

Johnson, R. C., N. S. Suzuki, & W. K. Olds. 1964. Phonetic symbolism in an artificial language. *J. Abnormal and Social Psychol. 69:* 233–236.

Köhler, W. 1947. *Gestalt Psychology.* New York: Liveright Publishing Corp.

Maltzmann, I., L. Morrisett, & L. O. Brooks. 1956. An investigation of phonetic symbolism. *J. Abnormal and Social Psychol. 53:* 249–251.

Markel, N. 1961. Connotative meanings of several initial consonant clusters in English. *Georgetown University Monograph Series on Languages and Linguistics 14:* 81–87.

Martin, S. E. 1964. Speech levels in Japan and Korea. In Dell Hymes (Ed.), *Language in Culture and Society,* pp. 407–415. New York: Harper & Row, Publishers.

Newman, S. S. 1933. Further experiments in phonetic symbolism. *Amer. J. Psychol. 45:* 53-75.

Sapir, E. 1929. A study in phonetic symbolism. *J. Experimental Psychol. 12:* 225–239.

Taylor, I. K. 1963. Phonetic symbolism re-examined. *Psychological Bulletin 60:* 200–209.

Taylor, I. K, & M. M. Taylor. 1962. Phonetic symbolism in four unrelated languages. *Canadian J. Psychol. 16:* 344–356.

Tsuru, S. & H. S. Fries. 1933. A problem in meaning. *J. General Psychol. 8:* 281–284.

Vetter, H. J., & J. A. Tennant. 1967. Oral-gesture cues in sound symbolism. *Perceptual and Motor Skills 24:* 54.

Weiss, J. H. 1963. Role of "meaningfulness" versus meaning dimensions in guessing the meanings of foreign words. *J. Abnormal and Social Psychol. 66:* 541–546.

Weiss, J. H. 1964a. Phonetic symbolism re-examined. *Psychological Bulletin 61:* 454–458.

Weiss, J. H. 1964b. The role of stimulus meaningfulness in the phonetic symbolism response. *J. General Psychol. 70:* 255–263.

Weiss, J. H. 1966. A study of the ability of English speakers to guess the meanings of non-antonym foreign words. *J. General Psychol. 74:* 97–106.

Whorf, B. L. 1956. A linguistic consideration of thinking in primitive communities. In John B. Carroll (Ed.), *Language, Thought, and Reality: Selected Writings of Benjamin Lee Whorf,* pp. 65–86. Cambridge, Mass.: The M.I.T. Press.

7

Biological
Bases
of
Language

The locus of all behavior is the organism. It follows, therefore, that an understanding of language behavior presupposes some basic comprehension of the structural and functional properties of the human organism, which does the behaving. As Lenneberg (1967) has noted, the study of language entails not only a description of language, not only a sociopsychological or experimental analysis of verbal learning, but an analysis of man as an organic system of interdependent variables. A full investigation of language, according to Lenneberg, "must not only study the organism that speaks but must also study the behavior itself —language—much the same way the zoologist who studies the badger must study its physique together with its habits in order to give a complete picture of that animal [p. 3]."

Linguistic functioning is a series of complex actions, which involve the integration of the central nervous system with the operation of auditory and vocal articulatory structures. Anatomical and physiological studies of these structures have contributed to our understanding of their functioning; especially important are such pioneering studies as those of Penfield and his associates (Penfield, 1965; Penfield and Jasper, 1954; Penfield and Perot, 1963; Penfield and Rasmussen, 1950; Penfield and Roberts, 1959) on the localization of speech centers in the brain. Additional evidence of a valuable kind has been gained from clinical studies of organic brain damage that results in aphasia, or of functional speech disorders such as stuttering. Still further contributions are made by physical anthropologists, whose efforts are directed toward the ways in which our biological heritage has shaped the species-specific characteristics of human language.

LANGUAGE AND EVOLUTION

In Chapters 2 and 3 we touched on the problem of when and how language may have developed. We saw that apes have a rudimentary ability in language which can be brought out under patient human tutelage. Modern apes may be brighter than their precursors some ten million years ago, when the human line seems to have diverged from that of the apes (Campbell, 1974), but it is still reasonable to seek the origins of language rather early in our evolution, when we were more apelike than we are today.

The distinctively human type of adaptation that depends on culture seems to have been launched some five million years ago with the appearance in Africa of a small, bipedal tool-making man-ape with the generic name of Australopithecus. There is a dispute over whether some of the early fossil material actually represents the genus *Homo* but for our purposes we may follow Campbell (1974), Washburn (Washburn and Moore, 1974) and others in considering all of the relevant materials to represent the australopithecines. That is, the general considerations relative to language are essentially the same no matter how the taxonomic issues are resolved.

Brain size, for example, is an important consideration. There is considerable overlapping in the range of the brain sizes of the great apes and Australopithecus, and if we look only at the approximate average brain size it is apparent that the advantage of the ancient man-ape was rather limited. Chimpanzees have a mean brain size of a little less than 400 cc., orangutans slightly more than 400 cc., gorillas barely more than 500 cc., and Australopithecus averages just under 600 cc. (Campbell, 1974). By comparison, Homo sapiens, or modern man, enjoys a weighty 1330 cc., while the intermediate form Homo erectus, sported a respectable 950 cc. (Campbell, 1974).

We cannot assume a direct correlation between absolute brain size and mental ability—let alone specifically linguistic ability—because several animals have larger brains than we do. There is one kind of whale, for example, with a brain of more than 10,000 cc. While we cannot usefully gauge the mental ability of such a creature, we have no reason to think it is within the human range, let alone six times as great. And as Washburn and Moore (1974) note:

> For all its great bulk, it constitutes only one gram of brain substance for each 8,500 grams of body, while modern man has one gram of brain for each 44 grams of body weight. But neither is the latter measurement an absolute. The capuchin monkey has one gram of brain for each 17.5 grams of body. The noted anthropologist Franz Weidenreich maintained . . . that a brain may be judged only by the use made of it and that cultural objects are the only reliable evidence of such use. [pp. 173–174]

Though neither absolute brain size nor the size of the brain relative to total body weight is a certain index of mental ability, there remains a general correlation. Up to a point, at least, cultural complexity has increased in proportion to increased brain size. The most obvious limit to the relationship is the fact that our brain size has been about the same for the last 300,000 years or so, while cultural complexity has been increasing at a fantastic rate in historical times, and particularly in the last few generations.

More important than brain size as such is the question of brain structure, though the two considerations are related because a great deal of our increased brain size is the result of new structures that have developed—structures that are critical for the distinctive cultural adaptation of humankind, including our ability in language. But some of the differences between our brains and those of infrahuman species, including those related to language and speech motor functions, involve not only the cerebral cortex but also subcortical and midbrain structures. Thus the capacity for language cannot be assigned to any specific neurological structure. Lenneberg (1967) suggests that insight into the language function of the brain could be gained more readily through the study of developmental processes and growth than through a study of mass. In Lenneberg's view language would have a biologically concrete structural basis in the sense that organization within the brain is itself a developmental process that has structural correlates on a molecular level.

But even in the more general sense, if we cannot say that the presence of certain gross features of the brain is proof positive of language ability, we can still approach the problem negatively. Thus Washburn and Moore (1974) see no evidence that the australopithecine brain had structures that would permit speech. We may assume that these man-apes had vocal, gestural, and postural signals, since the great apes have them; and we may assume that they were a little brighter, partly because of their very slight advantage in brain size and more importantly because they did leave evidence of culture, however rudimentary. Indeed, speculation on the language capability of our fossil ancestors depends to a considerable extent on how far we think cultural forms could develop in the absence of language.

Washburn and Moore (1974) are cautious in attributing language ability to the australopithecines, yet they do indicate that certain cultural forms may well have been present. The hunting bands of the australopithecines, they suggest, were too small to survive without intermating with other groups. "After some intermingling, it would be easy for a mother to suggest to her son that he might find a mate in the group from which she herself had come. Ties of custom and kinship would spring up [p. 151]." Of course, in the absence of language, it would not be easy for a mother to suggest anything. But given some intermingling of two small bands of the sort envisioned by Washburn and Moore (1974), it is not too difficult to imagine that male-female bonding could become customary between the two groups. It is doubtful that a kinship system of any great conceptual complexity could develop without the tool of language, but the basis for some of the social relationships which would later be verbally labelled could, and probably did, predate language. This is not a niggling qualification on our part, because speculation on the origin of language must be conservative in order to be sound. That is, if a custom, social relationship, technology, or conceptual system could reasonably have developed without language, it is prudent to assume that it did so. The subsequent verbal labelling of items, relationships, and events is easy enough to understand once the labelling concept became established.

Bernard Campbell (1974) suggests that by the early Pleistocene—toward the end of the australopithecine phase, that is—we "would expect *Australopithecus* to have a stable and well-adapted social system [p. 384]." We might suppose that cooperative hunting, for which there seems to be evidence, would imply the use of language. But while language would no doubt be a help, it is by no means required. Other animals, including baboons on occasion and chimpanzees (Campbell 1974), hunt cooperatively, and many animal species can be described as having stable and well-adapted social systems even though they lack language.

Direct evidence for the early use of language is not to be found in the archaeological record because the spoken word is ephemeral, while archaeological evidence necessarily is durable. The hard cultural evidence from the remote past does, however, provide a basis for judging complexity of social organization and cultural advance. It might be possible to discover a criterion for stating that a particular level of development could not have been attained in the absence of language. Organizational accomplishments on the order of those achieved by the social insects would no doubt meet such a criterion, given our general understanding of the different evolutionary course of the vertebrates and the particularly cognitive tendency of the hominids. Unfortunately this understanding does not help us pinpoint the origin of language. Our own only began to approach the complexity of social-insect organization in historical or near historical times, when language was already highly developed.

The examination of cultural history from this specific viewpoint may yet reveal an archaeologically verifiable aspect of culture for which there is a linguistic *sine qua non*. In the meantime, we have not exhausted the fossil evidence. We should expect an intellectual advance as significant as the development of language to have discoverable anatomical correlates. If this is so, there are several general periods in the past which may eventually prove particularly important. First is the period some millions of years ago when the australopithecines first appeared. But while they were clever enough to launch our cultural beginnings, these primordial fellows are not generally credited with anything that can properly be called language. A somewhat better bet, perhaps, would be the transition between Australopithecus and Homo erectus, since this was accompanied by an enormous expansion of the brain that peaked between one-half million to one million years ago (Campbell, 1974).

By 300,000 years ago, if Campbell (1974) is correct, the people living in Eurasia and Africa were physically indistinguishable from modern human populations except for their relatively long skulls and heavily built faces and jaws. Their brains were somewhat larger than ours. It may be that these Neanderthals were the first to develop language. Or the great step may have come with the reduction of the massive jaw and the slight reshaping of the skull that took place between 50,000 and 30,000 years ago, as Neanderthals disappeared and modern man (Homo sapiens sapiens) monopolized the human stage.

The last big change is of special interest because of the recent argument put forth by Lieberman (1973), who says that Neanderthal lacked the supralaryngeal vocal tract necessary for fully encoded human speech. The apes and Australopithecus show a similar lack. On the other hand, the female cranium found at Steinheim, which is thought to be 150,000 to 250,000 years old (Campbell, 1974), seems to have been suitably equipped with the necessary supralaryngeal vocal tract. Lieberman does not deny that Neanderthal may have communicated by means of language, but he does feel that by modern standards it would be greatly restricted, slow, perhaps supplemented by a gestural system, and best considered to be an intermediate form of language (Lieberman, Crelin, and Klatt, 1972).

Lieberman's conclusions have been challenged on methodological grounds by Carlisle and Siegel (1974), and while Lieberman and Crelin (1974) have offered a rebuttal, even on linguistic grounds their argument is somewhat questionable. That is, a great deal of their attention focuses on the specific quality of a very few sounds, and there is no obvious reason why any language should have to depend on a specific sound or limited set of sounds. Further, people who have had various of the "speech organs" surgically removed are often able to compensate for the loss sufficiently to speak more or less intelligibly. Still, Lieberman's approach is interesting as an example of the kind of ingenuity that can be turned loose on the problem of the origin of language.

CHARACTERISTICS OF SPEECH

According to a Pavlovian formula, vocal sounds make up another and more powerful "signaling system." In other words, they become *coded.* If words are used specifically and conventionally for external events, they can substitute for the visual, tactile, or other kinds of stimuli from these sources. Words, like gestures, can then be used to direct the sense organs of the hearer toward parts of the environment that he would not otherwise perceive, and to induce him to perceive at second-hand sectors of the larger environment that the speaker has perceived but the hearer has not.

As man's use of speech developed, the vocalizations that were uttered came to possess expressive as well as symbolic qualities. The qualities of vocal sounds that we call "expressive" specify types and subtypes of human emotions, moods, and feelings. The crying of a baby and the laughter of a young person are sounds that are unmistakable. There are moans of pain and sighs of relief, growls of anger and grunts of effort, shouts of triumph and murmurs of love. We must assume that these types of vocalization existed long before speech. It was probably from this repertory of spontaneous, unlearned utterances in our hominid ancestors that conventional speech sounds developed. It remains the function of these expressive qualities to reveal the mood, feeling, intentions, and temperament of the speaker.

Vocal speech also contains the symbols that express things in the common environment of all individuals. These symbols, according to Gibson (1966), enable men "to think of the same things, to have concepts in common, and to verify their concepts jointly [p. 88]." Symbolic meaning is on a different level from perceptual meaning. The cry "wolf" has an entirely different function from both the cry of alarm when one actually sees a wolf and the baying of the wolf itself.

The relation of a perceptual stimulus to its causal source in the milieu is of one genre, while the relation of a symbol to its referent is of another. The former depends on the laws of physics and biology, that is, on the "ecology of stimulation." The latter depends on a "linguistic community," which is a unique invention of the human species. The relation of perceptual stimuli to their source is an innate one; an example of this is projection. But the relation of symbols to their referents is an arbitrary one, governed by social agreement. The conventions of symbolic speech must be learned, but the child can learn one language just as easily as another. The connections between stimuli and their sources may well have to be learned in part, but they do not make a language. The language code is cultural, traditional, and arbitrary; the connection between stimuli and their sources is not.

PHYSIOLOGICAL ASPECTS OF SPEECH

The source of acoustical speech sounds is the human vocal apparatus, backed up by the human nervous system. This apparatus is one of the most complex sound-makers in the world. The sounds arise from a series of exhalations and inhalations produced by the breathing muscles of the chest and diaphragm. These may or may not be accompanied by movements of the mouth, jaw, lips, tongue, and velum (Gray and Wise, 1959). The series of concurrent movements produces what is called the "segmentation of speech"—that is, the segments in the flow of sound. This flow, voiced or unvoiced, is modified in spectral composition to make vowels. It is also cut by pauses, stops, and transitions, to make consonants. The vowels and consonants are the units of articulation.

The muscular movements that create phonemes tend to be stereotyped. If these phonemes are thought of as both the responses of a speaker and the stimuli for a listener, it can be predicted that each speaker of a community will be compelled to make the same phonemes as others, in order to be intelligible (Gibson, 1966). This phenomenon is generally viewed as part of what children do when they "learn to speak": they learn to pronounce in accordance with their language or their dialect, under social pressure from playmates, parents, and school.

In other words, the process of speech development could be conceptualized thus: at first the child possesses a large repertoire of speech sounds (many of which are not included in his native language). Gradually, through processes that seem to involve both maturation and learning, this repertoire is reduced to contain the sounds that are needed in his language; sounds that are not reinforced by the speech of his verbal environment are eliminated, and the child is left with a repertoire that contains his approximation of the sounds he hears. As the neuromusculature and the sound-discrimination processes mature, the child refines and polishes his repertoire into the sounds of his native tongue, gaining voluntary control over their production (Osborn, 1961). The sounds, having been stereotyped by the community, can be said to have a valid objective reality; according to Gibson (1966), they are "anchored in the habitual resonances, stops, frictions, and explosives of conventional articulation and specified by certain invariant properties of the wave trains of vibrating fields in the air [p. 94]."

One physiological process that plays a part in the way the infant learns to speak is referred to by Simon (1957) as "kinesthetic and auditory feedback." Buhler (in Brain, 1961), noting that the child hears the sounds that it produces, said:

> ... the psychologically important fact is the formation of strong associations between the auditory impression and the movements which produce it, for this is the essential basis of the later imitation of the sounds the child hears, in which it has to translate what it has heard into vocal movements of its own. [p. 154]

This approach represents an old theory, according to which the human infant, in the babbling stage of speech development, learns associations between the sounds of speech and the acts of speech, or conditioned reflexes that connect a certain auditory stimulus to a certain vocal response. This is taken to be the basis of vocal imitation, and to explain why deaf children do not learn to speak. It is assumed by association theorists, therefore, that children must learn that hearing and speaking correspond.

It is perfectly true that any single, elementary muscle contraction does not correspond to any single, elementary sensory datum. But the pattern of contractions and the change of nervous output at the muscles do correspond to the pattern of excitation and the change of nervous input at the cochlea (Gibson, 1966). There is no need for these to be associated, since they are identical. What probably happens during the babbling stage is that the child learns to differentiate pattern and change in muscular output, and makes a parallel differentiation of pattern and change in the cochlear input. As the child learns to articulate the invariants of sound, he learns to discriminate them. The practising of vocal-auditory activity permits learning, but it is not associative learning.

The function of auditory self-stimulation is, therefore, probably best understood if it is conceived not as a kind of audition, but as a kind of proprioception. It monitors the flow of speech in the same way as other modes of proprioception keep track of the flow of other types of behavior. It thus enables articulation to be controlled. The next syllable depends on the previous one; feedback yields a concurrent record of how far the speech has progressed.

NEUROPHYSIOLOGICAL ASPECTS OF SPEECH

From a neurophysiological standpoint, the expressive and symbolic qualities of language are merely manifestations of what Head (1926) considered to be the basic processes of symbolic formulation and expression. Brock and Krieger (1963) point out that in its most complete form, this symbolic thinking and expression becomes a function of the entire cerebral cortex. It is largely through the work of Penfield, however, that the true complexity of the speech mechanism has been revealed.

Penfield and Roberts (1959) have demonstrated that no two human cerebral hemispheres are ever the same in form and in the pattern of convolutions and fissures. At the time of birth, the motor and sensory areas of the brain are beginning to take on their function as transmitting stations. At that time the speech areas are "blank slates on which nothing has been written [p. 198]." Generally three cortical speech areas, shown below in Figure 7.1, will be developed in the left hemisphere. The right hemisphere may become dominant with respect to localization of the speech centers, but this is quite rare. In addition, a small lesion in infancy may produce some displacement of the expected location

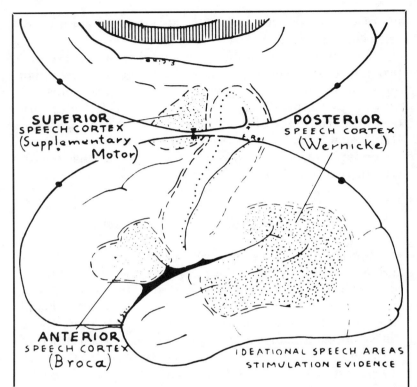

Figure 7.1. SUMMARIZING MAP OF THE AREAS OF CORTEX IN THE DOMINANT HEMISPHERE WHICH ARE NORMALLY DEVOTED TO THE IDEATIONAL ELABORATION OF SPEECH. Conclusions derived exclusively from the evidence of electrical speech mapping. (Reprinted by permission of Princeton University Press and the authors. Source: W. Penfield and L. Roberts, *Speech and Brain Mechanisms,* Princeton: Princeton University Press, 1959.)

of the areas within the left hemisphere. A large lesion in the posterior speech area may cause the whole speech apparatus to be developed in the right hemisphere, where the cortical areas will take up homologous positions.

In the cerebral cortex of the human adult certain areas are devoted to the control of speech musculature, and certain other areas are devoted to the ideational processes of speech. Each of these areas will be discussed separately.

Information about the motor mechanism of speech has been obtained by Penfield and others through the electrical stimulation of the cortex of conscious subjects. Vocalization (Penfield and Jasper, 1954) has been found to be the response of a small area between those governing the upper face movement and the lip movement on the precentral Rolandic gyrus (Figure 7.2). It was subsequently shown that vocalization could be produced in the supplementary motor area of either cerebral hemisphere (Penfield and Rasmussen, 1950). A gentle electric current in one of these specific cortical areas causes a patient who is lying fully conscious on the operating table to utter a long-drawn-out vowel sound, which he is completely unable to stop until he runs out of breath. Then, after he has taken a breath, he continues as helplessly as before.

One of the major differences between the cortical motor responses of man and animals is manifested in human voice control. The cortical area that governs control of the voice, including articulatory movements and vocalization, is located between the two principal areas that control ideational speech, one posterior and the other anterior (see Figure 7.1). It would appear that the Rolandic area of voice control on either side can serve the purposes of speech alone, since excision of one of the vocalization areas does not permanently interfere with speaking.

The areas of the cortex that are utilized in the ideational elaboration of speech have been determined by applying a gentle electric current to the relevant areas of the cortex of the dominant hemisphere in conscious human beings. The interfering current causes the patient to become aphasic until the electrode is withdrawn.

Three areas have been outlined (see Figure 7.1):
1. A large area in the posterior temporal and posterior–inferior parietal regions (Wernicke's area)

2. A small area in the posterior part of the third frontal convolution, anterior to the motor voice-control area (Broca's area)

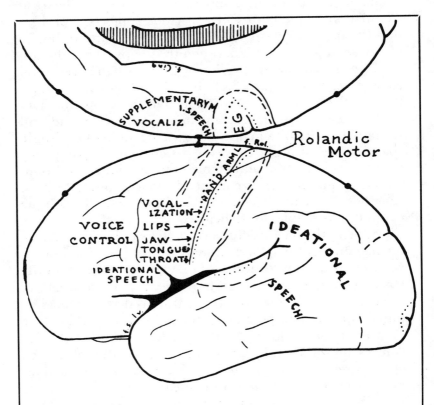

Figure 7.2. SPEECH MECHANISMS IN THE DOMINANT HEMISPHERE. Three areas are devoted to the ideational elaboration of speech; two areas devoted to vocalization. The principal area devoted to motor control of articulation, or voice control, is located in lower precentral gyrus. Evidence for these localizations is summarized from the analysis of cortical stimulation and cortical excision. (Reprinted by permission of Princeton University Press and the authors. Source: W. Penfield and L. Roberts, *Speech and Brain Mechanisms,* Princeton: Princeton University Press, 1959.)

3. A part of the supplementary motor area within the mid-sagittal fissure and just anterior to the Rolandic motor foot area (the supplementary speech area).

All three of these cortical areas, which are organized to function in one hemisphere only, play roles in the ideational speech mechanism under normal conditions. The primary function of these areas of the cortex is the "memory" of words.

In addition, part of the temporal cortex (chiefly on the superior and lateral surfaces of both lobes, and probably extending a little way into the parietal lobe) and parts of the hippocampal gyrus assume the function of interpreting experiences; hence they are known as the interpretive cortex. Referring to these areas, Penfield and Perot (1963) concluded the following:

> There is within the adult human brain a remarkable record of the stream of each individual's awareness. It is as though the electrode cuts in, at random, on the record of that stream. The patient sees and hears what he saw and heard in some earlier strip of time and he feels the same accompanying emotions. The stream of consciousness flows for him again, exactly as before, stopping instantly on removal of the electrode. He is aware of those things to which he paid attention in this earlier period, even twenty years ago. He is not aware of the things that were ignored. The experience evidently moves forward at the original pace. This was demonstrated by the fact that when, for example, the music of an orchestra, or song or piano, is heard and the patient is asked to hum in accompaniment, the tempo of his humming is what one would expect. He is still aware of being in the operating room but he can describe this other run of consciousness at the same time.
>
> The patient recognizes the experience as having been his own, although usually he could not have recalled it if he had tried. The complete record of his auditory and visual experience is not subject to conscious recall, but it is evidently used in the subconscious brain-transaction that results in

perception. By means of it, a man in normal life compares each succeeding experience with his own past experience. He knows at once whether it is familiar or not. If it is familiar, he interprets the present stream of consciousness in the light of the past.

There is, apparently, no overlap of the boundaries that separate the speech cortex, which endows one with memory of words, and the interpretive cortex, which gives one access to the memory of past similar experiences and thus enables one to understand the present (Penfield, 1965).

BIOLOGY AND LANGUAGE DEVELOPMENT

So far the only real evidence for the biological basis of language is the language universals: a common age of onset, the universality of the ontogenetic process of language, and the universality of syntactic structure (concatenation of morphemes in a nonrandom manner). The contention that language is biologically based seems well-supported, theoretically and experimentally, but this is only preliminary to the more basic question of what specific biological mechanisms are involved.

That speech habits emerge as a function of maturational changes within the growing child seems to be the best biological explanation of language, since a great variety of environmental conditions leave the age of onset unaffected. Furthermore, there is much evidence that language development is interlocked with other maturationally-based behavior such as stance, gait, and motor coordination, although it is independent of these other processes (that is, it is neither caused by, nor a cause of, these processes). Also, there is no evidence that training procedures can advance the rate of language learning. A critical period of language acquisition is linked with an initial lack of maturation; its termination is related to a loss of adaptability and of the capacity to reorganize in the brain; this is a function of the cerebral lateralization of function. As the specific neurophysiological correlates of language are still unknown, the emergence of the critical period of readiness for language cannot be attributed directly to any one maturational process. The prerequisite for the eventual discovery of these specific neural phenomena is a knowledge of the exact brain states before, during, and after this critical language period. Some factual evidence is available on which we can postulate that there is a correlation between full maturation of the brain and the end of the critical period, but a causal relationship cannot be inferred.

Aside from the correlational aspects of the process, just how does language develop? Lenneberg (1967) presents an argument that is more convincing on how it does *not* develop than on how it does. To say that language is a discriminatory learning process, or that it is a function of secondary reinforcement, or that it is mediated by stimulus generalization are oversimplifications that rest on hypothetical constructs and are contrary to the observed facts. There is some evidence that linguistic development is a process closely related to other biologically based principles of the organization of behavior. Sensory data are first of all grouped into undifferentiated global classes, and these are subsequently differentiated into more specific patterns. Both perceived patterns and self-produced patterns become organized in this way.

Concluding Observations

The outline of the neurophysiological basis of speech seems to be well-established. The three speech areas have been clearly mapped, and their function in word-recall has been described. Although the location may be different from person to person, their presence is certain. Penfield has demonstrated the existence of an interpretive cortex, which complements the function of the speech centers. It has the function of presenting a background of experience against which the individual can compare and interpret his present situation. Connecting pathways integrate these speech mechanisms, linking them to each other, to other areas of the cortex, and to the thalamus. It is the thalamus (plus the hypothalamus and limbic system) that functions as the integration center for all bodily functions.

The neurophysiological aspects of speech are still far from completely understood. As van der Berg (1961) has stated:

> The present data show a certain degree of specialization in the tremendous number of neurons and associated inter-connecting structures. A large number of 'centers' seems to be imbedded in a vast network of multi-purpose neurons. The topography becomes gradually better known and with it a rough outline of the channels interconnecting the 'centers,' but we are yet far away from the point where it would be possible to build an electrical analog. [p. 66]

Until further research is conducted and more facts are discovered, our understanding of the neurophysiological and psychological aspects of the production of speech will remain incomplete. A greater insight into the controlling mechanism of the subcortical structures and into the correlation of patterns of neural excitation with words and concepts is sorely needed.

REFERENCES

Brock, S., & H. P. Krieger. 1963. *The Basis of Clinical Neurology.* Baltimore, Md.: Williams & Wilkins Co.

Buhler, W. R. 1961. The neurology of language. *Brain 84:* 145–166.

Campbell, B. 1974. *Human Evolution.* (2nd ed.). Chicago: Aldine Publishing Co.

Gibson, J. J. 1966. *The Senses Considered as Perceptual Systems.* Boston, Mass.: Houghton Mifflin.

Gray, G. W., & C. M. Wise. 1959. *The Bases of Speech.* New York: Harper & Row, Publishers.

Head, H. 1926. *Aphasia and Kindred Disorders of Speech.* London: Cambridge University Press.

Lenneberg, E. H. 1967. *The Biological Foundations of Language.* New York: John Wiley & Sons, Inc.

Lieberman, P. 1973. On the evolution of language: a unified view. Paper presented at the IXth International Congress of Anthropological and Ethnological Sciences, September 2, 1973.

Lieberman, P., E. S. Crelin, & D. H. Klatt. 1972. Phonetic ability and related anatomy of the newborn and adult human, Neanderthal Man, and the chimpanzee. *Amer. Anthropologist* 74: 287–307.

Morgan, C. T. 1965. *Physiological Psychology.* New York: McGraw-Hill Book Company.

Osborn, S. S. 1961. Concept of speech development. *J. Speech and Hearing Disorders 26:* 391–392.

Penfield, W. 1965. Conditioning the uncommitted cortex for language learning. *Brain 88:* 787–798.

Penfield, W., & H. H. Jasper. 1954. *Epilepsy and the Functional Anatomy of the Brain.* Boston, Mass.: Little, Brown and Company.

Penfield, W., & P. Perot. 1963. The brain's record of auditory and visual experience: A final summary and discussion. *Brain 86:* 695–696.

Penfield, W., & T. Rasmussen. 1950. *The Cerebral Cortex of Man.* New York: The Macmillan Company.

Penfield, W., & L. Roberts. 1959. *Speech and Brain-Mechanisms.* Princeton, N.J.: Princeton University Press.

Simon, C. T. 1957. The development of speech. In L. E. Travis (Ed.), *Handbook of Speech Pathology.* New York: Appleton-Century-Crofts.

Van den Berg, J. W. 1961. Physiological basis of language. *Logos* *4:* 56–66.

Walker, E. 1938. The thalamus of the chimpanzee. IV. Thalamic projections to the cerebral cortex. *J. Anatomy 73:* 37–93.

Washburn, S. L., & R. Moore. 1974. *Ape into Man.* Boston: Little, Brown & Company.

8

The Theory of a Language

While most of us are startled to realize that *ghoti* can be pronounced "fish" (if we use the phonetic values of enou*gh*, w*o*men, and na*ti*on), we all acknowledge that our system of orthography is extremely cumbersome. We have at least a vague understanding that the problem lies in the fact that the same letters can stand for different sounds (*I*, mach*i*ne, m*i*tt), while given sounds may also be represented by different letters, as in the *ghoti* example. So even the linguistically naïve individual soon reaches the conclusion that an alphabetic script should represent rather closely the sounds of the language it depicts. A script that attempts to reflect pronunciation in detail is phonetic, and we might suppose that this is an ideal kind of writing system. In fact, a strictly phonetic script is neither feasible nor desirable for most purposes.

A number of attempts have been made to devise phonetic alphabets; the one most widely employed throughout

Extensive passages reprinted with the permission of © Ziff-Davis Publishing Company, 1973.

the world is the International Phonetic Alphabet (IPA) of the International Phonetic Association. The IPA was developed before the phonemic principle was well understood (Bloomfield, 1933; pp. 86–88), and great pains were taken to make fine distinctions. But there really is no practical way to represent the infinitely fine acoustical variations that mark speech, not only from one language to another, but even within the speech of a single individual. This will become clear shortly, when we consider some of the variations that occur in our own speech.

THE PHONEMIC PRINCIPLE

For most purposes, it is not the exact acoustical quality of a speech sound that must be graphically represented, but rather certain ranges of sound that are significant for a specific language or speech variety. This is the essence of the phonemic principle. A phoneme is an abstraction. We do not speak or hear a phoneme as such; rather we speak and hear specific representations of phonemes, which are known as allophones. We can illustrate this by considering the variations in the four words "cool," "school," "kill," "skill." There are two vowel phonemes, /uw, i/, and three consonant phonemes, /s, k, l/. But a closer look at the *k*- and *sk*- sequences shows that the value of the *k* differs in the two cases. In "cool" and "kill" a puff of air accompanies the *k*; this is missing in the other set, "school" and "skill." We can note the same contrast in the *p* of "pin" and "spin" and in the *t* of "tall" and "stall." We do not even notice this difference when speaking English, but it is a critical difference in some languages—as critical as the difference between *b* and *p* in English, for example. Thus Chao (1968) states that "the English word *pie* sounds like the word for 'to dispatch' in Chinese, while the *py* part of *spy* sounds like the Chinese word for 'to bow' [p. 3]."

Aspiration

Thus we simply say that the aspirated and unaspirated varieties of the *k* are allophones of a single /k/ phoneme, and we can further indicate that the aspirated form appears in the initial position and the unaspirated form occurs after a *fricative, s, z, f, v,* etc., where the flow of air is impeded by sufficient closure to yield audible friction, but is not stopped completely, as it is for *stops* such as *p, t,* and *k*.

Positioning

But we have not exhausted the allophones of /k/. If we compare "kill" and "cool," we can tell that with the *k*- before the *i,* the tongue presses the roof of the mouth further forward than in the case of the *k*- before the *oo.* One can feel this by forming the two *k*'s in the mouth, without actually saying the words "kill" and "cool:" the tongue is shifted back and forth. Again, we can predict that the front *k* will occur before *front vowels* (as in "kill," "keel," "care," "Kate," and "cat"), while the back *k* will anticipate the articulation of back vowels (as in "coops," "coat," and "couch").

It is obvious, then, that the phoneme /k/ always appears in some particular manifestation, which will contrast with other allophones. This is why we say that we do not actually hear or say a phoneme: the phoneme is an abstraction of all the allophones, and only one of the allophones can be uttered at a single time. We may also note that the quality of the -*l* differs after the front vowels in "kill" and "skill" and after the back vowels in "cool" and "school"; because the approach to the place where the /l/ is articulated is different in the two cases, and the lips remain rounded after the back vowel and unrounded after the front vowel. If we were to look in detail at all of the environments of /k/ (or of any other phoneme), we would find an enormous number of allophones. Fortunately, this is not necessary for most purposes. What *is* necessary is that we should identify the phonemes and then assign a single symbol to each one, rather than attempting to use a separate symbol for each phonetic variation.

Phonemes are important because they enable us to distinguish meanings. That is, when we find two strings of sound that are identical except for a single feature, we will say that the strings are identical if the feature in question is phonemic, and will not if it is not. Thus "nip" will be regarded as the same, whether or not the final -*p* is released with a puff of air.

Voicing

Thus aspiration is not critical, and we can say that we are dealing with allophones rather than with separate phonemes. But what of the difference between ni*p* and ni*b*? It happens that "nip" will characteristically end with a puff of air, while "nib" will not, but we have ruled out the aspiration as critical; and yet we know that the two sequences of sound have different meanings for us. If we attend carefully to what is happening, we will find that it is possible to prolong the sound of the -*b* but not the -*p*. What we hear when we prolong the -*b* is the vibrating of the vocal cords, or *voicing*. The vibration can be felt if we place the hand around the throat and sound the sequence of a very long s-z-s-z-s. That is, if we alternate between a hiss and a buzz, the absence of vibration when we are hissing is quite clear. So voicing is critical for certain consonant pairs (p-b, t-d, k-g, s-z, f-v, and so on).

Vowel Length

In some languages, such as Hawaiian and Japanese, vowel length is a critical, or distinctive, feature. In the latter language, for example, to lengthen the first vowel of *kofun* "burial mound" transforms the morbid meaning of the sequence into the much livelier *koofun* "(sexual) excitement." We are not used to the idea that vowel length is distinctive, and yet we regularly employ long vowels before voiced final consonants (as in "buzz," "pig," "bode") but short vowels before their unvoiced counterparts ("bus," "pick," "boat"). Yet if we artificially lengthen or shorten the vowels, we do not effect a change in the meaning.

Free Variation

Just as have to work a little even to hear the nondistinctive features that distinguish our allophones (such as the lack of aspiration in some phonetic environments or routine differences in vowel length), people who are learning English as a second language have the same sort of difficulty in distinguishing what are, for us, obviously distinctive sounds. How could anyone, for instance, confuse "loom" and "room"? Yet in some languages the *l* and *r* are in *free variation*. The Japanese *r* is usually described as a "flap" *r*, more like the Spanish sound than ours, but with many speakers the sound in question sounds like an *l* to us. In Japanese, it simply does not matter which way the articulation ends, because there is no linguistically significant difference between the two. And since the Japanese have grown up "tuning out" the differences within that particular range of phonological variation, when they find themselves in an English-speaking environment, they usually have considerable difficulty in learning to hear the distinction.

PHONEMES, MORPHEMES, AND SYNTAX

The development of the concept of the phoneme was something of a breakthrough in linguistic analysis, but in some ways it was too successful. The differences between phonemes could be demonstrated fairly neatly, and the same methodological approach could be applied to the smallest meaningful segments, morphemes, while longer stretches could be built up from morphemes. The striking success attained with phonemes focused attention on them almost to the exclusion of other features of language. This limitation was enhanced by the very useful work of missionaries who were primarily concerned to translate the Christian Bible into languages that had hitherto been without a script. Since the targets of this enterprise already knew their languages, the main job of the missionary/linguist was to identify and label phonemes. For various reasons, then, phonemes were the first order of business, and all too often the researcher ran out of gas, as it were, before he tackled the syntax. As Bolinger (1968) put it:

> What had started as a combination of practical necessity and historical accident was thus elevated to a theoretical precept: "Do not attempt to deal with syntax before morphology, nor with morphology before phonology; to do so is to *mix levels.*" Since the units of each lower level were the components of the units at the next higher one, it was impossible to move up until the proper foundation had been laid. [pp. 193–194]

We have probably implied that the identification of phonemes and morphemes is much simpler than it really is, but once the actual complexity of the task is appreciated, it is also easier to appreciate why so few attempts were made to deal seriously with syntax. The investigator of a tongue that is alien to him will hear a great number of exotic sounds, but some of these will be significant (phonemic) and some will not, while some of the acoustical distinctions he has been making all his life may not be relevant to the speakers of the alien language; thus we can imagine that even the description of a phonemic system can be a considerable undertaking. Yuen Ren Chao (1968) relates a surprise he received once:

> . . . I was watching some bargaining on a street market in Yunnan (where the dialect is a variety of Mandarin). I

couldn't be sure whether they were quarrelling or coughing. Listening more closely to what they were saying, I began to realize that the cough was simply the dialectal cognate of standard Mandarin aspirated *k*, the unaspirated *k*, as I knew, being a glottal stop in that dialect. [p. 24]

We should not be deceived into underestimating the task by anecdotes such as that offered by Chao (1968) about Edward Sapir, "who on our first meeting learned in little more than an hour not only the main phonemics of my native dialect Changchow, Kiangsu, but also what to say and when, and what expressive intonation to use [p. vi]." Very likely Sapir knew exactly what questions to ask, and Chao was able to respond immediately and knowledgeably; this is a rather different situation from that of an inexperienced linguist, uncertain of what he can expect, who is dealing with individuals who would not understand economical questions.

SUPRASEGMENTAL PHONEMES

We have mentioned some English phonemes; a more or less complete listing of phonemes for one speaker is given in Table 8.1. The *segmental phonemes,* including consonants, vowels, and semivowels, are probably clear enough —(at least in principle), thanks to our experience in writing and reading. That is, while our spelling seems highly imperfect, what we write consists of consonants, vowels, semivowels, and punctuation. Our punctuation marks only hint at another kind of phoneme, the *suprasegmental phoneme.*

Stress

In order to establish suprasegmentals (for example stress) as phonemes, it is necessary again to establish them as somehow critical. For many of us, the following constitute minimal pairs:

Table 8-1

ENGLISH PHONEMES AND SOME WORDS AND SENTENCES EXEMPLIFYING THEM[§]

33 Segmental Phonemes

20 Consonants		4 Semivowels	
		As	*In*
Occurring as initial, medial, or final:		*consonant*	*diphthong*

/b/ as in *buy*	/s/ as in *so*		
/d/ as in *do*	/t/ as in *toe*	/h/ as in *hoe*	*bah* /bah/
/f/ as in *foe*	/v/ as in *vow*		
/g/ as in *go*	/z/ as in *zoo*	/r/ as in *roe*	*err* /ər/
/k/ as in *key*	/θ/ as in *thigh*		
/l/ as in *lie*	/ŏ/ as in *thy*	/w/ as in *woe*	*now* /naw/
/m/ as in *my*	/š/ as in *show*		
/n/ as in *no*	/č/ as in *chow*	/y/ as in *you*	*boy* /boy/
/p/ as in *pay*	/ĵ/ as in *Joe*		

Occurring only as medial or final:

/ž/ as in *pleasure, rouge*
/ŋ/ as in *singer, thing*

9 Vowels

Simple vowel *+ consonant*	*Followed by semivowels*				
	/-y/	/-w/	/-h/	/-r/	/-yr/
/i/ as in *pit*	*pea*	*	*	*	*pier*
/e/ as in *pet*	*pay*	*	*	*	*pare*
/æ/ as in *pat*	*	*	/æh/†	*	*
/i̇/ as in *roses*	*	*	*	*	*
/ə/ as in *putt, but*	*	*	/əh/**	*purr*††	*
/a/ as in *pot*	*pie*	*now*	*pa*	*par*	*pyre*
/u/ as in *put, look*	*buoy*	*coo*	*boo!*	*poor*	*
/o/ as in *	*boy*	*low*	*oh!*	*pore*	*
/ɔ/ as in *	*	*	*law*	*war*	*

12 Suprasegmental Phonemes

4 Pitches: /¹/ (lowest), /²/, /³/, /⁴/ (highest).
4 Stresses: / ˈ / (primary), /ˆ/ (secondary), / ˋ / (tertiary), /ˇ/ (weak).
4 Junctures: / + / (internal), / | / (level), / ‖ / (rising), / # / (falling, terminal).

Table 8-1   (continued)

A Sample Transcription

He: /²dìʃə + sîyðə + ³hwáythàws³ ‖/
She: /²nów³ ‖²kəzay + wɔ́hntɨd + tə + vîzɨtðə + smìθsôwnɨyən +
myùw³zíyəm² |²ðə + lâybrərìyəv + ³káhŋgrìs³ |²aèn ðə + ĵéfərsən
+ mə³móhrìyəl² ‖⁴ ⁵hl² |²in + tûw + ⁴áwrz² #/
He: /²im⁴páhsɨbəl¹ #/

>   *He:* Didja see the White House?
>   *She:* No, 'cause I wanted to visit the Smithsonian Museum,
>   the Library of Congress, and the Jefferson Memorial—
>   (*excitedly*) all in two hours!
>   *He:* (*incredulously*) Impossible!

§After Carroll (1964, pp. 14–15). The phonemes are given as they occur in Carroll's Lower Connecticut Valley dialect.

*Does not occur as a monosyllable in Carroll's dialect, but may occur in other dialects of English.

†An interjection of frustration or disgust.

**The hesitation form.

††In Carroll's dialect, this is a single *r*-like vowel, but it fits best into the pattern if considered a diphthong with /ə/.

1. transport /trǽnsport/ /trænspórt/
2. import /ímport/ /impórt/
3. transfer /trǽnsfɨr/ /trænsfɨ́r/
4. increase /ínkriys/ /inkríys/

In all these cases, the shifting of the primary stress from the first syllable to the second shifts the meaning from that of a noun to that of a verb. This is enough to establish stress as phonemic in English. It is difficult to find minimal pairs which will demonstrate that there are more than two degrees of phonemic stress in English.

Nucleus and Intonation

We have what we can think of as normal stress patterns in English. Paul Roberts (1967) says that in English, a kernel sentence is made up of a nucleus and an intonation. The nucleus is represented by a word or several words, while the intonation is a combination of stress (loudness) and pitch (the high or low quality that depends on the speed of vibrations with which sounds are uttered). Any kernel sentence has a syllable that carries the main stress. More often than not, this stress falls on or within the last word in the sentence:

I bought a new *book.*

This carries no special implications: it is simply a casual sentence, which does not suggest a particular context. But if we shift the stress pattern, we change the meaning: we are answering different questions. "*I* bought a new book" tells who bought it; "I *bought* a new book" implies that the means whereby I acquired the book is in question; *a* answers the question of number; *new* rules out secondhand; and if we give an overstress to *book* we emphasize what it was that we bought. Joe Pierce (1966) thinks that overstress is not phonemic, serving only to call attention to that segment of the utterance; the fact that overstress alters the meaning (in that the utterance thereby answers different questions) would seem to indicate that it is, indeed, phonemic.

Pierce also suggests that because stress and pitch are so closely related, there are two "intensity" phonemes, rather than stress or pitch. The first is a phonemic stress-pitch and the second is a sentence stress-pitch. We need not choose sides here, but the argument depends in part on the claim that stress does not show up on the sound spectrograph even if it is "heard." Whatever the final decision may be so far as English phonemes are concerned, it is difficult to accept the idea that stress is altogether illusory; American students of Japanese, for example have to learn to avoid applying stress in Japanese, which relies on pitch accent. Americans must learn to make the right syllables higher in pitch, without at the same time making those syllables louder.

We have already shown that stress is phonemic in English, but so too is intonation. If, for example, we ask "Where?" with a rising intonation, we are asking to have the statement repeated, as if we did not hear it clearly or cannot believe the destination. But if "Where?" has a falling intonation, it means we want more detailed information. Suppose A says "I'm going shopping" and B asks "Where?" with a falling intonation: the name of a specific store would be an appropriate answer. If the "Where?" were asked with a rising intonation, a repeat of the statement would be the appropriate answer. Thus intonation contours are phonemic in English, but our use of them is relatively limited. In Mandarin Chinese, where theoretically every syllable has a characteristic tone (though in practice it works a little like our nuclei—a polymorphemic string will usually have a single syllable that predominates) the problem is more complex. As Robins (1964) describes the phenomenon, "The pitch levels or the rising and falling pitches are properties of the words as lexical items; the substitution of a different word in a sentence may change the pitch sequence, if the two words concerned are different in tonal composition [p. 112]." As an example, the sequence /ta/ in Mandarin may represent four different words, depending on its tone: "to raise" (level tone), "to penetrate" (rising tone), "to hit" (rising-falling tone), or "great" (falling tone). The local dialect of Hong Kong is more complicated; it has three tones in each of two registers (high and low).

Juncture

A moment ago we mentioned that not only stress and pitch, but also the intonation contour are phonemic in English. The intonation contour, however, is a combination of pitch and *juncture,* and at least one kind of juncture is phonemic and is not confounded by the question of pitch. This is the kind of pause that distinguishes "night rate" from "nitrate." The junctures are transitions that have a great deal to do with the rhythm of the language and its overall sound. Many speakers of Cantonese, for example, have a distinctly choppy sound when they tackle English, partly because they introduce too many *open* (or internal) transitions of the sort that separates the "night" and "rate" above. Some Spanish speakers, on the other hand, ignore certain open transitions in English, or else shift them: instead of saying an + ashtray, they may produce a + nashtray. We tend to think generally that the open transitions separate the words of an utterance (Sawyer and Silver, 1960), but this does not work out quite so neatly. In the sentence "Here it is," for example, the open transition (+) divides the vowel and consonant of "it."

We distinguish three other kinds of juncture in English. There is a rising juncture, represented by a double bar /II/, which usually comes at the end of a yes-no question ("Is he coming?"). One of the characteristics of many English speakers in Hawaii is that they use a falling juncture in this type of question. The falling, or terminal juncture, represented by a double cross /#/, marks the end of most of our sentences. Finally, there is a level juncture, marked by a single bar /I/, which is characteristically indicated by a comma when we write.

Morphemes

If we examine a corpus, or body, of material (a novel, for example), we will notice that it contains recurring partial similarities. The smallest units that occur this way are of course letters and punctuation marks, but having established that these are simply derived from phonemes, we may consider larger segments. We may see, for example, strings such as "word," "words," "wordy," "wood," "woods," "woody," and so forth. These six strings have four components: "word" and "wood," which may appear as independent units, and -*s* and -*y*, which appear only at the end of a string. We would have to modify the latter statement somewhat as we accumulated additional evidence (there are variations, as in "the park has a *woodsy* feeling about it, even though it is located in the heart of town.") But as a matter of convention we make the most complete, general statement that we can on the basis of our corpus. At any rate, we can in this way identify the minimal meaningful strings that we call *morphemes.* Strings such as "word" and "wood" we call *free* morphemes, and strings such as -*s* (indicating "plural") and -*y* (indicating "like" or "characterized by") we call *bound* morphemes, since they cannot appear as independent forms.

Allomorphs

Just as a phoneme represents various allophones, many morphemes have allomorphic variants. In the case of the plural, for example, we may note that typically there is an [s] sound after unvoiced consonants, except after some fricatives. Thus we get [s] after the [t] in "cat," or after the fricative [f] in "cliff," but after the fricative [s] of "bus," or the fricative *š* of "bush" we get [əz] or [ɨz]. The same mid-vowel + -*z* sound follows not only some fricatives, where the flow of air is forced through a constricted channel but is not quite stopped, but also some affricates. Affricates consist of a stop + fricative, as in "church," which begins and ends with a *t* + *š,* or "vex," which ends with a *k* + *s.* Elsewhere the plural is just the -*z* sound, without the preceding vowel. But this only accounts for the majority of noun plurals in English. There is also a zero allomorph of the plural, as in "sheep" or "deer," and there is another form that depends upon an internal vowel change, as in "man-men," "louse-lice," and so forth. There are also a few nouns that form the plural with -en, as in "oxen," or -a, as in "datum-data," or -i, as in "cactus-cacti."

When we consider all the problems with nouns (singu-lar versus plural, morphemes that make nouns into other forms such as adjectivals—book*ish*—or adverbials—mo-ment*arily*, and so forth) and the other so-called parts of speech, the study of morphemes becomes a little formida-ble. Some morphemic problems may not even come into focus until syntactic problems are tackled. In English we have a considerable number of two-part verbs, for example, but these are not very clear until we see how we can juggle the parts. We can turn off the road, and indeed we may have to turn off it if we come to a detour. But while we can turn off the audience with a poor speech, we cannot turn off it, no matter hard had we try. Thus we can use the pronoun "it" after the preposition "off" when "turn" is a one-part verb, but we cannot use "it" after the particle "off" when it is the second component of the two-part verb "turn off." We cannot say *turn it off* for "the road," or *turn the road off,* but "turn the audience off" is good English, if poor policy.

Immediate Constituent Analysis

Until 1957 the building-block approach to linguistic analysis held the field. One tackled phonemes, then mor-phemes, and then, as time permitted, so to speak, one tackled larger sequences such as syntax. One way or an-other, the interrelationships of the various elements in an utterance must be determined and described. To take an example from Gleason (1961: p. 129ff.), given the sentence "The old man who lives there has gone to his son's house," we can apply our intuitive knowledge of English to deter-mine that "old" and "man" belong together in a way that "man" and "who" do not; similarly, "has" and "gone" seem close. Our intuitions may differ on whether "his" and

*Indicates a hypothetical or grammatically impossible form.

"son's" go together better than "son's" and "house," however, and to the extent that we must depend on such intuitions (which, Gleason notes, are beyond the reach of the
foreign linguist, since he lacks the native's "feel" for the
language), the approach is weak. In the present case, however, it is possible to go beyond our intuitions by using the
phenomenon of substitutability. That is, for elements that
"go together," effectively constituting a single unit, we can
find a single-unit replacement that will still yield a grammatical sentence. Thus "oldster" can substitute for "old
man" and "that" will substitute for "his son's." With a little
ingenuity one can take successively larger segments and
substitute for them: thus one can substitute "Boston" for
"that house."

This seems to verify our feeling that "his" and "son's"
are closer than "son's" and "house" in this particular sentence. Gleason (1961, p. 130) carries the process to the
point at which "He" ultimately represents "The old man
who lives there," and "went" represents "has gone to his
son's house."

If we reverse the process, and ask what the basic division is in the sentence—what the primary constituents are
—we will again distinguish "The old man who lives there"
from "has gone to his son's house." And if we take each of
these sections and treat it as a construction, seeking its
immediate constituents, we will probably arrive at "The old
man" and "who lives there" in the first case, and "has
gone" and "to his son's house" in the second. Eventually,
we will show the relative degrees of closeness of the several
elements in the sentence.

But it is not always possible to get agreement on even
such a simple example as this, and there are two kinds of
sentence that immediate constituent analysis seems flatly
incapable of dealing with: ambiguous sentences and passive constructions. Langacker (1968, p. 99) offers the example of "Steve or Sam or Bob will come." If Bob is

coming for sure, then Steve and Sam constitute a unit, but we may only know that either Steve will come or both Sam and Bob will come; here the immediate constituents are different for the two cases. A sentence that is famous by now (thanks to Chomsky) is "Visiting relatives can be a nuisance;" here we do not know whether we are irritated by our guests or by our need to visit relatives.

The case of the passives is more technical, and we shall return to it later. In either case the traditional approach reflects a kind of building-block concept, and thus the task is to chop up an utterance and get at the basic elements. The implication of the traditional approach seems to be that language is a linear production.

Surface Structure and Deep Structure

But we do not begin an utterance by first thinking of a word with which to head the string, and then simply concatenating components until we need to draw a fresh breath. Complex rules govern the arrangement of the sounds of an utterance, and some segments that are destined to appear late have to be set up in advance by the inclusion of particular segments early in the utterance. To illustrate the point, we can contrast rules for typical yes-no questions in Japanese and in American English. In Japanese, one can convert most statements into questions by tacking the syllable *ka* onto the end of the utterance. But consider all the parts that have to be moved when we want to convert "he went" into a question. We have to begin with the auxiliary verb "do," which by beginning the utterance tells us that the utterance is to be a question of the yes-no variety. And the "do" carries the tense marker, which means that the tense marker is substracted from the main verb: "Did he go?" All these arrangements are set up before we actually produce the utterance; the utterance is a reflection of the arrangements of linguistic units that constitute its *surface structure.*

Morphophonemic Rules

This surface structure is not exactly the same as the utterance we hear, since it takes *morphophonemic* rules to convert strings of morphemes into strings of phonemes. (Chomsky, 1965, handles this differently, but the details need not concern us here.) Thus the plural morpheme will be in the surface structure, but the morphophonemic rules yield an /s/ sound in some cases, a /z/ sound in other cases, no sound at all in words such as "sheep," and so forth.

If we had to concern ourselves only with the surface structure, however, we would essentially be making an immediate constituent analysis. And we would still be hard-pressed to deal with ambiguities. Since an utterance of the sort "They are barbecuing chickens" can refer either to a kind of chicken being examined or to an activity that some people are engaged in, and since the speaker has one meaning or the other in mind before he speaks, the two meanings of the string must be separate somewhere in the system. Where they are separate is in the *deep structure* of the utterances. In the deep structure there are two quite different sentences. When we are talking about the kind of chicken, the main verb is the copula "are," and "barbecuing" is an adjectival expression that describes the chickens. When we are talking about what some people are doing, "are" is an auxiliary and the main verb is "barbecue."

TRANSFORMATIONAL GRAMMAR

To get from the deep structure down to the surface structure, we depend on *phrase structure* rules, which are (to state the matter a little too simply) expansions of ideas such as "main verb" or "noun phrase." And then, to achieve the final arrangement of the several components, we apply *transformation rules.* Thus it is a transformation rule that tells us that to make "he went" into a question, we must put the auxiliary "do" at the beginning of the utterance.

But just as the surface structure is not the actual end product of an utterance, the utterances do not actually begin with the deep structure. A myriad decisions have to be made before the deep structure can be set up. The first decision is whether to speak at all: individuals who incur sudden pain at a solemn moment are usually able to repress any "spontaneous" cry of pain, for example. If there is no psychological set to repress all sounds, so that the speaker has no inhibition against vocalizing, he must then select a code. If he is bilingual, he must draw on one language or the other. Once that decision is made, he must decide on a suitable level of politeness. If alone, he may curse; if in "polite" company, he may select a more innocuous expression. While an extremely intense pain may elicit a truly involuntary response, anything less will be subject to the kinds of decision just described.

The considerations that lead directly to the formation of the deep structure are whether to make an utterance interrogative, negative, passive, and so forth. Indeed, Charles Fillmore (1968) has gone so far as to propose a "case grammar," which depends on meaning-relations. As Crystal (1971, pp. 236ff.) puts it, Fillmore is referring to a set of concepts that have to do with the kinds of judgments that humans are capable of making about the events that occur around them: who did something, who it happened to, where it happened, and so forth. There are various possible descriptions for any given event. If "John opened the door with the key," for instance, the subject position is occupied by the actor or *agent* (John); if "the key opened the door," the subject slot is filled by the *instrument* by which the action was performed (the key); and if "the door opened," the subject slot is filled by the *goal* of the action (the door). Thus, Crystal states, "the function of the under-lying meanings in relation to the verb does not change from sentence to sentence, despite the surface differences; and it is this fundamental, semantic identity which is the important thing to recognize about these sentences, and the central fact which a system of grammatical analysis should explain [p. 237]."

At any rate, the new grammar promoted by Chomsky is known as transformational or generative (or generative-transformational) grammar. Such grammars do not depend on a fixed corpus; rather they aim to design rules that will generate all of the grammatical utterances of a language, while generating no nongrammatical utterances.

Linguistic Competence and Linguistic Performance

Viewing the matter in this way, we may readily understand why Chomsky, with one turn of phrase or another (1965, for example), has presented the idea that *grammar is a theory of language,* and a specific grammar is a theory of how a particular language works. This suggests that there are principles for the general case of language, which have applications to specific languages. In speaking of "language" here, we have in mind that Chomsky calls "linguistic competence," as against "performance." The competence is what one has to know (the rules) in order to produce and understand utterances. Performance is frequently marred by false starts, slips of the tongue, groping for the right word, and so forth. The distinction between competence and performance corresponds in part to the distinction between *langue* (language) and *parole* (speech), which was first made by the Swiss linguist de Saussure early in this century. But there is another aspect of *parole,* or speech, in which performance is governed by social considerations, as we shall see later. For the present we are concerned only with linguistic competence, the knowledge that we all rely on to engage in verbal communication.

As indicated above, the generative grammarians depend on two kinds of rule: phrase structure rules and transformational rules. The former are essentially instructions for expansions that will get us from deep to surface structure, while the latter deal with the arrangements of elements in the surface structure. Here we can do little more than hint at the complexity of the problem, and can provide only the roughest of conceptions of how the approach works.

Typically the transformationalist begins with the very abstract concept of the sentence, which is represented by an S. Then the S is expanded, to show that it consists of an optional sentence modifier and a nucleus. In order to gain some economy of presentation, a number of conventions are adopted. Optional elements are enclosed in parentheses, for example, and an arrow is used to indicate the appropriate expansion or category from which a selection is to be made. Thus S $\longrightarrow$ (SM) + Nuc means that S is to be rewritten or read as (Sentence Modifier) + Nucleus. The sentence modifier comes into play in the event that a sentence must be made negative or interrogative, for example. The nucleus can be written as a noun phrase plus verb phrase (Nuc $\longrightarrow$ NP + VP). The noun phrase, in turn, can be written (Det) N (Pl), which indicates that it must consist of a noun at the very least, but it may be preceded by a determiner ("a," "the," "those," for example), and it may be plural. The verb phrase consists of an auxiliary and a main verb, and may have various adverbials, as of manner, place, time, and reason: VP $\longrightarrow$ Aux + MV (manner) (place) (time) (reason). Liles (1971), on whom this section draws heavily, offers the example of "The man will drive carefully in town today because of the ice," where the NP is "The man," the Aux is "will," the MV is "drive," and manner is "carefully," place is "in town," time is "today," and reason is "because of the ice." We can see that if we begin at the end of the sentence and eliminate the optional elements one at a time, the essential integrity of the sentence is maintained. In fact, we can eliminate almost all of the optional elements without changing the essential meaning of the sentence; but there is one exception. If only "carefully" is omitted, there is a subtle shift in the meaning of the sentence, but a perfectly good sentence remains.

At first glance it might seem a little strange to say that the VP invariably contains an auxiliary as well as a main verb, because we think immediately of sentences such as "He ran," or "She is sad," but the rules of this approach specify that every auxiliary contains *tense*, and sometimes it consists only of tense. Thus the representation of the surface structure of "He ran" is *He past run.* If this seems a little cumbersome, consider an ambiguous example of the type "I beat him," which can refer to habitual action or to a specific event in the past; this shows us that one meaning or the other was present in the deep structure, and thus must be carried down to the surface structure.

The expansion of the main verb becomes a little complicated. It may consist of a verb and an optional noun phrase, V (NP), as in "[I present] understand (her)," or it can consist of "be" followed by a number of options: NP (is *a man*), Place (was *at home*), Adjective Phrase (is *very pretty*). In the last case the "very" is an optional intensifier.

The potential expansions of the main verb may thus be very economically represented by this formula:

$$\text{MV} \longrightarrow \left\{ \begin{array}{ll} \text{be} & \left\{ \begin{array}{l} \text{NP} \\ \text{place} \\ \text{AP} \end{array} \right\} \\ \text{V} & \text{(NP)} \end{array} \right\}$$

The "be" in the MV formula is a copula, and is not to be confused with the auxiliary "be." In the sentence "he isn't going," for example, the main verb is "go," while the auxiliary is Tense (be + ing). If we draw a tree for "He isn't going," the bottom line represents the deep structure:

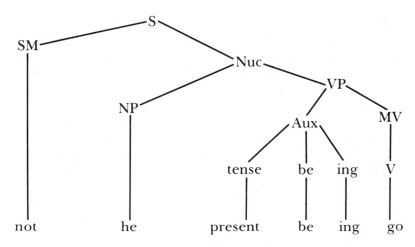

The rules that have been applied to this point are simply phrase structure rules which show the elementary structures that underlie the sentence. If we must rearrange, delete, or add structures, we will have to utilize *transformational* rules. In the present case we have to apply the negative transformation before we can arrive at the surface structure of the sentence. In particular, we have to have such a rule to show us how to put the SM "not" in the right place; the right place turns out to be the position following the first auxiliary after tense.

Thus the deep structure of "he isn't going" is *not he present be ing go.* The application of the negative transformation yields *he present be not ing go,* and all one must then do to arrive at the surface structure is to apply the affix transformation. That is, one must finally separate the *ing* from the auxiliary (be) and affix it to the MV (go): *he present be not go ing.* Morphophonemic rules yield the "is," and the joining of "is" and "not" yields *isn't.* As a matter of convenience, discussions of the surface structure are frequently handled as if the morphophonemic rules had already been applied. That is, the form we are accustomed to hearing or seeing in print is dealt with as the surface structure.

The "be" and the "-ing" go together, no matter what the main verb may be, so it is very economical to keep them together until the last step in the generation of the surface structure is reached. Similarly the past participle (en) goes with the auxiliary "have" (have + en), and it is again economical to keep them together as long as possible. Thus, before the affix transformation is applied, "He had been going" has the arrangement *he past have en be ing go,* and the affix transformation shifts the participles to the next unit in the sequence: *en + be* becomes "been," *ing + go* becomes "going." (A morphophonemic rule tells us that the past of "have" is "had".)

Ambiguous sentences provide one difficulty in immediate constituent analysis, and the passive construction provides the other serious difficulty. In a sense, the two problems are similar but opposite. That is, an ambiguous sentence represents a single surface structure for two deep structures, but for every passive construction there is an equivalent active construction, and either surface structure can be generated from a single deep structure. The passive transformation is characterized by the inclusion of *be + en* and *by.* That is, since the equivalence of the active and passive varieties is intuitively obvious and demonstrable, it is as important to find some way of relating the two structures as it is to clarify "They are barbecuing chickens." For a number of reasons (Chomsky, 1957) it is much more economical to derive the passive form from the active form of the utterance. Thus *the man past eat the food* becomes *the food past be en eat by the man;* there is a morphophonemic rule to ensure that *past be* is realized as "was," and the affix transformation shifts *en* to *eat,* "eaten." Again, the *en* is just the notation we use for the past participle, and the final form of the participle is subject to a morphophonemic rule that depends on the particular verb to which the participle is finally attached. The *en* takes the form *ed* in "The barn was painted by the farmer," for example.

GENERATIVE SEMANTICS AND BEYOND

One of the most significant features of the whole gen-erative-transformationalist movement has been the in-creasing concern with the role of meaning. Most recently, in fact, the concern with meaning has for some scholars supplanted the concern with syntax, somewhat analogously to the way the classic generative concern with syntax sup-planted concern with such lower-order events as phonemic analysis and description. Earlier, for example, we briefly remarked on the case grammar of Charles Fillmore (1968); another provocative statement from the same period was that of James McCawley (1968), who queried whether, in the quest to join semantic and phonological interpreta-tions, there was really a need to posit deep structure as a separate level. Indeed, at the other end of the model, there seems to be no need for the phoneme, if phonological analysis can be conducted without the concept (a view shared with McCawley by, among others, C. J. Bailey, ac-cording to a recent personal communication).

In general the problem that has led to the develop-ment of "generative semantics" is that, in the words of Wardhaugh (1972, p. 149), "Feature notation leaves many problems unsolved," including "that of specifying how the meanings of individual features and words somehow add up to produce the meanings of the total sentences." One approach to this problem is to develop "semantic-projec-tion" rules that would "provide semantic interpretations for syntactic structures into which meaning units had been inserted at some point or points" (Wardhaugh, 1972, p. 149). The syntax would thus remain the central generative component of the grammar, while the semantic component would synthesize the meaning in much the same way that the phonological component can be said to provide the sound. The generative-semantic approach, on the other hand, makes the semantic component the generative component and the syntactic component interpretive. Consequently, the deep structure of a sentence is a semantic structure rather than a syntactic one and syntactic restrictions and arrangements are completely determined by the semantic structure. [Wardhaugh, 1972, pp. 149–150]

The generative-semantic approach, according to Wardhaugh (1972), is intuitively attractive because, in addition to its various technical advantages, it takes into account the fact that what we put into sentence form are the meanings we wish to express, rather than the other way around. Chomsky (1972, for example) admits that his "standard theory" (essentially represented by Chomsky, 1965) is inadequate and needs modification. But the necessary modifications, he feels, are included in his "extended standard theory." Many of the differences that seem to exist between the extended standard theory and generative semantics are more apparent than real, as when the differences are basically terminological. Perhaps the "only fairly clear issue with empirical import that distinguishes these theories," Chomsky (1972) suggests, "has to do with the ordering of lexical and nonlexical transformations" (p. 136). In essence, Chomsky is defending deep structure as a well-defined notion which is better retained than dropped or bypassed.

We cannot here lay out the arguments in detail, but it is not likely that the classical generative grammar is going to be abandoned altogether. It is still useful even to the most avantgarde of the theoreticians, and even if it is an imperfect system, it is, at any rate, a complete one. Lakoff's repeated challenges on the other hand do not comprise a complete system and Lakoff admits that many other kinds of rules must yet be formulated, prompting Chomsky (1972) to remark that "to say this is not to provide an alternative theory" (p. 142).

Finally, generative semantics seem now to be becoming engrossed with what Lakoff (1973, for example) calls "fuzzy grammar." Philosophically, the concern is with the fact that things are rarely tidy. We define categories and describe their membership. But just as some blues are bluer than others, some men more masculine and some women more feminine than others, so, too, in grammar some nouns are more noun-like than others and some sentences are more incontestably grammatical than others (see Lakoff, 1972).

One of the lead scouts through the morass of fuzzy grammar is John Robert Ross, who has armed himself with a conceptual weapon that he calls a "squish" (Ross, 1972). In place of fixed, discrete syntactic categories, Ross posits quasi-continua (squishes) that include within a category space variable categories (verb > adjective > noun) that may even be quantifiable. That is, it may be possible to develop a measure of nounness or verbness, and so forth. To illustrate variability at the level of the sentence, we may take an example from Lakoff (1973). In the eleven sentences that follow, all but the last would be grammatical if the adverb for time appeared at the end of the sentence. But if the adverb is preposed, Lakoff asserts, only a few of the sentences are clearly grammatical (the first four, which lack an asterisk). The next sentence, which is marked by a question mark, he tends to accept, but is fully aware of its fuzziness; the one after that is marked by an asterisk, indicating that it is not grammatical, yet there is a residual uncertainty in his mind, so he has added a question mark. The remainder, all marked by asterisks, he finds clearly ungrammatical.

a. Tomorrow John will leave.
b. Tomorrow I think John will leave.
c. Tomorrow Bill says he'll be able to do your tax return.
d. Tomorrow I know Bill will be in his office.
e. ?Tomorrow I realize that Bill will be in his office.

   f. ?*Tomorrow I found out that tax returns are due.

   g. *Tomorrow I'm surprised that Bill will be in his office.

   h. *Tomorrow I believe the claim that Bill will be in his office.

   i. *Tomorrow John married Mary and will leave on his honeymoon.

   j. *Tomorrow I knew the girl who John will marry.

   k. *Tomorrow John will see Bill and the day after.

The sentences are listed approximately in accordance with their degree of grammaticality for Lakoff (1973, p. 275). The last differs from the others in that the adverb cannot come at the end either, but must be immediately in front of "and the day after" in order to be clearly grammatical. The discovery and formulation of rules to account for such variability seems likely to occupy the neogrammarians for some time to come, and their findings could enormously enhance our understanding of the relation between language and mind, even if they never generate a thoroughly new theory of language.

References

Bloomfield, L. 1933. *Language.* New York: Henry Holt & Co.

Bolinger, D. 1968. *Aspects of Language.* New York: Harcourt, Brace & World, Inc.

Chao, Y. R. 1968. *Language and Symbolic Systems.* London: Cambridge University Press.

Chomsky, N. 1957. *Syntactic Structures.* The Hague: Mouton & Co.

Chomsky, N. 1965. *Aspects of the Theory of Syntax.* Cambridge, Mass.: The M.I.T. Press.

Chomsky, N. 1972. *Studies on Semantics in Generative Grammar.* The Hague: Mouton & Co.

Crystal, D. 1971. *Linguistics.* Baltimore, Md.: Penguin Books, Inc.

Fillmore, C. J. 1968. The case for case. In E. Bach & R. T. Harms (Eds.), *Universals in Linguistic Theory.* New York: Holt, Rinehart & Winston, Inc., p. 1–88.

Gleason, H. A. 1961. *An Introduction to Descriptive Linguistics.* New York: Holt, Rinehart & Winston, Inc.

Lakoff, G. 1972. Hedges: a study in meaning criteria and the logic of fuzzy concepts. *Chicago Linguistic Society, Regional Meetings Papers.* 8: 183–228.

Lakoff, G. 1973. Fuzzy grammar and the performance/competence terminology game. *Chicago Linguistic Society, Regional Meeting Papers.* 9: 271–291.

Langacker, R. W. 1968. *Language and Its Structure.* New York: Harcourt, Brace & World, Inc.

Liles, B. L. 1971. *An Introductory Transformational Grammar.* Englewood Cliffs, N.J.: Prentice-Hall, Inc.

McCawley, J. 1968. The role of semantics in a grammar. In E. Bach & R. T. Harms (Eds.), *Universals in Linguistic Theory.* pp. 124–169. New York: Holt, Rinehart & Winston, Inc.

Pierce, J. 1966. The supra-segmental phonemes of English. *Linguistics.* 21: 54–70.

Roberts, P. 1967. *Modern Grammar.* New York: Harcourt, Brace & World, Inc.

Robins, R. B. 1964. *General Linguistics: An Introductory Survey.* London: Longmans, Green & Co., Ltd.

Ross, J. R. 1972. The category squish: endstation Hauptwort. *Chicago Linguistics Society, Regional Meeting Papers.* 8: 316–328.

Sawyer, J. O., & S. Silver. 1960. *Conversations and Pronunciation Drills for Foreign Students of English.* (Rev. ed.) Berkeley, Cal.: California Book Company, Inc.

Wardhaugh, R. 1972. *Introduction to Linguistics.* New York: McGraw-Hill Book Co.

9

Derived Systems

Linguists consider language to be primarily a system of vocal communication, but it can be transposed into nonvocal forms in various ways. The transpositions may correspond rather closely to the spoken forms; in our writing system, for example, we may say in a very general way that each graph (letter) corresponds to a sound, and the sequencing of the graphs corresponds to the sequencing of the sounds in the spoken form of the message. On the other hand, the transposition may be very global; a signal may correspond to a whole message, as in our legendary warning to Paul Revere that one signal light would indicate that the British were approaching by land, while two lights would indicate that they were approaching by sea. One could argue against describing this sort of case as a transposition of language, but we shall keep the example as marking one extreme (the other being, perhaps, a very precise phonetic transcription of a spoken message). Among the types of derived system to be discussed here are scripts, the manual communication system of the deaf, various kinds of secret language, "Pig Latins," drum and whistle languages, and glossolalia, which is a kind of pseudolanguage.

SCRIPTS

The first attempts at graphic communication may have been of the global variety, rather than being isomorphic with spoken language. The magnificent cave paintings from the Upper Paleolithic period in Europe, which date from about ten to fifteen thousands years ago (Clark, 1967), imply very strongly that mimetic magic was used. The famous masked dancer known as The Sorcerer, for example, who is wearing a wolf's tail and a deerhead mask, seems to be prancing in a ritual dance, which Hoebel (1972, p. 187) compares with the Deer Dance that is performed today by Pueblo Indians. In the same vein, Clark (1967) looks to the Australian aborigines to show that primitive hunters seek an edge in survival and reproduction, and that art is used as a magical device to get that edge.

Of course Upper Paleolithic art does not reflect language, but in the Near East, within a few thousand years, pictures had become pictograms, and had formed the basis for a true system of writing: what Trager (1972) describes as "any conventional system of marks or drawings or analogous artifacts which represents the utterances of a language as such [p. 180]." The oldest such system, so far as we know, was the cuneiform writing of the Sumerians, developed some five to six thousand years ago (Trager, 1972, p. 193). The cuneiform messages consisted of wedge-shaped components that were formed into conventionalized pictograms and scratched into clay tablets. Figure 9.1 shows how pictograms (at the top of each sequence) developed into the cuneiform characters. The slightly more recent and perhaps independently invented Egyptian hieroglyphs (Trager 1972, p. 19) remained more obviously pictorial

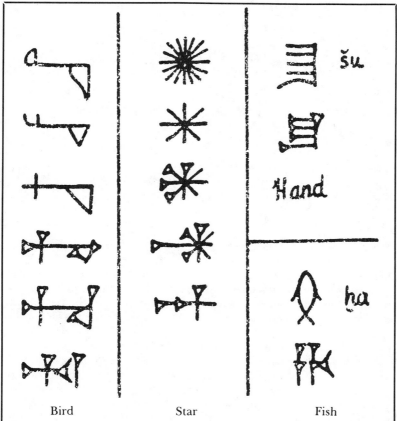

Bird   Star   Fish

Figure 9.1. OLD SUMERIAN PICTOGRAMS AND THEIR DEVELOPMENT INTO CUNEIFORM SYMBOLS. From Friedrich, *Archiv Orientální*, Vol. 19, Table XI. (Reprinted by permission from J. Friedrich, *The Extinct Languages*. New York: Philosophical Library, 1957, p. 34.)

(Figure 9.2), and were painted onto surfaces, including paper (papyrus), with a brush and ink. By four thousand years ago the Chinese were inscribing pictographic characters on bones for purposes of divination, and by the beginning of the Christian Era the Maya were inscribing and painting characters that were basically pictographic, but in

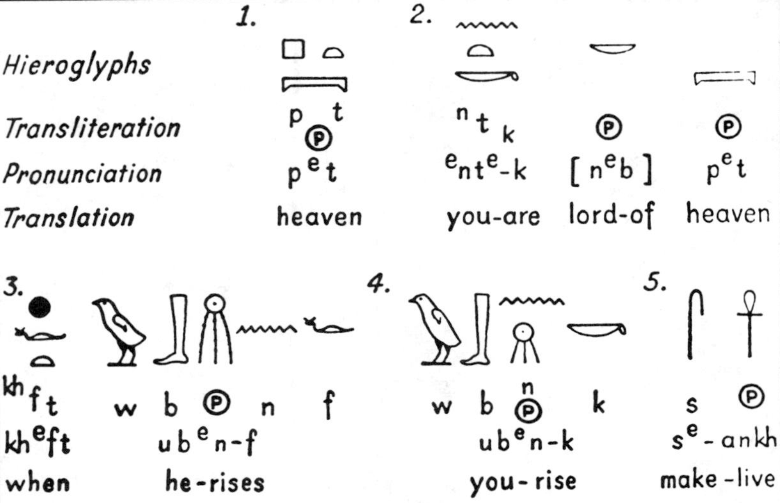

Figure 9.2. MIXED PICTOGRAPHIC AND PHONETIC ELEMENTS IN EGYPTIAN HIEROGLYPHS. Phrases from a page of Egyptian hieroglyph papyrus. The circled **P** denotes a pictograph or ideograph; the rest of the writing is by pictorial *consonantal letters*. In 1, heaven is written alphabetically and confirmed by a conventionalized pictographic "determinative" (the vault of heaven); in 2, by pictograph alone. The first words of 2 and 3 are wholly phonetic: pictographs for the ideas of "when" and "you are" would be hard to devise. The grammatical suffixes -*l* and -*k* added to *uben*, "rise," in 3 and 4 illustrate another reason for the development of consonant letters. In the first of these, the confirming pictograph (sun with rays) is put in the middle of the stem *uben;* in the second, between it and the suffix. In the first words of 2 and 3, the letters in the word read downward; elsewhere, mostly horizontally. The true alphabet was devised by a process of *segregative reduction* out of mixed-method writing such as this. (Reprinted by permission from A. L. Kroeber, *Anthropology: Race, Language, Culture, Psychology, Prehistory.* New York: Harcourt Brace Jovanovich, 1948, p. 371.)

many cases were so stylized as to render interpretation difficult or impossible. Trager (1972) and Kroeber (1948) both give helpful discussions of the Maya system; Friedrich (1957) deals with most of the Old World early writing systems, including many that have never been appreciably deciphered. Trager (1972) gives the most comprehensive and concise recent treatment of the nature and development of scripts; Gelb (1963) has produced the classic study of writing systems from a theoretical, as against a historical-descriptive, standpoint, but Trager (1972) cautions against Gelb's conclusions, while conceding that the factual material Gelb has assembled is useful.

In both the Near and the Far East, pictographic writing developed into a kind of rebus system, in which a picture could be used for its phonetic value. Rebus writing based on English would include, for example, successive drawings of an eye, a tin can, and waves (to imply the sea), to render the sentence "I can see." We do this now for entertainment, but in the development of scripts this was a valuable move toward the development of systems based directly on the graphic representation of sound: syllabaries and alphabets.

Kroeber (1948) called the rebus writing a mixed -phonetic or transitional system, in which pictures of "ideographs" were used alongside other pictures that were used for their phonetic value. Such systems are very cumbersome, of course, by comparison with alphabetic systems, yet custom has been powerful enough to foster long-term retention: the Egyptians retained theirs for three thousand years (Figure 9.2), including a thousand years after their neighbors had begun to use alphabets (Kroeber, 1948, p. 512). In the case of China, retention has been even longer —some four thousand years and counting.

Chinese characters are frequently described as having a general semantic component (there is a "wood radical" under which many characters are classified, for example, and they include words for the names of trees and for various objects that are or have been made of wood, as well as words that lack any obvious "wood" meaning) and also phonetic components. Historically, each character represented a word; hence the script is technically described as *logographic.* When the Japanese borrowed the Chinese script, which they began to do perhaps 1500 years or so ago, they simply read and wrote Chinese. Eventually, around the eighth century, they began to use the characters to render Japanese, which is quite a different kind of language. This involved the use of markers to indicate the order in which the characters were to be read, so as to get them into Japanese syntax; at about the same time, characters which for the most part had already been used for their phonetic values were deliberately selected and simplified into two forms of a syllabary (which is reasonably convenient for Japanese). Karlgren (1923) gives a lucid account of how the Chinese script developed; the introduction of the Chinese script into Japan has been readably described by Sansom (1928); and the general problem of how Chinese writing was used by surrounding groups is discussed by Trager (1972).

Some Egyptian hieroglyphs were used for their consonantal value, independently of whatever pictographic value they may have had before. Various surrounding Semitic peoples carried the phonetic principle further, developing the alphabetic principle between perhaps 2000 B.C. and around 1200 B.C., when the form we recognize as "ancestral" (that of the Phoenicians) became established. Virtually all forms of all the alphabets found in the world can be traced back to this period in the Near East, though which specific group, Phoenician or some other, deserves credit for the idea of an exclusively phonetic use of graphs may never be known with certainty. Once the idea was established, however, that idea could generate alphabets which bear no formal resemblance to the ancestral form. The Cherokee Indian Sequoya, an illiterate of the early nineteenth century, got the idea of an alphabet from seeing how books were used by literate Americans, and used the letters of our alphabet to depict the sounds of his native Cherokee

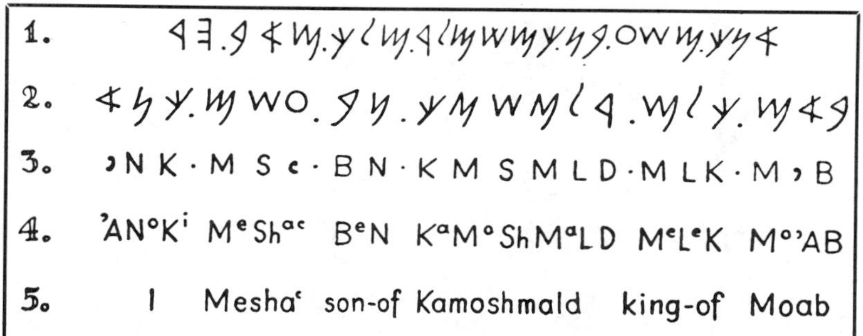

1. ᐊᗺ.Ꭾ ⳤ ⱦ.y ⟨ⱦ.◁ ⟨ⱦwⱦy.ⱨᎮ.OWⱦ.yⱨⳤ

2. ⳤⱨy.ⱦWO.Ꭾy.yⱦWⱦ⟨◁.ⱦⱦ⟨y.ⱦⳤᎮ

3. ꜀N K · M S c · B N · K M S M L D · M L K · M ꜋ B

4. 'AN°Kⁱ MᵉShᵃᶜ Bᵉ N Kᵃ M° ShMᵃ L D Mᵉ Lᵉ K M° 'AB

5. | Meshaᶜ son-of Kamoshmald   king-of Moab

Figure 9.3. INSCRIPTION ON MOABITE STONE, 860 B.C. 1, First line of
actual inscription, read right to left. 2, Same, reversed, left to right,
words slightly spaced. 3, Transliteration into modern Roman capitals. 4,
Unwritten vowels supplied, to give full pronunciation. 5, English translation.—Note resemblance of letters of line 2 with those of 3 and 4, slightly
disguised by originals facing opposite from ours (B, D, K), lying on side
('A, S), extra stroke or lengthening of a stroke ('A, D, M). (Reprinted by
permission from A. L. Kroeber, *Anthropology: Race, Language, Culture,
Psychology, Prehistory.* New York: Harcourt Brace Jovanovich, Inc., 1948,
p. 470.)

language (though, of course, the values he assigned to
these letters had nothing to do with the phonetic values
that we assign to them).

One of the earliest examples of the Phoenician alphabet is on the famous Moabite Stone of King Mesha (see
Figure 9.3). Note carefully the familiar forms of some of the
original letters, such as the A that heads line 2 (though it
is on its side from our standpoint). The actual inclusion of
specific letters for vowels was a Greek contribution, but
that original sign for the glottal stop is the character that
later became our A. Then compare the letters on line two
of Figure 9.3 with the letters in Figure 9.4, which is a passage in Manchu. (The Manchu form of the alphabet is virtually the same as that of the Mongols, from whom they
received it, adding a few diacritical marks; the Mongols, in
turn, received the alphabet from the Uighurs, and they

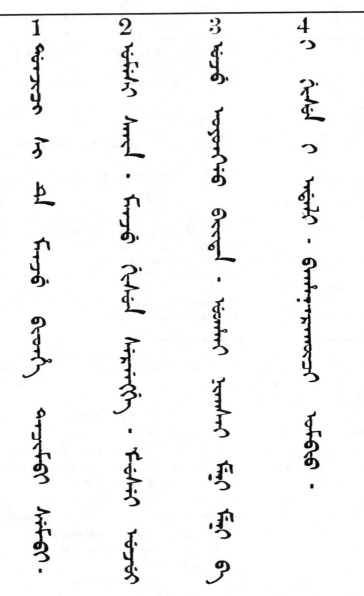

Figure 9.4. PASSAGE IN MANCHU. (Reprinted from P. G. von Möllendorff, *A Manchu Grammar.* Shanghai: American Presbyterian Mission Press, 1892, p. 15.)

SENIOR. So I hear you are studying Manchu, eh? that's right. Manchu is with us Manchus the first and foremost of essentials; it is to us, in short, what the language spoken in his own part of the country is to a Chinese; so it would never do to be without a knowlwdge of Manchu, would it?

donjiei, Condit. tense (6) of *donjimbi* to hear: I hear, but I am not sure, whether it is so

si thou

te now

manju Manchu

bithe book

tacimbi Present Tense (2) to learn

sembi (2) to say, here merely closing the report he heard

umesi very

sain good

manju Manchu

gisun word, speech

serengge Future Part. of *sembi* to say, namely

musei we, with genitive affix *i*, of us

manjusai Manchus, gen. plur. *sa-i*

ujui first, with genitive affix *i* ⎫ the first of
uju first   ⎬ the first
                                       ⎭

oyonggo important @INS,34

baita thing, matter

uthai therefore, it is as @INS,36

nikasai, pl. of *nikan* Chinese *(nikasa)* with gen. affix *i* of the Chinese

meni meni every @INS,38

ba place

i genitive affix

gisun word, speech

i genitive affix

adali alike, similar to

bahanarakūci Fut. (5) of *bahanambi* to comprehend, with negation *akū* and *oci* Conditional (6) of *ombi* to be, if you should not know

ombio Pres. Tense (2) of *ombi* to be, with interrogative *o*, will that do?

185

received it from the Sogdians, who received it from the Aramaeans; Aramaean was probably the language of Christ, since Hebrew had already ceased to be a spoken vernacular by that time.) For example, in Figure 9.4 the initial letter of the first word of the first line (read top to bottom, left to right) is D. The initial of the second-last word in line 4 is a B, while the word just above it begins with a double-toothed A, which is the form it takes in initial position; after the D (which is also a little different when not initial) there is another A, which would look quite similar to the A on line two of Figure 9.3 if it were carved in the older, wood-block style. The L of the same word still resembles the original on line 2 of Figure 9.3, as does the M (line 1, word four; line 2, word three, etc.). The S may be a little less obvious (line 1, word two), but the resemblance is there. The extended example is offered simply to demonstrate the ultimate affinity of our alphabet and one as exotic as that of the Manchus (which is one of the few that Trager does not describe).

Scripts, if they are to be maximally serviceable, must be transparent representations of language. Of course no script is immediately transparent—we must learn to equate the vocal units with the graphic units, and this is more difficult with some scripts than with others. The Spanish and Finnish alphabets, for example, are employed in a way that poses minimal difficulties, because they do a pretty good job of reflecting the phonemic realities of their languages. Our spelling, on the other hand, presents difficulties even to native speakers of English, because of its departures from the principle that one symbol should represent one significant unit of sound (the unit here is the phoneme; we are ignoring the suprasegmentals, which ideally would also receive graphic expression). But any alphabetic system is probably potentially more serviceable than a nonalphabetic script. Syllabic systems such as the *kana* of Japan may work well enough for the languages to which they have been adapted, but no technical difficulty would be involved in substituting an alphabet; there might be psychological problems, simply because change is involved, but an alphabet would do the job at least as well as the syllabary alone. In practice, the Japanese use their syllabary in conjunction with the Chinese characters, which has the advantage of disambiguating homonyms, but the syllabary offers no advantages over an alphabet in the matter of homonyms. Furthermore, in the case of loanwords from languages with different sound patterns (English words taken into Japanese, for example), an alphabet provides the necessary flexibility. Even Chinese, which has phonemic tones that are theoretically part of every syllable (though only a few syllables in each spoken sentence may receive full tonal value), can be handled easily with the alphabet. The student of Chinese writing must learn hundreds of characters to gain even a minimal understanding of Chinese printed materials, and a highly literate individual will number his inventory in thousands of characters.

Why have the Chinese not cast aside such a cumbersome system in favor of the alphabet? The main reason is of course the force of tradition, but the visual diversity of characters also has some advantages. We can perhaps appreciate the visual advantage of spelling differently the homophones "pair," "pare," and "pear," which a truly phonemic spelling would obscure. The American student of Chinese may be confronted with pseudo-problems, because of the ways in which Chinese is frequently Romanized. The Yale system depends on diacritical marks to indicate tones, while the Wade-Giles system uses superscript numbers. In both cases, the tendency of the student is to learn the letter groupings (as we all do with the Chinese names that appear in the newspapers—Mao, Shanghai, and so on), and then try to recall what the appropriate tones are. This might be nearly as cumbersome for the Chinese as it is for an American, but the National Romanization System employs an ingenious notion, which Chao (1947) attributes to Lin Yutang: the spelling is varied to indicate difference in tone. Thus *mai, mae,* and *may* would in other systems be spelled the same, and diacritics or superscripts would indicate the tones. In the National Romanization Systems the *-ai* indicates a high rising tone, the *-ae* a low rising tone, and the *-ay* a falling tone, no matter what the initial consonants may be. In this case *mai* is "to bury," *mae* is "to buy," and *may* is "to *sell*" (Chao, 1947, p. 10). Chao's students, at least, seem to remember tones relatively easily with this system, but not even the current Chinese government, which emphasizes mass education, has managed to replace the traditional logographic system with an alphabet. Perhaps because characters serve so well to symbolize· the Chinese identity, the administration seems content for the present to simplify characters and to restrict their variety.

Secret Languages

While most scripts aim at maximum clarity (given the restrictions of tradition), secret languages are designed to obscure meanings for the outsider. In his recent general treatment of secret languages, Joyce Hertzler (1970) was concerned more with their social than their linguistic aspects. Socially, Hertzler distinguishes codes that enhance and support the mystery, grandeur, and exclusiveness of all kinds of secret societies, and codes that consist mainly of the cants of the half-world and the underworld. After considering some aspects of such argots, we shall look at some more high-powered disguises of communication.

Argot

Argot is the secret language of thieves and tramps (Fowler, 1926, p. 307). Its colorful and often intricately contrived vocabulary serves to mask the meaning of communications that take place between members of the "ingroup," particularly those that occur in the presence of the uninitiated, but it has the additional purpose of promoting feelings of security and camaraderie among those who employ such verbal camouflage. Fowler notes that in earlier usage, the term "cant" was the English equivalent of argot, the designation for the "special vocabulary of the disreputable," although its current meaning is more restricted to "the insincere or parrotlike appeal to principles . . . that the speaker does not believe in or act upon, or does not understand [p. 307]."

One of the most famous varieties of argot, *jobelin,* the secret language of the medieval crime society called the "Coquillards," was immortalized in the poems of François Villon. Six *ballades* composed in argot have been recognized by scholars as the authentic work of Villon; another group of five *ballades en jargon,* of the Stockholm Manuscript, were published for the first time in 1884 by A. Vitiu, but the authenticity of these works has been seriously challenged (Sainéan, 1913).

The secret language of the Coquillards was racy, earthy, occasionally quite bawdy, and thoroughly appropriate to the society of the *coquille* (meaning shell, or more figuratively the rounded hilt of a sword), whose members, according to Wyndhan-Lewis (1928), included "the best card-sharpers, brigands, footpads, dice-coggers, crimps, Mohocks, mumpers, pimps, ponces, horse-stealers, confidence-men, bruisers, thugs, lock-pickers, coin-clippers, house-breakers, hired assassins, and all-round desperadoes in Europe [p. 6]." Perhaps its most outstanding characteristic, as exemplified in Villon's work, was the richness of its metaphors, which recall the characterization of slang as the poetry of everyday language. Thus criminals whose ears had been lopped off were described as having been "circumcised of their handles" (*des ances circoncis*), a figure of speech which, as Fox (1962, p. 106) observes, seems particularly appropriate in a language whose word for head had originally meant "earthenware pot." The *jobelin* was especially given to irony. Fox notes:

> . . . *le mariage* meant "hanging"; *montjoye* ("Hill of Joy," originally the name given to a hill near Paris where St. Denis was martyred) meant "gibbet"; *un ange* was a hangman's assistant; *dorer* meant "to lie," literally "to cloak beneath a bright exterior"—a little like English "to gild the pill;" a *vendeguer* was a thief, as was also *gagneur,* recalling the euphemistic use of "to win" in modern English. [p. 106]

There are some remarkable parallels with modern English slang. *Ne pas sçavoir oignons peller* seems to have meant much the same as "not to know your onions," and *estre sur les joncs* ("to be on the rushes") meant "to be in prison," an expression that is close to the English "to be on the mat" (to be in trouble).

Although some of the *jobelin* terms are rather obvious (e.g., *le coffre* for prison, *la dure* the ground), we can only guess at the meanings of many of the words that Villon used in poems such as this:

Spelicans

Qui en tous temps

Advancez dedans le pogois

Gourde piarde

Et sur la tarde

Desbousez les povres nyais,

Et pour soustenir vos pois

Sans faire haire

Ne hault braire,

Mais plantez ils sont comme joncs

Par les sires qui sont si longs.

Similarly, we can catch tantalizing glimpses of illicit activity in W. E. Henley's verse:

Fiddle, or fence, or mace, or mack,

Or moskeneer, or flash the drag;

Dead-lurk a crib, or do a crack,

> Pad with a slang, or chuck a fag;
> Bonnet, or tout, or mump and gag,
> Rattle the tats or mark the spot:
> You cannot bag a single stag,
> Booze and the blowens cop the lot.

Villon, one believes, would have agreed fervently with the hedonistic fatalism of those last two lines, for he had often enough "dropped a big score" on booze and broads himself.

The insular and isolated life-style of the professional criminal tends to preserve intact many terms of the argot vocabulary. A good deal of the language used by the professional thief even in the twentieth century resembled the argot spoken by members of the Elizabethan underworld (Aydelotte, 1913; Judges, 1930). Elizabethan professional criminals ("conny-catchers") were subjects of interest to Shakespeare, whose character Autolycus in *A Winter's Tale* is the most noteworthy example of the pickpocket in English literature. As Judges (1930) points out, some of these argot terms (for example, "cut-purse" for pickpocket) can be traced back to the time of Geoffrey Chaucer and the emergence of the English language itself, and perhaps even further back, to an Anglo-Saxon root.

We are indebted to the work of David Maurer (1940, 1941, 1969) for more recent studies of argot among professional pickpockets, forgers, and confidence men. Pickpockets ("cannons") belong to a "whiz mob" and speak the "whiz lingo." The training process whereby a youth is indoctrinated into the whiz subculture and instructed in the use of its argot is part of an apprentice-journeyman relationship between a "new stall" and a "tool." Maurer (1960) describes it thus:

> Many a night in a hotel room they *punch gun* or *punch whiz* and the whole lore of the subculture is gradually made clear to him. "Guns like to punch whiz when they get together and they tell funny things about eggs they have pushed around.

Peter men don't punch much guff as a rule, but sometimes
the scat will loosen them up . . ." [p. 450]

The tool may have more than one prospect, or protégé, that
he is grooming to become a "class cannon." He may "muz-
zle around" a bit "single o," then come back to complete
the training of the "new stall." Now, as Maurer puts it:

The boy has *busted out*. He has been *joined out*. He is part of
a mob. He has *mobbed it up,* though he might be stretching
this phrase a bit to apply it to a boy making his debut in a
two-handed *outfit.* He is a *cannon* now and *on the whiz*. [p.
450]

As a secret language, argot is devoid of any features
that would be of compelling interest to the linguist. The
etymologist would undoubtedly find his curiosity aroused
by problems of word origins, in the case of some of the
more obscure terms and phrases in argot; and the literary
analyst cannot help being intrigued by the expressive use
of simile and metaphor in which the argot abounds. But
apart from purely lexical considerations, the argot poses no
linguistic challenges at the syntactical level. It is this aspect
of the matter, together with the obvious problems involved
in gaining access to the criminal subculture that employs
the argot, that has largely accounted for the relative dearth
of linguistic studies in this area.

Drum Language

While drum messages in Africa may be limited to
phrases such as "danger, return to village" and "end of
danger" (van Valen, 1955), and thus need not depend on
the forms of spoken language, the drums are more commonly used for any type of message, including gossip, an-
nouncements, hunting calls, jokes, and entertainment.
Doob (1961, p. 284) has described the awe and mystery
that may surround the drums associated with high office
among the Nhole of Uganda; Armstrong (1954) has de-

scribed how drums are used to instruct the dancers in the warlike secret societies of the Oglemye or Ichahoho.

In the groups described by van Valen (1955), every male member of the community may have a drum name, with three components: first, a drum phrase or epithet characteristic of the individual; second, the first part of the father's name; and third, the village of maternal origin. The name is given either at initiation ceremonies or when the boy is first old enough to understand the drum (around five or six years old). In the latter case the name is sometimes changed at his initiation. The drum name for a woman consists of the expression for "girl" or "wife" plus the drum name of either the father or husband. Most women understand the drum language but do not send messages, and thus never touch the drums.

The chief of a tribe may have the prerogative of silencing all other drums in the area by sounding his special name, to ensure the clear transmission of his message. In some areas only the chiefs and their close male relatives are permitted to use the drums at all. A complete message usually consists of five parts (van Valen, 1955):

1. a signal for attention or a chief's refrain
2. the name of the desired recipient (repeated three or four times)
3. the name of the sender (omitted if the chief's refrain is used)
4. the message itself (repeated three times or more)
5. the signal for the end, either a single sharp beat or a series of low notes.

There are regional variations, of course; the entire message usually takes 5 to 15 minutes, but it may continue for an hour if the drummer is in the mood to play the drums for effect.

The maximum audible range for one drum is usually 5 to 7 miles, though under optimum conditions (especially early in the morning or late in the evening, when thermal convection currents are reduced), the messages may carry as far as 20 miles (Carrington, 1949). It is theoretically possible to relay messages hundreds of miles, but this rarely happens, because most messages do not warrant it, and it would require what in effect are bilingual drummers.

The drums themselves may be grouped into two major types: the more common all-wood slit drums, which are usually called gongs (or bells, by Herzog, 1964) since they have no tensed membranes, and those that have a skin. The latter often occurs in pairs and are called, appropriately enough, twin drums. The types vary regionally, but each tribe customarily uses only one variety for signalling purposes. For more technical accounts of the drums, see Good (1942), Armstrong (1954), Herzog (1964), or the summary in Vetter (1969).

The general principle that governs the actual language of the drum seems to lie in the tonal quality of most of the spoken languages: the drum reproduces the tones, stresses, and number of syllables in the various utterances (Armstrong, 1954). That is, every syllable has its own tone, subject to variations in accordance with grammatical and phonological contexts. What the drums transmit, then, is an abstraction from the total speech utterance; thus it is not usually a code or cipher. The messages seem to be analogues of the suprasegmentals of the spoken forms. Messages tend to be standardized and fairly long, since short, nonstandard transmissions are more likely to be ambiguous unless there is a sufficient social context to make their meanings clear.

Van Valen (1955) distinguishes *grammatical* tone, which evidently has an analogous function to that of intonation and stress in English, and *semantic* tone (the tonal character of the words themselves); the semantic tone is typically more important than the grammatical tone.

Each syllable has a definite relative pitch or tone, which is either high or low, although one or more middle levels may be related in some way to these. The tone is part of the word, so that if we let (') represent a high tone and (.) represent a low tone, we can see how the tones are phonemic: in one area *lisaka* (. . .), *lisaka* (. .'), and *lisaka* (.") mean respectively "puddle," "promise," and "poison."

Since the drum beats are discontinuous, problems arise in the representation of tonal glides and vowel length, which are phonemic in many of the languages concerned. The Luba of the Belgian Congo try to avoid words that contain tonal glides, but when that is impossible they reduce them to one of two register tones; the Yaunde, when in the same situation, use two quick successive strokes that represent the termini of the glide (Stern, 1957, p. 497). For vowel length the Yaunde use two short strokes, which are distinguished from successive short vowel representations by the tempo with which they are administered; the Tshi signals of the Ewe indicate length by extending the interval between strokes (Stern, 1957, p. 497).

The range of individual styles is about the same as that in the speech of individuals (Clarke, 1934).

Herzog (1964) has provided a useful case study of how the drums are used to transmit messages by the Jabo of Eastern Liberia. Jabo is essentially monosyllabic and tonal; vowel length and voicing are also phonemic. Where duration is critical, it is customary to speak of the duration of a short vowel as consisting of one *mora,* while a long vowel might be one-and-a-half or two *morae* in length. In Jabo drum language, then, each beat on the wooden signal drum represents a single *mora.* If two full vowels follow each other, one beat may be omitted or both beats may be shortened. In addition, a technique called "scraping" is sometimes used to represent duration. This consists of two quick beats, given by the two sticks in alternation. Since the scraping occasionally occurs when the drum grammar does not seem to require it, it seems to have an element of style or artistry about it. Scraping is also used to represent true diphthongs, though a single beat is more common, and the variation again may be governed by aesthetic qualities.

While the spoken language of the Jabo is basically a four-tone system, in the drum language the two lower tones are generally treated as if they were one (yielding a three-tone drum language), even though the two lower tones could be kept distinct without too much technical difficulty. The two higher tones are less frequently treated as the same on the drums, and the two middle tones are consistently distinguished. The correlation and variation of the spoken tones and the drum tones led Herzog (1964) to conclude that the Jabo four-tone language grew out of an older three-tone system, with the splitting of the lower register. Most of the surrounding tribes, including the Grebo, from whom the Jabo derived their signalling system and much of their music, employ a three-tone language.

On the true, or skin-covered, drum, only the two middle tones are reflected, probably for technical reasons. Since considerable force is required to beat the drums effectively, the drummer tends to make his strokes with the right hand and left hand alternately, which leads to a mechanical alternation of the two middle tones. In any event, because of the concomitant simplification of the sound patterns, most messages tend to be stereotyped, or coded.

In the Jabo area there are comparatively few drummers, and they tend to be specialists; but in other regions of Africa, for instance the Cameroons or the Congo, many men know how to play the signal drum.

Whistle Speech

Whistle speech, which is employed by the male speakers of several tonal Indian languages in Oaxaca, Mexico, shares some interesting parallels with the drum languages of Africa. For example, in both cases the underlying languages are tonal, so that it is the suprasegmental pattern that provides the basis of communication. Again, it is typically the prerogative of the male to engage in whistle language, though the women understand it. In both cases, since the segmentals are absent, there is considerable danger of ambiguity. And in both cases the derived systems tend to be employed over distances that are not suitable for normal conversation.

The whistle language seems to have greater flexibility than drum language, however. At least among the Mazateco, in Oaxaca, all males use the whistles regularly, not only in the fields and in other areas where they are separated by considerable distance, but even when within conversational range (Cowan, 1948). Cowan provides several examples of business and social transactions of some complexity that were conducted without difficulty by means of whistles, and he was able to get consistent translations from different informants for his whistle texts.

One of the most common occasions for ambiguity is the whistling of proper names. This follows, Cowan says, from the way in which Spanish names are assimilated into the Mazateco tonal system.

> The stressed syllable of the Spanish word becomes semi-high in tone, syllables preceding the stressed syllable become semi-low, syllables following the stressed syllable become low. The word loses its Spanish stress on the last syllable of the word. Thus names such as *Modesto, Gustavo, Frederico,* and *Ricardo* would all take an identical tone pattern: semi-low, semi-high, low. There is no way, aside from the context of the company present, to tell which name is being whistled. [p. 283]

For a more extended discussion of this interesting phenomenon, with some technical elaboration, see Cowan (1948).

Pig Latins

Hertzler (1970) notes that linguistically, the secret languages of so-called primitive societies are variations on the everyday language, rather than completely novel systems. In the case of the Eskimo and Dakota Indian secret languages, for example, ordinary speech is modified by unusual accentuation, the use of special figurative or symbolic expressions, and the addition of archaic words and phrases.

Most of us have had experience at some time in our childhood with some form of "Pig Latin," or *igpay atinlay,* in which the initial consonant or consonant cluster is removed from the initial position and suffixed with /ey/ to the end of each word, or in the case of a word that begins with a vowel sound, the /ey/ or /yey/ is suffixed alone to achieve the thin disguise. The conversion of normal speech to Pig Latin is essentially a matter of applying a simple morphophonemic rule, linguistically a very low-order event—far less complex than applying the interrogative, negative, or "do" transformations in everyday speech. Yet, as Saporta (1967) has pointed out (following the discussion in Halle, 1962), Pig Latin would differ from normal English in having infixes where English has suffixes, as in [óyzbey] rather than [bóyz] for the plural of *boy.* Further, Pig Latin lacks initial and final consonants, but has extremely complicated medial clusters and so forth. The point is worth emphasizing, because typologically English and Pig Latin would seem rather different, even though their actual language differences are minimal, as measured by the number of rules required to convert English into Pig Latin.

The composition of "secret" languages through the application of a simple morphophonemic rule seems to be rather widespread throughout the world, even though the phenomenon has not received a great deal of attention in the literature. Very likely there are several such systems even within the United States. College students at Oglethorpe University in Atlanta, Georgia, for example, were using "Easy Talk" in the 1950s. Before words that begin with a vowel, [iyəz] is employed as the initial; otherwise it follows each consonant sound except a final one. Thus,

"This is a table" would be [ɖiyəzis iyəzəz iyəzə tiyəzeybiyəzl]. On the island of Hawaii, a [g] plus reduplication of the preceding vowel is used, so that "Book" would be [buguk], "Nothing" would be [nəgəθigiŋ], and so forth.

One form found in Japan simply requires the insertion of *nosa* after every syllable but the last. Thus *kono hon*, "this book," becomes *konosano honosan* (final *n* is syllabic in Japanese). It requires very little practice to catch on to such a simple system, even though it can seem quite alien the first time it is encountered. Jeffreys (1956) has compiled several passing descriptions, from various sources, of low-order systems of disguised language in Africa. A number of accounts refer to languages that are spoken backwards, but it is unlikely that whole utterances of sentence length are precisely reversed. A Swahili system is approximately the reverse of our own Pig Latin: the final syllable of each word is prefixed to the beginning. Also, some of the Congo peoples are said to reverse the syllables of their words. But reversing syllables or transposing a final syllable to the first position of a word is not the same as speaking backwards. The difference can be illustrated with our word "backward": [bǽkwɨrd] would have to become [drɨwkǽb], not an impossible switch, of course, but rather difficult to handle fluently, especially if longer sequences are involved. On the other hand, [wɨrdbæk] is relatively simple; this is an operation that can be applied automatically to one word at a time, rather quickly. A sentence-length reversal would require conscious control of the whole sequence before one started.

At any rate, in all cases where details are spelled out at all, it is apparent that relatively low-order rules are applied. The Boloki of the Congo seem to have a system very similar to the Japanese secret language described above: *sa* is inserted after each syllable. While working with Ibo groups in Nigeria, Jeffreys came across many allusions to such secret languages, but he was unable to obtain particulars. This is, of course, one of the hazards of trying to investigate something that is supposed to be "secret." Of potential interest, however, is the remark that the secret speech of one town is unintelligible in the next town, and the secret speech of one age group might even be unintelligible to another age group. In the absence of clear evidence to the contrary, we would be wise to assume that any "secret" language that can be learned quickly and used fluently involves only a few, very low-order linguistic rules.

Codes and Ciphers

There really are some secret languages of a very high order of sophistication. Most notably these are found in use between diplomatic and military posts. There are many levels of system, including the theoretically unbreakable one-time pad system, which depends on the use of additive pages that are never reused, and thus do not provide the outsider with the kinds of statistical information that provide the key to breaking lesser systems. Cryptanalysts rely on a knowledge of letter frequencies /e/ is the most frequent letter in written English, so the most frequently occurring symbol in the cipher text is likely to be an /e/, and so forth) and a familiarity with stereotyped expressions, particularly at the beginnings and ends of messages. But only the very simplest systems can be carried in the head of the user, and any system as simple as that will be broken very quickly by the expert, with relatively little data. To devise high-level systems, on the other hand, requires nearly as much ingenuity as is required to break them.

On November 19, 1941 the Japanese Foreign Ministry cabled the Japanese Embassy in Washington, saying that if an apparent weather message, "East wind, rain," were inserted in the middle of the daily Japanese language news broadcast, all code papers and the like were to be destroyed, because Japanese-American diplomatic relations would have reached the breaking point (Wohlstetter, 1962, p. 51). The three-word weather message was a code, in which a limited signal represented a whole message; there was no direct representation of the language of the message in the signal that was to be concealed in the news broadcast. As with other codes, the recipient must have the inventory of messages or message components (words and phrases that equate to the arbitrary signals) in advance of transmission. Since the code units are representations not of language, but rather of messages or message units (note the use of international codes of various sorts, such as flags to indicate weather conditions, or semaphore signals, which can be interpreted the same way by speakers of different languages), they are not of particular interest here.

Ciphers are quite a different proposition. Ultimately the signal units represent the language units. The Chinese Telegraphic Code Book, for example, contains approximately 9,999 four-digit numbers, which correspond to that number of Chinese characters. A message that consists of four-digit numbers converts directly into a message of Chinese characters, which are read as if the message had originally been transmitted in the Chinese script. By far the most common systems, however, depend on ciphers that convert to alphabetic letters and directly represent the language of the message. The breaking of ciphers depends on a practical understanding of specific features of written language, such as letter frequencies and frequencies of letter sequences; and of course specific frequencies will vary from one language to the next. Gaines (1956) gives examples:

> Finding, for instance, an unexplained cryptogram in which a count of the letters show that about 40% of these are vowels (with or without Y), we may classify it, not only as a transposition, but as one enciphered in English or German, since one of the Latin languages can hardly be written with

so low a vowel percentage. Then, if we note the occurrences of the letter *E,* and find that this makes up about 12% of the total number of letters we may discard the possibility of German, in which the letter *E* is far more likely to represent 18% of the text. Or, if the vowel percentage is high enough to point to one of the Latin languages, French would be distinguished from the others by the outstanding frequency of its letter *E,* sometimes as great as that of the German *E,* while the Spanish, Portuguese, or Italian language will not always show it as the leading letter, its place having been taken by *A.* In the Serb-Croat language, the letter *A* always predominates, and in Russian the letter *O.* [pp. 14–15]

Gaines (who wrote originally in 1939) mentions only European languages, but obviously the logic would apply to any language that is alphabetically rendered. On the matter of sequences of letters, lists of the digrams, trigrams, and commonest words in English are readily available (see the appendices in Gaines, 1956, for example). Thus "the" is far and away our most popular word, being more than half again as frequent as the next most popular, "of," and 15 times more frequent than "this" or "my." The English trigram *the* is about three-and-a-half times more frequent than the next most popular, *ing.* The frequency of *the,* of course, reflects not only the popularity of the word with that spelling, but also words such as "these," "there," "breathe," and "mother."

It is easy to see, then, that a monoalphabetic substitution system, in which the letters are given an arbitrary but consistent value, would hardly stump a third-grader who was armed with even the most elementary statistical information on his language. The problem became more interesting, however, around the middle of the fifteenth century, when the Italian architect Leo Battista Alberti introduced the notion of multiple alphabets (Kahn, 1966). Alberti began with a scrambled alphabet, say *rpqemy* . . . , from which the first letter of the message would be taken. Suppose we want to send the message "Face them down." The *f* would be represented by *y;* then to get the second value, the scrambled alphabet would be shifted one place to produce a second scrambled alphabet. Thus the second alphabet would begin *pqemy . . . r,* and the *a* in "Face" would be represented by *p.* Shifted again, the alphabet becomes *qemy . . . rp,* and the *c* in "Face" is represented by *m;* so "Fac . . ." would appear in the enciphered message as "Ypm. . . ." On the basis of a single scrambled alphabet, shifting yields as many alphabets as there are letters in the alphabet being used (in this case, obviously, 26).

Since each letter of the alphabet will have 26 values, it would be necessary to have a lot of traffic (messages) in order to compute the letter frequencies, and very likely the starting point for the sequence of alphabets would be changed periodically. The original alphabet *(rpqemy . . .)* might be used for the first letter of the messages on the first of the month, but the second alphabet might be used to begin messages on the second of the month, and so forth, for 26 days, after which the cycle might begin anew. But certain shortcuts in deciphering are provided by our tendency to use stereotyped beginnings. If, for example, we were intercepting messages from Naval Headquarters for the Pacific Theater, and had reason to believe that the majority of messages originating there would begin "Cincpac" (Commander-in-Chief, Pacific), we would assume that if a majority of messages on a given date all began "Xaqibbs" we might have our foot in the door for seven alphabets. Then, if we knew that a fair number of Cincpac messages contain the word "directive" followed by a number, we would have a lead on another nine or more alphabets. The different letter sequences that would represent these same assumed values on succeeding days would provide the means of calibrating the several alphabets, and this would lead eventually to the recovery of the whole sliding-alphabet table.

This overly casual description should not deceive the reader into underestimating the ingenuity needed to devise and break code and cipher systems. The polyalphabetic system was modified in the sixteenth century by Belasco (Kahn, 1966), so that an easily remembered keyword was repeated over the plain text for encipherment, to indicate the specific alphabet to be used, and according to Kahn it remained essentially impregnable for 300 years. Today there is an international battle of computers among the major powers, each of which is seeking more clever systems for itself and more effective ways of breaking the systems of the other powers.

While considerable genius has been involved in the development and solution of ciphers, there has been little systematic exploitation of them for any psychological insights they may contain. We know that there is remarkable consistency in an individual's letter frequencies. Kahn (1967) notes the _tour de force_ of Wright (1939), who wrote a 267-page novel without using the letter _e_. The difficulty of the task can be appreciated when one realizes that Wright had to avoid most verbs in the past tense, because they end with /-ed/; he could not use such popular words as "the," "there," "these," "those," "when," "then," "more," "after," or "very"; the pronouns "he," "she," "they," "we," "me," and "them" were out; and certain forms of "be" and "have," which function both as main verbs and auxiliaries, had to be ducked—namely "be," "have," "are," "were," or "been." And Wright was a sufficient purist to avoid using the numbers 7 through 29 inclusive, because if they were spelled out, they too would contain at least one _e_, and for the same reason he avoided the abreviated forms "Mr." and "Mrs."

Ignoring letter-frequency statistics can result in such economic outrages as our standard typewriter keyboard. Thus, as Kahn (1967) notes, 56% of the action is on the left-hand side, even though ours is largely a right-handed world; and 48% of all motions for successive letters use only one hand rather than two.

> Thus words like _federated_ and _addressed_ force the left to leap
> frantically among the keys while the right hand languishes

in unemployed torpor. Much more efficient is the even rhythm of the two-handed *thicken*. As if to emphasize the problem, touch-typing places the two most agile fingers of the right hand directly on keys for two of the least frequent letters of the alphabet, *j* and *k*. [p. 741]

Certain more recently designed keyboards, which take into consideration the relative frequency of letters, can cut the learning time in half. Samuel Morse, on the other hand, assigned his dot-dash values to letters on the basis of his count of the letters in a Philadelphia newspaper's typecase: thus *e* is simply one dot, *t* one dash, and so forth. Kahn (1967) maintains that because Morse was so rational in his approach, it is possible to handle nearly 25% more traffic on a telegraph line in a rush period than would have been possible if Morse had made up his code haphazardly. As to why the manufacturers of typewriters do not mend their ways and produce rational keyboards, the answer is simple enough. Typists who have learned the old system are not much interested in learning a new one, and the people (especially in business) who own typewriters are not much interested in making the expenditure necessary to obtain the new machines. The problem is perhaps similar to that of our spelling system: we all recognize that it is cumbersome, but there is too much lethargy in the system to permit a change.

Anyone interested in the history of codes and ciphers should consult David Kahn's (1967) *The Codebreakers*, an enormous volume (containing nearly a thousand pages of text) written for the layman. For those who would try their hand at some cipher systems, Gaines' (1956) little introduction is useful; it contains problems—and solutions!

GLOSSOLALIA

One of the (socially) more interesting "secret" languages is not really a language at all. This is glossolalia, or the practice of "speaking in tongues." In the United States the so-called gift of tongues was until recently found mainly among various Pentecostal groups (Samarin, 1972), but now enthusiastic glossolalists are to be found among Catholics, Lutherans, Baptists, Presbyterians, Pentecostals, Episcopalians, and even the "Jesus People" (Grabbe, 1971). Very briefly, the speaker of tongues vocalizes in a way that is unintelligible to most listeners, and perhaps even to himself, but the vocalization is presumed to be divinely inspired, and typically there is someone in the audience who renders a "translation" of the glossolalia.

Glossolalia is of greater social and psychological than linguistic interest, since the vocalizations do not constitute language (Samarin, 1969, 1972; Goodman, 1969a). Jaquith (1967) has provided two samples of glossolalia, which were produced by a young, white, adult male, raised in a large Midwestern city, a product of Anglo-American and Pentecostal traditions. The first of 13 strings marked by a terminal contour was "kow hi na ya ka yow a na"; the last was "pa rey ney ə kə rey ə rey ne ki ya la re ya na la re a ro o re ne kiy ya le ya ka tuw." (Only the segmental phones, syllable boundaries, and contour-final junctures have been indicated; stress, vowel length, and intonation are unmarked, to simplify presentation.) All of the phones in both samples occur in the casual speech of the informant, and the distribution patterns of the phones are compatible with those of his ordinary speech. Jaquith correctly notes that the strings are not amenable to phonemic analysis, precisely because they are not examples of language. The "translations" are unitary semantic blocks, nearly always a very generalized praise of God, and could in no way be treated as languages are when translated from one to another (morpheme by morpheme or phrase by phrase).

A useful survey of glossolalia and of similar phenomena in non-Christian religions has been conducted by May (1956). There seems to be some disagreement on the extent to which glossolalia is associated with a trance or some other special psychic state. Worldwide, of course, we should expect to see considerable variation, but even within the American Midwest there seems to be significant variation. Goodman (1969b), for example, maintains strongly that trance is the type of state associated with glossolalia, but Jaquith (1967) saw little evidence of this in his material (see also Hine, 1969). Again, it need not be the case that one investigator is correct and another mistaken. Very likely there is actual variation, depending on cultural considerations and even local social expectations. But if Kildahl (quoted by Grabbe) is correct, it is at least necessary that the individual should be able to relinquish some measure of mental self-control. The following rather detailed account of glossolalic behavior, gathered by Salas (1967), is probably typical of many experiences.

The account is that of a young woman who was first exposed to the Pentecostal religion when she was eight years of age, in the Spanish Harlem section of New York City.

> It has been five years since I stopped speaking in tongues. I do not know what I meant when I was speaking, but I do know that I said repetitions of syllables, vowels, and consonants. To acquire the gift, I was told by a young preacher . . . to repeat rapidly several praises to the Lord, as *Cristo*, *Dios mio*, and Halleluja. I felt afraid, because the people who were seated next to me expected me to start speaking in tongues right away. The lady next to my father kept saying *pecado, pecado*. I could not let my father think I was in sin, so I did what (the preacher) told me to do. I began repeating Halleluja, and *Cristo*.

Gradually, as she repeated the phrases, her vocalizations underwent a change, until they became unintelligible, as if she were a babbling baby.

> I just felt large amounts of energy pouring from my system. The joy I felt made me jump all over the church. I fell on the floor, but it would not hurt me.

While thus possessed she would from time to time take hold of someone, with her eyes closed, and pull him to the altar. This implied that he was in sin, and if he was not, then he would have to testify to that effect in public.

The atmosphere of the church seems to have had a great deal to do with whether or not glossolalia would occur. One evening, in an unfamiliar Pentecostal church, she noted that few people were present, the pace of the service was slow, the opening prayer was delivered without much energy, and the hymns were all subdued. No tongues were spoken that night, but a week later the situation was quite different. There was a large congregation, the music was spirited, and even the prayers were rather lively.

> Even the children were attentive. The hymns sung were full of life, and so cheerful and hearty that on the singing of *El espiritu de Dios se mueve,* a lady came out of the back seat with the Holy Spirit, and began throwing herself all around the place and speaking in strange tongues. I could not understand it, but this language sounded beautiful, very loud and clear.

Soon many voices were heard, particularly those of women and children, and the lively atmosphere was maintained by continued singing and praising of the Lord.

Visits to various Pentecostal churches in New York, including some in the Bronx and Brooklyn, all revealed the same experience. When the service was lively and a sense of unity held the congregation, someone would begin to speak in tongues, and the rest would soon join in. When the service was very slow there was no speaking in tongues. Further, glossolalia was most likely to begin while hymns were being sung, especially the fast ones and those that mentioned the Holy Spirit, for example *Ese cielo azul es mi cielo, es la biblia sagrada mi historia, el Espiritu Santo me guia, y con Cristo me voy a la gloria.*

We can gather from this young woman's experience that there may be a considerable anxiety component among those who do not engage in glossolalia, because they fear they will be accused of sin by the glossolalists. When the glossolalia begins, there is a sudden increase in traffic to the rest rooms—particularly, it seems, on the part of teenagers, who show a sudden urgent need to comb their hair and wash their hands. Those who cannot escape in this fashion are strongly motivated to speak in tongues. In one congregation of approximately 60, nearly half were speaking in tongues at the same time.

Children in the churches could be observed looking around, attending to those speaking in tongues, and then they would imitate them. One little girl said that she liked to speak in tongues, because people in the church were always so nice to her afterwards. Older people generally treated glossolalic children with respect, and even their nonglossolalic peers treated them deferentially, usually declining, for example, to tell dirty jokes in front of them.

In brief, in this woman's experience, glossolalia is unlikely when the congregation is small, the preacher is not lively in his presentation, the singing leader is monotonous, and the hymns are slow; and individuals are not likely to participate if they are unduly troubled. Given the proper atmosphere and even a minimal exposure to the phenomenon, anyone who is interested in developing the techniques of glossolalia can do so. Samarin (1969) maintains that "the only necessary, and perhaps sufficient, requirement for becoming a glossolalist seems to be a profound desire on the part of an individual for a new or better religious experience." Perhaps a small qualification of both of these statements is required. Some of Goodman's informants never seemed to catch on, and Jaquith's informant seems to have sought the experience for many years before gaining it. In view of Kildahl's argument that the individual must relinquish some measure of conscious control over his behavior, perhaps we should say that the individual must be able

to free himself of any inhibitions he may have with respect
to relinquishing that control.

REFERENCES

Armstrong, R. G. 1954. Talking drums in the Benue-Cross River
region of Nigeria. *Phylon 15:* 355–363.

Aydelotte, F. 1913. *Elizabethan Rogues and Vagabonds.* London:
Clarendon Press.

Carlisle, R. C., & M. I. Siegel, 1974. Some problems in the interpretation of Neanderthal speech capabilities: a reply to Lieberman. *American Anthropologist* 76: 319–322.

Carrington, J. F. 1949. *Talking Drums of Africa.* London: Cary
Kingsgate Press.

Chao, Y. R. 1947. *Cantonese Primer.* Cambridge, Mass.: Harvard
University Press.

Clark, G. 1967. *The Stone Age Hunters.* New York: McGraw-Hill
Book Company.

Clarke, R. T. 1934. Drum language of the Tumba people. *Amer.
J. Sociology 40:* 34–48.

Cowan, G. M. 1948. Mazateco whistle speech. *Language 24:* 280–
286.

Doob, L. W. 1961. *Communication in Africa.* New Haven, Conn.:
Yale University Press.

Fairservis, W. A., Jr. 1955. *Cave Paintings of the Great Hunters.* New
York: Marboro Books.

Fox, J. 1962. *The Poetry of Villon.* London: Thomas Nelson and
Sons Ltd.

Fowler, H. W. 1926. *A Dictionary of Modern English Usage.* London:
Clarendon Press.

Friedrich, J. 1957. *Extinct Languages.* New York: Philosophical
Library, Inc.

Gaines, H. F. 1956. *Cryptanalysis.* New York: Dover Publications,
Inc. (Originally published in 1939.)

Gelb, I. J. 1963. *A Study of Writing.* (Rev. ed.) Chicago: University
of Chicago Press.

Good, A. L. 1942. Drum talk is the African's wireless. *Natural
History 50:* 69–74.

Goodman, F. D. 1969a. Phonetic analysis of glossolalia in four cultural settings. *Journal for the Scientific Study of Religion 7:* 227–239.

Goodman, F. D. 1969b. The acquisition of glossolalia behavior. Paper presented at the 68th Annual Meeting of the American Anthropological Association, New Orleans, November 20, 1969.

Grabbe, L. L. 1971. Glossolalia: The new "tongues" movement. *The Plain Truth 36* (No. 10, October): 20–24.

Halle, M. 1962. Phonology in a generative grammar. *Word 18:* 54–72.

Hertzler, J. O. 1970. *Laughter: A Socio-Scientific Analysis.* Jericho, N.Y.: Exposition Press, Inc.

Herzog, G. 1964. Drum signaling in a West African tribe. In Dell Hymes (Ed.), *Language in Culture and Society,* pp. 323–329. New York: Harper & Row, Publishers.

Hine, V. H. 1969. Pentecostal glossolalia: Toward a functional interpretation. *Journal for the Scientific Study of Relegion 7:* 211–226.

Hoebel, E. A. 1972. *Anthropology: The Study of Man.* (4th ed.) New York: McGraw-Hill Book Company.

Jaquith, J. R. 1967. Toward a typology of formal communicative behavior: glossolalia. *Anthropoligical Linguistics 9* (No. 8): 1–8.

Judges, A. V. (Ed.) 1930. *The Elizabethan Underworld.* London: Routledge.

Jeffreys, M. D. W. 1956. Letter on disguised languages to *Man 56* (No. 19): 15–16.

Kahn, D. 1966. Modern cryptology. *Scientific American 215* (No. 1): 38–46.

Kahn, D. 1967. *The Codebreakers.* New York: The Macmillan Company.

Karlgren, B. 1923. *Sound and Symbol in Chinese.* London: Oxford University Press.

Kroeber, A. L. 1948. *Anthropology.* New York: Harcourt, Brace & World, Inc.

Lieberman, P., & E. S. Crelin. 1974. Speech and Neanderthal Man: a reply to Carlisle and Siegel. *American Anthropologist 76:* 323–325.

Maurer, D. W. 1940. *The Big Con.* Indianapolis: Bobbs-Merrill Co.

Maurer, D. W. 1941. The argot of forgery. *American Speech 16:* 243–250.

Maurer, D. W. 1969. The skills and training of the pickpocket. In Donald R. Cressy & David A. Ward (Eds.), *Delinquency, Crime, and Social Process.* New York: Harper & Row, Publishers.

May, L. C. 1956. A survey of glossolalia and related phenomena in non-Christian religions. *American Anthropologist 58:* 75–96.

Mollendorff, P. G. 1892. *A Manchu Grammar.* Shanghai: American Presbyterian Mission Press.

Sainéan, L. 1913. *Les Sources de l'Argot Ancien.* Paris: Champion.

Salas, J. E. 1967. Learning to speak in tongues. Unpublished paper.

Samarin, W. J. 1969. Glossolalia as learned behavior. *Canadian Journal of Theology 15:* 60–64.

Samarin, W. J. 1972. Glossolalia. *Psychology Today* (August): 48–50, 78.

Sansom, Sir George. 1928. *An Historical Grammar of Japanese.* London: Oxford University Press.

Saporta, S. 1967. Linguistics and communication. In Lee Thayer (Ed.), *Communication Theory and Research,* pp. 4–27. Springfield, Ill.: Charles C. Thomas, Publisher.

Stern, T. 1957. Drum and whistle language: An analysis of speech surrogates. *American Anthropologist 59:* 487–506.

Trager, G. L. 1972. *Language and Languages.* San Francisco: Chandler Publishing Co.

Van Valen, L. 1955. Talking drums and similar African tonal communication. *Southern Folklore Quarterly 19:* 252–256.

Vetter, H. J. 1969. *Language Behavior and Communication.* Itasca, Ill.: F. E. Peacock Publishers, Inc.

Wohlstetter, R. 1962. *Pearl Harbor.* Stanford, Cal.: Stanford University Press.

Wright, E. V. 1939. *Gadsby, a Story of Over 50,000 Words Without Using the Letter E.* Los Angeles: Wetzel Publishing Company.

Wyndham-Lewis, D. B. 1928. *François Villon.* New York: Coward-McCann.

10

The
Ontogenesis
of
Language

Slobin (1971) claims that until recently, "behavioristic psychology looked upon language, and the task of first language learning, as just another form of human behavior which could be reduced to the laws of conditioning," and thus were "governed by variables such as frequency, recency, contiguity, and reinforcement [p. 40]." Perhaps the most elaborate presentation of this view was made by Skinner (1957), and the most detailed rejection of it is by Chomsky (1959). Others concede that the approach has inadequacies, but seem reluctant to abandon it (DeVito, 1970), perhaps for want of a more satisfactory theory and because the extreme in the other direction denies that first language acquisition even involves learning.

A middle ground, which admits the inadequacy of the stimulus-response approach, while insisting that evidently innate language acquisition capabilities do reflect learning, has been proposed by Hebb, Lambert, and Tucker (1973).

By allowing for the concepts of one-trial- and latent learning (the latter does not require more or less immediate reinforcement) and of perceptual learning, and by making liberal allowance for the concept of simultaneous learning at various levels of abstraction (to learn that "finger" can be pluralized is to learn at the same time that "thing" can be pluralized), Hebb *et al.* avoid the more simplistic views that were mentioned above. The logic of their argument may not persuade those at either extreme, but if the theory can be more minutely articulated and proves to be experimentally productive, it may acquire a strong following.

In the meanwhile, the view that seems to inform most researchers on first language acquisition is in accord with the description provided by Slobin (1971), of "a child who is creatively constructing his language on his own, in accordance with innate and intrinsic capacities—a child who is developing new theories of the structure of the language, modifying and discarding old theories as he goes [p. 40]."

In the past few years the view has been growing also that language is a little more than something that is simply acquired, like the ability to operate a helicopter or to play a piano. Lenneberg (1967), Smith and Miller (1966), and others have posited that humans have an innate predisposition for acquiring language. Vetter and Howell (1971) have gone further, suggesting that language ability is part of a more general ability to deal with extremely complex patterns of stimuli, and Lenneberg (1971) has also extended his view to include the human ability to know arithmetic. What remains distinctive about language, however, is that it is everywhere a complex phenomenon, which is invariably elaborated. That is, many people and many cultures leave their arithmetic and other abilities relatively undeveloped, but this is never true of language. Even in the case of the profoundly deaf, who must rely on manual articulation, the system is typically highly complex and developed.

The idea that language is a peculiarly human ability is not new, of course; as Chomsky (1968) expresses it, Descartes (1596–1650) correctly observed that "language is a species-specific human possession, and even at low levels of intelligence, at pathological levels, we find a command of language that is totally unattainable by an ape that may, in other respects, surpass a human imbecile in problem-solving ability and other adaptive behavior [p. 9]."

Given that the normal youngster has a genetic predisposition for language-learning in general, he has no such predisposition for learning a specific language. He will in a matter of three or four years gain a mastery of the language appropriate to his cultural and linguistic environment. The essential independence of race, language, and culture has long been established in anthropology (Boas, 1949; Kroeber, 1948; Linton, 1936; Sapir, 1921). A black youngster raised in Paris will grow up speaking Parisian French; a Navaho Indian child raised in Peking will grow up speaking Mandarin Chinese; a Muscovite child raised in the appropriate part of Africa will grow up speaking perfect Swahili.

The fact remains, however, that the child must *learn* his language, and how this is accomplished is one of the most interesting questions in psycholinguistics. Rather than reviewing those arguments that seem inadequate in modern perspective, we shall simply outline some of the methodological and theoretical approaches that are employed by most researchers today.

First of all, the sound system of the child and the set of rules he uses to form sentences are described in their own terms; that is, they are described independently of the model presented by the adult community. A second aspect of the modern approach is that attention is devoted to the successive steps through which the child passes on his way toward mastery of the system employed by the adults around him (Ervin and Miller, 1963).

PRELINGUISTIC VOCALIZATION

Eisenson, Auer, and Irwin (1963) have suggested that there are five stages of prelinguistic vocalization: undifferentiated crying, differentiated crying, babbling, lallation, and echolalia. The vocalizations of deaf and hearing children are indistinguishable in the first three months, and it is only after the age of six months that there is a decrease in the range of sounds uttered by the deaf (Lenneberg, 1964). For the normal infant, babbling begins by the third or fourth month of life, but it is only at about six months of age that the vocalizations become typically differentiated into vocalic and consonantal components (Lenneberg, 1967).

Babbling is normal infant behavior, but it does not lead to normal language development in the case of the profoundly deaf, and it is not critical for the later development of linguistic competence. At least one youngster who was incapable of speech articulation because of a congenital neurological defect was able to demonstrate normal comprehension of speech (Lenneberg, 1962). The period that features *lallation,* the child's imitation of his own accidentally produced sounds, begins at around six months of age, while *echolalia,* the imitation of sounds produced by others, begins around the ninth or tenth month (Eisenson *et al.,* 1963). There is little reason to doubt that these exercises provide the infant with helpful practice in learning to control his vocalizations, but there is little evidence to suggest that the rehearsals are systematically related to the production of sounds that will eventually constitute the youngster's phonemic system.

There is no direct progression from a stage in which all sounds are random to the stage at which all sounds and sound sequences match those of the model; hence it should not be assumed that linguistically relevant behavior does not occur during the months prior to the production of unmistakable words. Weir (1966) and Eleanor Maccoby of Stanford sampled the vocalizations of infants between six and eight months of age in households in which the primary languages were Mandarin Chinese, Syrian Arabic, and American English respectively. They were usually able to identify the Chinese infant by his distinct pitch patterns, but were unable to distinguish the two Arabic babies easily from the American one.

A subsequent, more extensive study along the same lines was undertaken by the same investigators, and some very preliminary observations were reported by Weir (1966). At approximately six months of age, very different patterns could be seen developing for a Chinese baby, an American baby, and a Russian baby. Weir (1966) notes:

> The utterances produced by the Chinese baby are usually monosyllabic and only vocalic, with much tonal variation over individual words. A neutral single vowel with various pitches is also typical of another six-month-old Chinese infant, as well as of a still different seven-month-old one. The Russian and American babies, at six and seven months, show little pitch variation over individual syllables; they usually have a CV (consonant-vowel) syllable, often reduplicated or repeated at intervals several times, with stress patterns occurring occasionally and intonation patterns usually over a number of syllables.

On the basis of this and other evidence cited in Weir (1966), it appears that the first unmistakable steps toward the acquisition of a specific language are taken around the sixth or seventh month, with the acquisition of tonal or intonation patterns that depend on particular linguistic environments for their distinctive characteristics.

While it is likely that the majority of students of language acquisition prefer to begin their studies at the period when the child has "at least two systematically contrasted meaningful words, a point usually reached by the end of the first year" (Ervin and Miller, 1963; p. 109; see also Slobin,

1971; p. 41, who favors beginning with the two-word sequence), it is apparent that a great deal of important preparatory activity has taken place before intelligible sounds are produced.

LINGUISTIC DEVELOPMENT

First Stage

There is no clear point at which we can say without fear of contradiction that true linguistic behavior has begun and that all previous behavior, however vocal, is nonlinguistic. Intonation patterns, which in English constitute one aspect of the phonemic system, show the influence of the linguistic environment around the sixth or seventh month. Yet it is the use of *symbols* that more than anything else distinguishes language from other forms of communication, and the most elementary manifestation of this process is naming, or labeling. This means using words, where there is no intrinsic association between a sound sequence and its referent. Thus there is reason to designate the use of unmistakable words as the first stage of linguistic behavior.

Second Stage

If one-word utterances mark the first stage of linguistic development, then the first sequencing of words, the use of two-word utterances, is a convenient marker for the second stage. Of course there is no clear differentiation between the one-, two-, and multiword stages, and after a period in which two-and three-word utterances are pretty typical, events move swiftly. Not only is there a sharp increase in the vocabulary, but the grammatical patterns used increase in number and complexity. By the age of four years the normal child has acquired the essential patterns of daily verbal interaction. There is no final stage, of course, since many adults continue to refine their use of the language and add to the range of utterances they can comprehend. After treating the development of the phonemic system, we shall consider the stages that are characterized by one-word utterances, two-word utterances, and multiword utterances, and (rather briefly) some of the problems that arise through the study of reading and writing.

PHONOLOGICAL DEVELOPMENT

As we have already seen, we cannot identify phonemes until we have at least two consistent sound sequences that can be established as differing in meaning. Since babbling sounds have no direct bearing on what will become the phonemic system of the youngster, many sounds are produced that are later dropped, and some of them will have to be acquired again later, because they are significant in the model, they need not be considered here. Intonation is relevant and seems to appear early, but we lack sufficient evidence to relate it usefully to a general discussion of the phonemic system as it develops later, beyond Lenneberg's (1967) observation that the child reacts to whole patterns rather than to small segments. This appears to explain why babies of Chinese-speaking parents show a markedly different intonation pattern from that shown by the babies of English-speaking parents, as early as about six months (Weir, 1966). The difference is generally of the sort that we might expect to see developing in a potential speaker of a tonal language, as against the pattern for a potential speaker of a nontonal language.

One of the interesting, yet vexing, problems in the study of early language acquisition is the description of a *collapsed phonemic system.* Thus a three-year-old boy in the process of abandoning Japanese and acquiring English had a single initial /d/ for English /d/ and /l/. He would accordingly, say *I dike you* where we would say "I like you." In the present case it was obvious that his performance and his competence differed, because he would not accept imitations of his system. That is, if adults tried to employ a /d/ where the adult model called for /l/ (*dove* for "love," for example), the child indicated by means of headshaking and other signs that the substitution was inappropriate.

In general, it seems that the younger the child is, the broader the sound categories will be that constitute his phonemic system. This can considerably obscure the identification of vocabulary items, and can even delay recognition that the one-word stage has been reached. Who but an experienced linguist, for example, would be able to recognize the following pattern reported by Morris Swadesh (in Ervin and Miller, 1963) for his son's phonemic system?

> Final and medial consonants of the adult's words were dropped by the child. The initial consonant was replaced by a nasal if a noninitial nasal was found in the adult's word; a labial was replaced by the labial nasal /m/, and a nonlabial was replaced by /n/: *blanket* /me/, *green* /ni/, *candy* /ne/. Complicated substitutions of this type are not at all uncommon, but they are ordinarily not recognized by the parent. [p. 115]

The final mastery of the adult model phonemic system may take a considerable time. Templin's (1966) data suggest that most children have mastered all the phonemes of English by the age of eight years; any gross distortion of a phoneme or substitution of one phoneme for another is considered to indicate a speech (articulatory) problem.

Distinctive Features

Phonemes can be described in terms of distinctive features, which are identified through the use of mininal pairs (different words that differ only in the feature under investigation). Jakobson (1941, cited in Carroll, 1960) has suggested that the child may learn to produce the distinctions required by the model in a definite developmental sequence. The order of learning is said to reflect the prevalence of the contrasting features in the various languages of the world. The distinctive features that occur most rarely in the world's languages tend to be the last mastered by the children who speak those languages. Thus the distinction between the initial sounds of *free* and *three* is required in English, but in very few other languages, and it appears to be one of the distinctions learned relatively late by English-speaking children. (We might expect the same pattern to develop in language-contact situations, including Creole languages. In the Hawaiian Creole, for example, the fricatives in bro*th*er and *th*rough are replaced by their corresponding stops: [brədə], [truw].

Once a contrast has been learned, it tends to permeate the whole phonemic system. When Joan, a child described by Velton (1943, cited in Ervin and Miller, 1963), learned to contrast *p* and *b*, she also learned to contrast *t* and *d*. That is, when she learned to distinguish the *p* and *b*, she was not simply sorting out two phonemes that had formerly been one in her system; she was developing a more abstract distinction—voiceless versus voiced stops. In this way, a child could double his repertoire of consonants with each pair of contrasting features learned. According to Ervin and Miller (1963), "The theory presents an economical process of learning since the number of contrasting features is much smaller than the number of phonemes. Radical changes in the system come at once rather than through the gradual approximation of the adult phonemes one by one [p. 112]."

SYNTACTICAL DEVELOPMENT

For about half a year, between the ages of 12 and 18 months, the vocalizations of the child typically consist of single words. There are phonological, syntactic, and semantic differences between these utterances and those of the model: this Lenneberg (1967) sees as evidence not only of maturational factors, but also of a difference in learning strategy. The child learns patterns and structure first, rather than constituent elements. Most adults who are learning or teaching a second language seem to begin with particular attention to the phonetic skills required, and take up the problems of syntax and semantics later. Krech and Crutchfield (1958) have reported studies of the relative effectiveness for adults of learning complex skills and a whole process, as against mastering specific processes that are constituents of the whole and subsequently trying to join them into a single process. Their evidence suggests that the former approach is more effective.

The one-word utterance seems to be a universal stage, and most students of child language clearly prefer to begin the study of their grammar with a consideration of utterances of two words or more. But Lenneberg (1967) seems to have a point well taken when he suggests that "if we assume that the child's first single word utterances are, in fact, very primitive, undifferentiated forms of sentences, and that these utterances actually incorporate the germs of a grammar, a number of phenomena may be explained [p. 283]."

If Lenneberg is correct, it would seem that more attention should be paid to this stage than has been customary. It is apparent that "daddy" will not represent the same expansion of deep structure every time it appears, for example, and a study of the pitch contours with which it is associated in different contextual circumstances should provide further clues to the grammar of the one-word utterance. Not only may the one-word utterance represent a kind of sentence that will vary with different presumed deep structures, but there may yet be some validity to the more prevalent assumption that they are mere labels. That is, some one-word utterances may be labels in which the grammatical question simply is not relevant. And to the extent that one-word utterances serve reference functions, they are important to our understanding of early concept formation (Vetter and Howell, 1971).

Evidence from Comparative Linguistics

Our lack of adequate comparative material from non-Indo-European languages obscures several questions. First, different languages codify experience in different ways, and that may have implications for the kinds of problem encountered in first-language learning. Any normal child can learn any language as his native tongue, but all languages may not be equally easy or difficult to learn. It would seem likely that a language with a relatively simple phonemic system, such as Spanish or Hawaiian, would pose fewer problems of articulation than a language with a more complex phonemic system, such as Korean or English. This in turn would imply that the performances of beginning speakers of languages with simple phonemic systems should be more readily interpreted by those attending them. That is, there would be less need to puzzle out collapsed phonemic systems, and this in turn would mean that certain kinds of communication should be simpler at the early stages. The Japanese term *mamma* "food" is a term spoken by and to children, and is learned very early, probably before the first birthday in most cases. It conforms essentially to the phonemic pattern of the model, is easy to articulate, and serves very effectively in adult-child communication. In English, on the contrary, there seems to be nothing that quite corresponds to this. At least, we are not aware of common examples of terms for "food," "milk," or "bottle," or of any linguistic term that would be functionally equivalent. Our experience is that the youngster tends to cry, and thus leaves it to the ingenuity of the parent to determine what his response should be.

Another problem that we need comparative material to resolve is the effect of different morphosyntactic structures on the problems of first-language learning. Word order is more critical in English than in Russian, which has a highly developed inflectional system, yet the Russian child typically relies on the subject-object-verb order until around the end of the second year, when subject-verb-object begins to predominate. At first both languages are unmarked for tense, gender, number, and so forth, but we might reasonably expect that the Russian child would first learn the morphological markers for subject, object, and verb, and then combine them in any order, since they are exposed to such a variety of word orders by their linguistic environment. Slobin (1966) says, however, word order is as inflexible for Russian children as it is for American children.

The extent to which different language structures condition different learning patterns remains an important problem area. Kluckhohn (cited by Casagrande, 1948) felt that Navaho children take longer to learn their extremely complicated language than English-speaking children, whose task appears easier, take to learn theirs. Even in English there is a great deal to be learned about one-word utterances, but what of languages in which even the simplest words consist of several morphemes? In English, "open" is a single morpheme, but in Japanese the simplest equivalents are marked for aspect or tense, and contain two morphemes: for example, *akeru* means "will open," *aketa* means "opened," and as a request (imperative) *akete* is common in the speech of the Japanese child. Whether or not one chooses to treat these as equivalent to our one- or two-word utterances, it may be that the sequencing of *morphemes* is a more important general consideration than the sequencing of *words*. Indeed this conclusion *has* been reached also on the basis of the evidence of English (Brown, 1973).

Sequencing

In English, at least, the sequencing of two words marks a new stage of development, which usually begins at around 18 months of age. A two-word sequence is more than a mere joining of two independent entities. As Brown and Bellugi (1964) have indicated, single-word utterances carry primary stress and have a terminal intonation contour, but when two such words, for example "push" and "car," are put into a single construction, "push car," the "push" will carry a lesser stress and a lower pitch, and will lose its terminal contour, while the "car" will retain its primary stress and terminal contour, and will gain a higher pitch.

Form Classes

In addition to tactical rules such as this, which become evident at the two-word stage, there are also different *form classes*. There is an open class, which has a large membership, consisting of many of the words that had formerly comprised the one-word utterances (Slobin, 1971). Words of the other class are variously called *modifiers* (Brown and Bellugi, 1964; Brown and Berko, 1960; Brown and Fraser, 1964), *operators* (Ervin, 1963, 1964), or *pivot words* (Braine, 1963). This is a relatively closed class: it has few members, but each member gets a greater piece of the verbal action.

With some exceptions, a two-word sequence may be generated by taking any member of one class and placing it in sequence with any member of the other class. In some constructions the pivot word comes first: "a coat," "a Becky," "a celery," "more nut," "dirty knee" (Brown and Bellugi, 1964). In the other major construction the pivot word is in the second position: "boot on," "tape on," and so forth (Slobin, 1971). The former construction contains sequences that seem to correspond to the sequences in the adult model, but some in fact do not. We use the indefinite article "a" only to modify common count nouns in the singular, and we consider it inappropriate before proper nouns (*a Becky) or mass nouns (*a celery). Similarly, we require the plural when "more" modifies a count noun, so that we would not consider "*more nut" to be grammatical for us. (Again the asterisk marks theoretical forms.)

In a manner somewhat analogous to the notion of a collapsed phonemic system, the child's form classes are collapsed, in that there is a class of words that must ultimately be divided into subclasses such as the definite article, indefinite articles, demonstrative adjectives, possessive pronouns, and so forth. It is reasonably clear that some of the surface structures reflected in the two-word utterances represent different deep structures. Slobin (1971), on the basis of examples provided in Bloom (1968), suggests that such nonpivot structures as "cup glass," "party hat," "Kathryn sock," "sweater chair," and "Kathryn ball" represent five different semantic relationships. Thus the first may show conjunction, "a cup *and* a glass"; the second attribution, the *kind* of hat in question; the third possession, *whose* sock; the fourth location, *where* the sweater is; and the fifth a subject-object relationship, *who* will throw *what*. Of course a very careful examination of the context in which the utterance occurs is necessary before the semantic relationships can be guessed with any confidence. As Slobin points out, the semantic relationships are usually clear in the adult speech, because the syntactic forms are fully developed. But the youngster is limited to very short utterances, which cannot make the relationships explicit: "An important aspect of grammatical development, therefore, is the ability to produce longer utterances in which subparts of the utterance bear grammatical relations to one another [p. 47]."

IMITATION AND EXPANSION

A word about imitation is in order, since it has played such an important part in the older theories of language acquisition, and of course it still has some intrinsic interest. We have already indicated that in matters of phonology the productions of the very young child bear little direct relationship to those of the adult model. Even from the brief examples of two-word utterances just given, it should also be obvious that the early grammar of the child is not immediately related to that of the model.

Imitations may be made by the parent, in which case the parent typically expands the child's utterance, as when one mother expanded her son's "There go one" into "There goes one" (Brown and Bellugi, 1964). In this study, the mothers were found to respond to the speech of their children with expansions about 30% of the time. In general, the expansions consist of the original word order plus whatever additions are necessary to transform the child's utterance into an appropriate and grammatically acceptable equivalent in the adult model. The imitations of adult speech by the child tend to be reduced; for example, he may convert "That's an old time train" to "old time train." In both cases the imitations tend to preserve the word order of the original, while the omissions and additions are likely to be of function words (the words that serve to show the relationships among the lexical or content words).

One point of particular interest in the matter of adult expansions of infant speech is concerned with the development of what Bernstein (1966) calls *restricted* versus *elaborated* codes. To oversimplify a bit, the elaborated codes are what we think of as the grammatically complex speech associated with the more advantaged parts of the speech community, and the restricted codes are more typical of the culturally deprived and working classes. Ward (1971) has given a useful description of mother-child interaction in a black Louisiana community. Telegraphic expressions such as "It a bus?" are virtually never expanded into a form typical of Standard English, such as "Is it a bus?" Instead of focusing on the speech form, the mother advances the dialogue and thereby ends it. Mama initiates the conversation, determines the topic and the direction it will take, and terminates it. So far as the adults are concerned, the children in this community are not suitable companions in a conversation.

Ward appears to feel that her material casts doubt on some of the theories that have been advanced, partly on the basis of the expansions that are typical of white middle-class mothers. But many of the features that are missing in the youngster's speech, such as the copula, are also missing in the adult vernacular. That is, many potential expansions would be appropriate for the middle-class white model, but would not be appropriate for the local vernacular.

A final word on imitation is in order. Labov (1972, pp. 304–305) has noted that most models and studies of language acquisition focus on the mother-child interaction and tend to exclude the influence of the peer group. We learn that a child has acquired a particular feature, but we do not know with whom he has been interacting in the interim. Perhaps the key point in Labov's argument is that the children of immigrants almost always speak as their age-mates speak rather than as their parents speak, (so far as English is concerned, at any rate). Indeed, so long as very young children interact with their age-mates in any linguistic environment, it is probably impossible to keep them from speaking in the local vernacular, and the parents need never learn even the most elementary features of that language—as with many American parents abroad, for example.

CHARACTERISTICS OF CHILD LANGUAGE DEVELOPMENT

There are a number of interrelated processes that appear to typify child language development in general. These include analogical formations, overgeneralization, the expansion of telegraphic speech, increase in the length of utterances, and the increasing mastery of rules that relate syntactic units.

Analogical Formations and Overgeneralization

Analogic formations involve generalization of the sort that goes from "cat/cats" to "coat/coats," but overgeneralization can yield forms that are not found in the model, such as "foot/foots," or "hit/hitted" (by analogy with "pit/pitted"). The "incorrect" forms imply strongly that the child is demonstrating mastery of a rule: a rule for generating the plural in "foots" and a rule for generating the past tense in "hitted."

This problem was investigated in Jean Berko's (1958) imaginative study of the acquisition of English morphology. If a young child can supply the correct ending for the plural of an ordinary noun, it may be merely a demonstration that he has memorized the correct form. If, on the other hand, he is able to give the correct plural ending /-z/ for a nonsense word (for example, gutches as the plural of gutch), this suggests that the child has internalized a working system of plural allomorphs and conditional variants, and is able to generalize to new cases and select the right form.

Berko was also interested in the manner in which these morphological rules evolve. Is there a progression from simple, regular rules to more irregular and qualified rules that are adequate to describe English fully?

The experiment began with an examination of actual vocabulary. The 1,000 words most frequently found in a first-grader's vocabulary were selected from a standardized list. These were examined to see what features of English morphology were commonly represented in the vocabulary of a child of this age. On the basis of actual vocabulary samples, estimates were then made of the kind of morphological rules that children might be expected to have acquired, and from these items a list was constructed. In order to gather some idea of the notions that children form about compound words in their language, it was decided to ask them directly about a selection of such words.

Thus, from within the framework of a child's vocabulary, a test was devised to explore the ability to apply morphological rules to new words. Subjects were called upon to inflect, derive, compound, and analyze words.

Nonsense words were made up according to the rules for possible sound combinations in English. Pictures were then drawn on cards to represent these nonsense words. There were 27 of these pictures; they were brightly colored, and depicted objects, cartoon-like animals, and men performing various actions. Several actual words were also included. The text, which omitted the desired form, was typed on each card. The following is an example of the card used to test for the use of the regular plural allomorph /-z/. Each child was brought to the experimenter, introduced, and told that he was going to look at some pictures. The experimenter would point to the picture and read the text. The child was asked to supply the missing item, and his responses were phonemically transcribed. After all the pictures had been shown, the child was asked why he thought the things denoted by the compound words in the list (such as newspaper, Thanksgiving, fireplace, airplane, and so on) were so named. The general form of these questions was, "Why do you think a blackboard is called a blackboard?"

This is a wug.

Now there is another one.

There are two of them.

There are two ————.

Figure 10.1. Illustration of Berko's Method for Eliciting Inflections. (Reprinted by permission from R. Brown and C. Fraser. The acquisition of Syntax. In U. Belliyi and R. Brown (Eds.), *The Acquisition of Language.* Monograph, Society for Research in Child Development 29, No. 1, 1964.)

If the child answered, "Because it's a blackboard," he was asked, "But why do you think it's called that?"

The answers given by the children were not always correct so far as the English language is concerned, but they were consistent and orderly answers. The evidence strongly supports the conclusion that children in this age group operate with clearly delimited morphological rules. The children did not treat new words according to idiosyncratic patterns. They did not model new words on patterns that appear infrequently. Where they provided inflexional endings, they did best with those forms that are the most regular and have the fewest variants. With morphemes that have several allomorphs, they could handle forms that called for the most common of those allomorphs long before they could deal with allomorphs that appear in a limited distribution range.

It frequently happens that a youngster will initially have the correct irregular plural or past forms, and will later drop these for the overgeneralized forms. Presumably the initial use of the irregular form implies the learning of specific words, as against the generation of forms on the basis of abstract rules. Essentially the same sort of overgeneralizing has also been reported for Russian children (Slobin, 1966).

Slobin has traced the order of development and subdivision of grammatical classes in Russian children learning their language, and showed the importance of the semantic and conceptual aspects of the classes. His analysis suggests that in English, we might also expect to find that the grammatical devices which carry the greatest personal significance for the child are learned first, even though they may be relatively less important in the adult grammar as a whole. Brown and Bellugi (1964), for example, noted that conversations in which the child is involved are highly contemporaneous, without references to events at other times and other places.

Bellugi (1966) has conducted an analysis of the development of questions, in which she sees three stages. First, a string of words may be turned into a question by a gradual rise in pitch; Slobin (1971, p. 45) notes that yes-no questions can be produced by pronouncing any two-word sentence with a rising intonation in English, German, Russian, Samoan, and Luo (in Kenya), but not in Finnish. And according to Melissa Bowerman (cited by Slobin, 1971), in the case of Finnish child language the emergence of yes-no questions is very late. Here we might note, incidentally, that the Hawaiian Creole differs from Standard English in that it marks yes-no questions with a falling rather than a rising intonation, but to date there has apparently been no systematic study of child language in Hawaii to see if the yes-no question there also develops quite late.

Even when the child is learning to use a rising intonation to mark a yes-no question, negatives are indicated by the simple addition of "no" at the head of the string. At this stage, it appears that the child does not understand the construction of certain types of question. In the second stage the questions are still produced by the rising intonation or by the use of question words ("what," "how," and so on), but the essential competence appears to have been achieved; this is indicated by the appropriateness of answers to questions. The third stage appears around 10 months after the youngster has begun to form two-word utterances. It coincides with the appearance of functional auxiliary verbs and negative sentences, and is characterized by the production of well-formed questions.

One interesting observation noted by Bellugi was that there is a limitation on the number of transformations under control in the third stage. If a negative and a question appeared in a single utterance, only one or the other aspect was under good control. One child could ask "Can't it be a bigger truck?" in which it appears that he understood the negative question in both respects, but the same child revealed that the question aspect was less well controlled than the negative aspect when he failed to make the necessary inversion in the question "Why the kitty can't stand up?" After giving numerous examples from the speech of the child under study, the author concluded: "In his responses, all affirmatives were inverted, all negatives were not. The interpretation again fits the notion of a limit on the permitted complexity at one stage [Bellugi-Klima, 1968, p. 40, quoted by Slobin, 1971, p. 52]."

TOWARD A THEORY OF LANGUAGE ACQUISITION

The ability to induce meanings and to structure them is present very early in the ontogenesis of language. It should be apparent by now, even after this very cursory look at a few of the problems, that no theory that bases language acquisition on the concept of simple imitation is going to be very useful. An adequate theory will have to account for the structuring process. The child induces the grammatical and referential meanings from the utterances in his linguistic environment; these form the basis of his linguistic competence. But his linguistic performance is different from that of the adult, whose performances usually provide a more immediate demonstration of his competence, and frequently correspond precisely with the model if the adult is given adequate time to prepare his utterances (that is, if his speech is not spontaneous).

The principal concern of the linguist is competence rather than performance, *la langue* rather than *la parole,* the abstract language code rather than the particular speech events. The child develops rules of his own, which the investigator can deduce from the child's performances, while the child's competence is always tested in terms of the model of the adults. Since we know the future result of the child's operations—mastery of the adult model—this probably creates no serious difficulties.

In brief, then, an adequate theory of language ontogenesis must account for the original and creative bridges constructed by the child to get from his original experimental and maturational limitations to the rules that underlie adult linguistic performances. Such a theory will have to include and go beyond a theory that accounts for adult competence and performance, since that is only the final stage of ontogenesis. Very likely such a theory will have to be keyed to theories of cognitive development, what Carroll (1964) has described as "a child's capacity to recognize, discriminate, and manipulate the features and processes of the world around him [p. 31]."

REFERENCES

Bellugi, U. 1966. Development of negative and interrogative structures in the speech of children. In Thomas Bever and William Weksel (Eds.), *Studies in Psycholinguistics.* New York: Holt, Rinehart & Winston, Inc.

Bellugi-Klima, U. 1968. Linguistic mechanisms underlying child speech. In E. M. Zale (Ed.), *Proceedings of the Conference on Language and Language Behavior.* New York: Appleton-Century-Crofts.

Berko, J. 1958. The child's learning of English morphology. *Word 14:*150–177.

Bernstein, B. 1966. Elaborated and restricted codes: An outline. *Sociological Enquiry 36:* 254–261.

Bloom, L. M. 1968. Language development: Form and function in emerging grammars. Unpublished doctoral dissertation, Columbia University.

Boas, F. 1949. *Race, Language, and Culture.* New York: The Macmillan Company.

Braine, M. D. S. 1963. The ontogeny of English phrase structure: The first phase. *Language 39:* 1–13.

Brown, R. 1973. Development of the first language in the human species. *American Psychologist 28:* 97–106.

Brown, R., & U. Bellugi. 1964. Three processes in the child's acquisition of syntax. In Eric Lenneberg (Ed.), *New Directions in the Study of Language,* pp. 131–161. Cambridge, Mass.: The M.I.T. Press.

Brown, R., & J. Berko. 1960. Word association and the acquisition of grammar. *Child Development 31:* 1–14.

Brown, R., & C. Fraser. 1964. The acquisition of syntax, In Ursula Bellugi and Roger Brown (Eds.), The acquisition of language, pp. 43–79. *Monographs of the Society for Research in Child Development 29:* 1–191.

Carroll, J. B. 1961. Language development in children. In Sol Saporta (Ed.), *Psycholinguistics*, pp. 331–345. New York: Holt, Rinehart & Winston, Inc.

Carroll, J. B. 1964. *Language and Thought*. Englewood Cliffs, N.J.: Prentice-Hall, Inc.

Casagrande, J. B. 1948. Comanche baby language. *Internat. J. Amer. Linguistics 14:* 11–14.

Chomsky, N. 1959. Review of B. F. Skinner's *Verbal Behavior*. *Language 35:* 26–58.

Chomsky, N. 1968. *Language and Mind*. New York: Harcourt, Brace & World, Inc.

DeVito, J. 1970. *The Psychology of Speech and Language*. New York: Random House, Inc.

Eisenson, J., J. J. Auer, & J. V. Irwin. 1963. *The Psychology of Communication*. New York: Appleton-Century-Crofts.

Ervin, S. 1963. Structure in children's language. Paper presented at the International Congress of Psychology, Washington, D.C.

Ervin, S. 1964. Imitation and structural change in children's language. In Eric Lenneberg (Ed.), *New Directions in the Study of Language*, pp. 163–189. Cambridge, Mass.: The M.I.T. Press.

Ervin, S., & W. Miller. 1963. Language development. In *The Sixty-Second Yearbook of the National Society for the Study of Education*. Part I. *Child Psychology*, pp. 108–143. Chicago, Ill.: University of Chicago Press.

Hebb, D. O., W. E. Lambert, & G. R. Tucker. 1973. A DMZ in the language war. *Psychology Today 6:* 55–62.

Jakobson, R. 1941. *Kindersprache, Aphasie und allgemeine Lautgesetze*. Uppsala, Sweden: Uppsala Universitaets Aarsskrift.

Krech, D., & R. Crutchfield. 1958. *Elements of Psychology*. New York: Alfred A. Knopf, Inc.

Kroeber, A. L. 1958. *Anthropology*. New York: Harcourt, Brace & World, Inc.

Labov, W. 1972. *Sociolinguistic Patterns*. Philadelphia, Pa.: University of Pennsylvania Press.

Lenneberg, E. H. 1962. Understanding language without ability to speak: A case report. *J. Abnormal and Social Psychology 65:* 419–425.

Lenneberg, E. H. 1964. Speech as a motor skill with special reference to nonaphasic disorders. In Ursula Bellugi and

Roger Brown (Eds.), The acquisition of language, pp. 115–126. *Monographs of the Society for Research in Child Development 29:* 1–191.

Lenneberg, E. H. 1967. *Biological Foundations of Language.* New York: John Wiley & Sons, Inc.

Lenneberg, E. H. 1971. Of language knowledge, apes, and brains. *J. Psycholinguistic Research 1:* 1–29.

Linton, R. 1936. *The Study of Man.* New York: Appleton-Century-Crofts.

Sapir, E. 1921. *Language.* New York: Harcourt, Brace & World, Inc.

Skinner, B. F. 1957. *Verbal Behavior.* New York: Appleton-Century-Crofts.

Slobin, D. I. 1966. The acquisition of Russian as a native language. In Frank Smith and George A. Miller (Eds.), *The Genesis of Language,* pp. 129–148. Cambridge, Mass.: The M.I.T. Press.

Slobin, D. I. 1971. *Psycholinguistics.* Glenview, Ill.: Scott, Foresman & Company.

Smith, F., & G. A. Miller (Eds.). 1966. *The Genesis of Language.* Cambridge, Mass.: The M.I.T. Press.

Templin, M. 1966. The study of articulation and language development during the early school years. In Frank Smith and George A. Miller (Eds.), *The Genesis of Language,* pp. 173–180. Cambridge, Mass.: The M.I.T. Press.

Velton, H. V. 1943. The growth of phonemic and lexical patterns in infant language. *Language 19:* 281–292.

Vetter, H. J., & R. W. Howell. 1971. Theories of language acquisition. *J. Psycholinguistic Research 1:* 33–64.

Ward, M. C. 1971. *Them Children: A Study in Language Learning.* New York: Holt, Rinehart & Winston, Inc.

Weir, R. H. 1966. Some questions on the child's learning of morphology. In Frank Smith and George A. Miller (Eds.), *The Genesis of Language,* pp. 153–172. Cambridge, Mass.: The M.I.T. Press.

11

Speech
Pathologies

The study of speech irregularities and problems of comprehension provides valuable clues toward an understanding of normal linguistic behavior; it also provides clues with which to trace the neurological correlates of speech, and frequently it has implications for learning theory.

The simplest type of irregularity is the nongrammatical pause, which may be silent or accompanied by an empty filler of the sort that we usually represent as "er" or "uh." The investigation of such phenomena helps us to deduce the processes that take us from concept to utterance. From a consideration of such normal aberrations of speech, we shall move into rather complex problems, such as the types of performance that result from brain damage and from severe emotional disturbances.

HESITATION AND PAUSAL PHENOMENA

In the course of a normal conversation we not only pause, but we also start to say something, break off in the middle of an utterance, and start over or head off in a completely different direction; we repeat ourselves, and in general present the listener with a highly fragmented stream of sounds. Thanks to his linguistic competence, the listener is usually able to follow the sense of the errant stream and make some suitable response.

Obviously the listener depends on a sufficient context to make his interpretation, but how does the speaker generate an utterance? The most naïve psychological theory is that the speaker responds to some stimulus with a word, with which the stimulus has been associated previously, and then that first word serves as a stimulus for the elicitation of a previously associated second word, and so forth.

Lashley's classic statement on serial order in behavior (1951) and Chomsky's criticisms (1957) have stilled most concepts explicitly based on the notion that language is simply a matter of unit-by-unit sequencing, yet the central place of transition probabilities in discussions of hesitation phenomena and the idea that pauses are attributable to the relative unavailability of the next word suggest that the older line of thinking still persists, even if in somewhat altered form (Goldman-Eisler, 1958a, 1958b, 1961a, 1961b; Maclay and Osgood, 1959).

Transitional Probabilities

In analyzing an extensive corpus of spontaneous speech, Maclay and Osgood (1959) noted that pauses occurred more often before content words (nouns, verbs, adjectives, adverbs) than before function words (connectives and other expressions that relate the more substantive words to each other grammatically). This suggested that the unfilled pauses were the result of difficulty in selecting the next lexical, or content, word. Supposedly the lexical items are not used as often as the function words, and thus are not as readily available to the speaker. To illustrate very briefly, we have a very common construction that contains "to" plus a "verb" (to go, to sing, to rape, and so on); hence it is obvious that the function word "to" is going to be used much more frequently than any single verb. Thus, because of the practice we have had, we should find it easier to produce "to" than, say, "sing" or "rape."

A very similar idea had been advanced somewhat earlier by Goldman-Eisler (1958a, 1958b), who was influenced by certain notions derived from information theory. She argued that hesitations seemed to occur before the relatively less predictable words in a sentence, the words that have a relatively low transition probability. Actually, her findings were somewhat contradictory, since pauses do often precede an increase in information, but it is just as frequently increased without a preceding pause (Goldman-Eisler, 1958a, 1958b). Subsequently (1961a, 1961b, 1961c) she attributed the silent (unfilled) pauses to the speaker's monitoring his own speech and to his verbal planning (see Bernstein, 1962). Using a somewhat different approach, Boomer (1965) also challenged the transitional probability theory of hesitations.

HESITATION AND SPEECH PRODUCTION

To test the specific hypothesis that hesitations were to be attributed to the unavailability of the next lexical item, Howell and Vetter (1968) demonstrated that very low-frequency nouns could be employed as readily as high-frequency nouns; thus supporting Deese's (1961) notion that once a word has been thoroughly learned, it remains available.

In the Howell and Vetter (1968) study, word frequency as such was much less important than the semantic and grammatical contexts of the words. The technique employed was this: a word was said to the subject, and the subject had to produce a sentence that contained the stimulus word. The time it took to begin the response (the preliminary hesitation time) was measured, and the length and placing of subsequent pauses were recorded. A very low-frequency word such as "caboose," which should have been troublesome if Maclay and Osgood (1959) had been correct, posed no problem. But a much more frequently used word, such as "grief" or "consequence," was very likely to involve obvious hesitation. This seemed to be due to the relatively elaborate verbal context that had to be created for such words, while "caboose" could be put into a highly stereotyped frame: "It's a. . . ." Thus the construction of a sentence around some words involved more difficult grammatical and semantic considerations, while word frequency as such was not a consideration.

If word frequency does not account for most of the hesitation phenomena that characterize our speech performances, what does? The idea already mentioned, that monitoring of verbal planning was involved, seemed reasonable, so Howell and Vetter (1969) tried explicitly to relate hesitations to the cognitive complexity of utterances. As in the previous experiment, subjects were to form sentences from unambiguous stimulus nouns. The words were presented 1, 2, and 3 at a time, and 10 sentences were elicited in each sequence.

The actual time spent *vocalizing* was directly related to the number of stimulus words in the sequence: 1 second (on the average) of actual vocalizing for sentences produced in response to a single word, 2 seconds for those containing 2 stimulus words, and 3 seconds for those with 3 stimulus words. But the hesitations increased dramatically for the three conditions. The ratio for preliminary hesitation was 3:1. Thus about 3 seconds elapsed before subjects began sentences containing 1 stimulus word, 6 seconds before they began those containing 2 stimulus words, and 9 seconds before those containing 3 stimulus words.

The preliminary hesitation seemed clearly to be taken up with verbal planning, so we can say that the verbal planning time was a linear function of the cognitive complexity of the task.

The amount of pausing after the sentence was begun was roughly parallel to the vocalization time, but the important consideration was not the precise character of the word following the pause, but the relationship of the stimulus word to the utterance as a whole. Thus, in the one-word series, hesitation might occur before or after the stimulus word was uttered; the chances for either were about even. About half the time the subject began his sentence with a phrase that included the stimulus word, then hesitated before tacking on another phrase to conclude the sentence. And about half the time, the subject began with a phrase that did *not* include the stimulus word, paused, and then tacked on a concluding phrase that did include the stimulus word.

For the two- and three-word sequences, hesitation rarely followed the production of the final stimulus word. That is, the last stimulus word tended to be in the concluding phrase. In both of the complex series, the favorite way of handling the stimulus words was one at a time. A phrase that contained the first stimulus word would be produced, and after a pause the second phrase would be uttered with the second stimulus word; and in the three-word sequence an additional pause would be followed by a concluding phrase, containing the last stimulus word.

Here the hesitations are very clearly related to the time required to construct a suitable context for the given words, and in the complex sequences, the construction of contexts that would accommodate all three stimulus words could be a little difficult (for example, with the sequence "mustang," "wisteria," and "zither"). An even more open-ended demonstration of the relationship between hesitation and cognitive complexity was provided by Goldman-Eisler (1961a), who compared the amount of hesitation observed when subjects described cartoons and when they had to abstract the meaning behind the cartoons; the latter task required a great deal of hesitation.

Blocking and Blending

While monitoring and verbal planning appear to account for most of the hesitation phenomena in normal speech, within this general framework there are two additional notions to be treated: blocking and blending. Blocking is primarily a recall problem, which ranges from the unhappy inability to recall the name of a *very* dear friend and colleague, through the vexing failure to find "just the right word" to gain purchase on a concept, to the difficulty of recalling imperfectly learned material of the sort that characterizes typical verbal learning experiments.

Blending operates on the phonological level, as with tongue twisters (say "toy boat" rapidly several times, and you may arrive at "toy boyt") and spoonerisms (as that of the poor radio announcer who tripped in extolling the virtues of the "best in bread"), and the simple errors of anticipation, which are familiar to those of us who type with greater speed than accuracy. Blending also appears on a much higher level, where it involves two ways of saying virtually the same thing. This might be called *pragmemic* blending. A friend, for example, recently said "Yeh, I gotta quit layin' off," in response to a comment on the hazards of smoking. The blend appears to involve two equivalent utterances: "Yeh, I gotta quit smoking" and "Yeh, I gotta start layin' off [cigarettes]."

Blocking and blending both involve response competition; normally both are detected by monitoring, and both necessitate new verbal planning. Blends are particularly useful for the study of the structures that underlie utterances, though they have not as yet been systematically explored to this end. A similar phenomenon may illustrate the point. Youngsters seem frequently to begin with the wrong kin term, as "Mommy" when addressing "Daddy," and parents may call their children by a wrong name. In such cases it seems that the social identities are the relevant consideration (the parent, one in authority, etc., versus the child, one who is subject to orders, etc.). The higher-order event is the social identity, and sometimes the alternative realizations are confused in the speech performance.

In the following section the same themes will recur, even though the focus shifts from what we consider to be "normal" to what are considered exceptional situations with regard to the emotional state of the speaker.

HESITATION AND ANXIETY

We have argued that in normal, spontaneous speech, pauses are mainly a function of verbal planning, but the spate of studies made on this subject during the last 15 years was largely stimulated by clinical observations that pauses appeared to be closely correlated with states of anxiety. There is no necessary contradiction in these views; the implication is that during the clinical interview, there may be more cognitive activity, which is not directly reflected in the patient's speech. Toman (1953), for example, asked subjects to relate their life histories for five to ten minutes, then later asked them about the pauses in their narration. A certain amount of affect-laden material, frequently related to childhood memories, thus came to light. Presumably the hesitations were largely devoted to the editing of these intrusions. If this is indeed the case, it would appear to constitute an extension of what we have described as monitoring.

Mahl and Schulze (1969) cite a number of sources to the effect that prolonged silences (rather than brief hesitations) seem to reflect the inhibition or suppression of aggressive and erotic impulses, an editing out of the linguistic expression of such impulses, and an attempt to elicit responses from the therapist. In general, their interpretation is that long pauses imply conflict, fear, and anxiety. While the psychotherapy situation contains complexities that may not be directly relevant to more casual conversational situations, these observations again are not inconsistent with the concepts of monitoring and verbal planning. The differences seem largely to lie in the content of the cognitive activity that is not to be reflected in verbalization.

STUTTERING

When the repetition of a phoneme, syllable, or word occurs so frequently that it interferes with otherwise easy communication, we say that the speaker is stuttering. In addition to the repetitions, blockings, prolongations, and hesitations of the stutterer, speech tends to be too rapid, too restricted in pitch range, overtense, lacking in expressive coloring, and generally clumsy in articulation (Johnson and Moeller, 1967; Van Riper, 1971, 1972, 1973).

Theories of Stuttering

Theories of stuttering fall into three main categories. *Breakdown* theories view stuttering as a momentary failure of the complex coordinations involved in the production of speech. *Repressed need* theories maintain that certain neurotic needs are being satisfied when an individual stutters. *Anticipatory struggle reaction* theories assume that the stutterer anticipates difficulty in speaking, tenses the vocal apparatus, and thus precipitates the condition he has anticipated.

Most breakdown theories assert that a child must be predisposed to stuttering in some way before his speech can disintegrate. Van Riper (1971), for example, believes that the nervous system of the child who begins to stutter is less capable of coordinating the speech musculatures when subjected to the pressures of communication; and Bluemel (1957) assumes that a child is prone to disorganized speech due to the nature of his personality. But it is generally thought that the problem has a genetic basis (West, 1958), and may be part of a grosser syndrome that Lenneberg (1967) discusses briefly under the rubric of "congenital language disability."

No matter what the underlying genetic problems may be, however, stutterers do not encounter difficulty every time they vocalize. Most can be quite fluent in the absence of an audience, in the presence of an audience that poses no threat to the ego (household pets, small children), or when performing anonymously, as when singing or reciting aloud in a chorus (Eisenson, 1938). Thus stuttering is not simply a physical problem.

One of the more interesting theories is that of cerebral dominance, which postulates that if one hemisphere is not sufficiently dominant over the other, the two hemispheres tend to function independently, thus yielding poor synchronization and a consequent breakdown in speech production (Travis, 1931, 1957). The theory is particularly useful in that it accounts for the popular observation that stuttering is frequently associated with changing the handedness of children, as when naturally left-handed children were forced to write with the right hand. The right-hand training supposedly built up the strength of the originally subordinate hemisphere, and thus reduced the relative dominance of the other hemisphere.

More recent research, however, has failed to demonstrate that stutterers are particularly distinguished either by left-handedness or by ambidexterity, as the theory would seem to require. Moreover, the vast majority of children whose handedness had been changed by parents or teachers did not stutter. Thus the validity of the Travis theory is open to serious question; but the notion of cerebral dominance will recur in connection with language when we deal with aphasia.

Anticipatory struggle reaction theories typically depend on the assumption that stuttering develops from the normal hesitation phenomena found in children's speech (Bloodstein, 1958). According to Bluemel (1935, 1957), if the child's attention is unduly drawn to such normal phenomena, he becomes self-conscious and thus becomes a stutterer. Johnson and Moeller (1967) see the problem rather as developing out of a "hesitation to hesitate," which appears if the child has adopted the anxiety-tensions of the parents (if they have interpreted the normal hesitation phenomena as abnormal).

The repressed need theories are largely psychoanalytic; they draw on the concept of the infantile need for oral erotic gratification, or see stuttering as either an indirect expression of hostility or a manifestation of an unconscious desire to suppress speech. The last is particularly interesting, due to its obvious connection with the idea of verbal planning. If this theory is correct, the child fears that in speaking he will reveal forbidden wishes or feelings, or he may see the very fact of speaking as aggressive, and fear retaliation. Such theories find most of their support in clinical observations, but to date they find little support from other sources.

Operant Conditioning Studies

Whatever the psychological causes of stuttering, the problem is essentially one of articulation, and it has been attacked in the laboratory by various researchers who rely on the principles of operant conditioning (Brutten and

Shoemaker, 1967; Flanagan, Goldiamond, and Azrin, 1958; Goldiamond, 1965; Martin and Siegel; 1966; Shames and Sherrick, 1963). The basic idea, stated very simply, is that behaviors which are rewarded are likely to recur, while behaviors that are punished are likely to disappear. By systematically rewarding (verbally or otherwise) intervals of vocalization without stuttering, and/or punishing (verbally, electrically, or otherwise) instances of stuttering, it is usually possible to effect some reduction in the frequency of stuttering. Once outside the laboratory, however, the stutterer has a tendency to revert to his usual level. To cope with this tendency, some researchers gave the subjects a recording apparatus that re-creates some aspect of the laboratory situation, and thus permits the stutterer, in effect, to carry his treatment with him.

Stuttering and Linguistic Research

Linguistically, stuttering offers some interesting research possibilities. Virtually any type of speech sound can be involved in stuttering, to judge from the range discussed by Moore, Soderberg, and Powell (1952), but as with most of the traditional work on verbal learning and verbal behavior in psychology, the research possibilities offered by stuttering have not been fully explored, due to the lack of linguistic sophistication. Notice, for example, the problems of interpretation that result from the rather typical excerpt found in Moore *et al.* (1952):

> I . . . I . . . I went to . . . to . . . to the suh . . . suh . . . suh . . . suhcus (circus). We . . . we . . . well we had our suh . . . suh . . . suh . . . suppur (supper) theuh (there). The an . . . an . . . animals an . . . animals all ate all . . . all they ate too. It wuh . . . wuh . . . was . . . was . . . f . . . fun.

It is not clear from this, for example, whether in the speech of this five-year-old boy a blockage can occur after a vowel or, indeed, whether a word can begin with a vowel. It is conceivable that in the absence of any other consonant, a word will begin with a glottal stop. The spelling *theuh* for "there" implies that this is some sort of regional speech, perhaps a variety that lacks the off-glide that marks most regional standards for the first person pronoun—that is, /a/ instead of /ay/ for "I." We will not labor the point by giving additional examples from even this short excerpt; the question that cannot be answered in the absence of a phonetic transcription is whether interrupted syllables are typically closed by a consonant. It may be, on the other hand, that blockages occur typically after sounds that *can* be continued, such as vowels, semivowels, nasals, fricatives, or liquids. This seems very likely, in view of the relative infrequency of reported blockages *after* stops. In the passage above, for example, there is no blockage after wen*t*, ha*d*, a*te*, or i*t*, and there seems to be little difficulty with medial stops, as in su*pp*er, even though the /p/ as an initial sound frequently gives trouble.

A careful study of stuttering in different language areas is necessary not only for a fuller understanding of the linguistic events involved, but also for a more perfect understanding of the cultural and/or genetic basis of stuttering.

The incidence of stuttering in the United States population generally is about 7 per 1000, or 0.7% (Conner, 1970). Similar figures have been reported for Denmark, Hungary, Belgium, Great Britain, and other European countries, yet the claim is made that stuttering is rare or absent in so-called primitive societies (Bloodstein, 1969).

In view of the indisputable emotional aspects of the problem, it is reasonable to speculate that the absence of stuttering implies a lack of the kinds of social situation that seem to foster stuttering. On the other hand, if stuttering depends on genetic predisposition, it should be possible to trace the distribution of the gene(s) responsible. If it is indeed true that stuttering is virtually nonexistent among preliterate peoples, such people would surely serve as an excellent control for any investigation of the origins of the disorder.

It is more likely, however, that the shortage is not of preliterate stutterers so much as of reports addressed to the question. Most ethnographers go into the field to seek general social or cultural information, and probably would see no reason to comment on the existence of one or two stuttering children in a tribal group of several hundred. Also, if the worldwide incidence should prove to be less than 1% of the population, there is a strong likelihood that no stutterers would be present in a small tribal sample. Finally, ethnographers all too frequently have a limited command of the language of the people they are studying, and in any event they tend to rely on a small number of adult performers for their data. Thus the odds are against the appearance of reports that note stuttering among pre-literate peoples. The information could be obtained, of course, if the ethnographer would make the necessary inquiries and were prepared to observe instances of stuttering.

Social factors appear to be critical in stuttering. In the United States, at least, public-school speech therapists report that in large metropolitan areas, the "better" neighborhoods have a disproportionately high number of stutterers. Similarly, college students show an incidence two or three times higher than that of the grade-school population. Thus in the United States, stuttering seems to be mainly a middle- and upper middle-class problem (Bloodstein, 1969).

In addition to the factors of social class and parental pressures that promote stuttering, the disorder is most typical of childhood and is predominantly found among males. There is some variation with the age and educational status of the groups surveyed, but generally there are two dozen male stutterers to one female stutterer; and males tend to experience a more severe form of stuttering than females, and are less likely to grow out of it (Schuell, 1946).

Aphasia

The study of speech disorders that result from damage to central structures of the nervous system is one of the most promising lines of research for a better understanding of speech production and comprehension. If a given aberration can be correlated with damage to a specific part of the brain, we may conclude that the relevant structures are responsible for whatever linguistic processes have been disrupted.

Since head wounds are often untidy, involving damage to more than a single area of the brain, the most controlled opportunity for study appears in the course of brain surgery, when aphasic behavior can be induced by electrical stimulation of specific areas. Penfield and Roberts (1959) have provided a map of the localization of functions in the brain, based on a survey of the clinical literature on aphasia (see Figure 7.1 in Chapter 7).

Two gross categories of aphasia are illustrated by the following samples from Goodglass (1968). The first is commonly associated with damage to Broca's area (shown in Figure 7.1):

> Yes . . . ah . . . Monday . . . ah . . . Dad and Peter Hogan [pseudonym for speaker], and Dad . . . ah . . . Hospital . . . and ah . . . Wednesday, nine o'clock and ah Thursday . . . ten o'clock ah doctors . . . two . . . two . . . an doctors and . . . ah . . . teeth . . . yah. And a doctor . . . an girl . . . and gums, and I. [p. 178]

The speech is telegraphic, with few inflectional endings or function words, and a virtually complete loss of syntactic complexity. That is, there is little in the way of coordinating and subordinating constructions.

This "agrammatic" aphasia contrasts with a "fluent" variety, in which the most striking characteristic is difficulty in producing specific words, usually nouns:

> Well, I had trouble with . . . oh, almost everything that happened from the . . . eh, eh . . . Golly, the word I can remember, you know, is ah . . . When I had the . . . ah biggest . . . ah . . . that I had the trouble with, you know . . . that I had the trouble with, and I still have a . . . the ah . . . different . . . The things I want to say . . . ah . . . The way I say things, but I understand mostly things, most of them and what the things are. [p. 179]

It would be most convenient if we could simply assign the first type of disorder to Broca's area and the second to Wernicke's area (see Figure 7.1), but the matter is not that simple. Penfield and Roberts (1959) argue that there are no really pure forms of defect. The aphasic may be relatively less capable in one aspect of language than the other, but he is seldom completely capable in any aspect. Moreover, the popular idea that multilingual aphasics may suffer disturbances in one language while having normal control of speech in another language is very doubtful. At least Penfield is convinced (Penfield and Roberts, 1959, p. 221), on the basis of 30 years' experience with French-English bilinguals in Montreal, that careful testing always shows defects in both languages. The point is important to the issue of whether different areas of the brain are used for different languages.

The whole of the cerebral cortex seems to participate in the various language processes, but not all locales are equally important in this respect. The superior cortical speech area (see Figure 7.1) is most dispensable. If this area in the dominant hemisphere is removed, the result is an aphasia that disappears in a few weeks. If Broca's area is removed, the resultant aphasia eventually clears up completely in some cases, but possibly not in all cases. On the other hand, any large destruction of the posterior (Wernicke's) area has lasting and serious effects. In the case of a child, a major lesion in the posterior speech cortex or in the underlying thalamus results in the transfer of language processes to the opposite hemisphere. In the case of adults, it is doubtful that a similar transfer is possible. We are again reminded of the recurring argument that puberty marks important developmental changes in language ability.

The terminology found in discussions of aphasia is bewildering, but we have already seen that there are at least two characteristic problems of language production: grammatical and lexical. In addition, we should expect to see problems of comprehension. Jakobson (1966) has indicated some important differences between the tasks of the aphasic speaker and the listener. The speaker begins with certain basic notions, represented by his content words, and must then build a context for these by means of the function words. The agrammatic type of aphasia disturbs the second part of the process, while the fluent type disturbs the process of selecting the content words, but leaves the basic syntactic constructions intact. The use of content words in the absence of a grammatical context is what gives the agrammatic type the appearance of telegraphic speech. While the speaker knows what he wants to say, the listener depends on the whole to understand the parts. The listener, says Jakobson,

> is a probabilist to a much greater extent than the [speaker]. Thus there are no homonyms for the speaker; when he says 'bank' he knows perfectly whether he is speaking about the shore of a river or a financial establishment, whereas the listener, as long as he is not helped by the context, struggles with homonymy and has to use a probability test. The identification of the constituents is the second stage.

Thus the speaker may have trouble dredging up his key words, or he may be able to produce the words but not to relate them grammatically. In the first case the listener must guess the missing lexical items, and in the second he must guess how the items are supposed to be related.

Studies of the sort conducted by Goodglass and Hunt (1958) and Goodglass and Berko (1960) seem particularly well suited to an attack on the question of how encoding (speaking) and decoding (interpreting or listening) are related. In the former study, 24 aphasic subjects answered questions based on a statement read to them by the examiner:

Examiner reads: "My sister lost her gloves." (This is repeated.)

Question 1. What did she lose?

Question 2. Whose gloves were they?

The subjects thus have to understand the statement and respond to two aspects of it. The first requires production of the plural marker (gloves); the second requires production of the possessive marker (sister's). According to their interpretation of Jakobson's position, Goodglass and his associates felt that patients with agrammatism (contiguity disorder, telegraphic speech) should have more trouble with the possessive than with the plural; and as predicted, the possessive /s/ was much more frequently omitted than the plural /s/. While it may not be critical, it should be noted that the sample item given above (from Goodglass, 1968) requires that the subject just repeat the plural form of the original, while the possessive does not appear in the original, and thus must be supplied as well as articulated by the subject.

By asking subjects to indicate whether certain sentences are correct or incorrect, it is possible to determine whether aphasics can realize that various features are missing, such as the missing plural marker in "three book," the missing possessive marker in "ship anchor," or the missing third person marker in "he run." On the basis of these and similar experiments, Goodglass concluded that there was no correspondence between the inability to use a form and the inability to recognize it auditorily. The two processes appear to be somewhat independent.

Earlier, Jakobson (1955) had suggested that in aphasia, grammatical features are lost in the opposite order to that of acquisition. That is, the features mastered last by the child are the first to be lost through aphasia. This is usually called the "regression hypothesis" (but see Wepman and Jones, 1964, for another regression hypothesis). Jakobson's hypothesis received some support from experiments conducted by Goodglass and Berko (1960), but Goodglass (1968) found that aphasics also "showed a wide range of difficulty with grammatical operations that had already been well mastered by Berko's young children [p. 188]."

The question of whether there really are different types of aphasia has also been linked to the old but continuing argument over the "equipotentiality" versus "localization" of brain functions. Howes (1967), depending on experiments that were based on written rather than spoken forms of language, concluded that there are two distinct types of aphasia, and at least one of the neural systems that underlie these types must be an equipotential system. (Equipotentiality is implied when recovery takes place because the functions of the damaged tissue have been taken over by some other tissue.)

As Lenneberg has pointed out (in Wepman and Jones, 1966), in addition to the problems of grammatical relationships and lexical availability, there is an emotional component. Some patients do better when alone or relaxed, while others do better when greatly exercised. In one case, a patient with global injuries and severe disturbances of both types, who could say nothing, was about to be sent home to a relative whom he could not stand: he became very excited and suddenly spoke quite fluently.

Goldstein (1948) has argued that brain damage involves a drop in the level of thought and language from the abstract to the concrete, a point that is hard to demonstrate conclusively. Of greater interest is the argument posed by Luria (1959, 1962), that it is not so much the signals that are lost as the *significance* of the signals. Jakobson (1966) expounds the idea thus: there is "no question of inability to hear or articulate vowels of longer or shorter duration [in languages such as Czech or Hungarian]; what is lost is the distinctive semantic value of the difference between long and short signals in the phonemic code [p. 71]."

SCHIZOPHRENIC SPEECH

The other major area of speech pathology is the range of disturbances associated with schizophrenic disorders. In the case of stuttering or aphasia, we assume that the speaker desires to communicate in normal terms, and that the cognitive processes are essentially intact. In the case of schizophrenia, the cognitive processes frequently appear to be disrupted, and there is reason to doubt that the patient desires to communicate in the normal sense.

Many clinicians would probably subscribe to Ferreira's (1960) notion that the schizophrenic manipulates or disguises his language, in order to conceal thoughts known to be dangerous and forbidden: "In the privacy of his language, the schizophrenic finds the much looked-after opportunity to say a piece of *his* mind about a relationship the nature of which he could not state publicly [p. 136]."

Bateson, Jackson, Haley, and Weakland (1956, 1963) have advanced the theory that schizophrenia has its origin in the "double bind" in which a youngster finds himself when a parent consistently conveys simultaneous but incongruent messages. That is, the mother says words to the effect, "Come here, I love you," but at the same time communicates rejection by her tone of voice, gestures, and other subtle cues. If the child discriminates accurately between the messages, he will be punished by the realization that his mother does not really love him, but if he does not discriminate accurately between them, and takes the verbal message at face value, then he will approach her. When he approaches she will become hostile, so he will withdraw; then she will rebuke him for withdrawing, because that signified that she was not a loving mother. Either way the child loses, and thus is in a double bind.

So far the double bind concept has been pretty well received, and if Bateson *et al.* are correct, it may be more than a coincidence that schizophrenic verbalizations are frequently ambiguous, difficult, or impossible to interpret. That is, the schizophrenic frequently offers difficult messages to those with whom he *appears* to be interacting.

The schizophrenic's apparent flatness of affect, inappropriate expression of affect combined with withdrawal, or loss of interest in the social and physical environment, are probably the most widely cited characteristics of the disorder. It is typically withdrawal that seems to be expressed in schizophrenic speech. Tangential responses and the pursuing of irrelevant details are easily interpreted as an avoidance of direct communication.

The omission of transitional expressions and joining of disparate ideas (called *scattering*) is less readily interpreted in the same way, though the effect is still poor communication. The following written example of scattering (from Maher, 1966) seems almost like a third or fourth approximation to English:

> If things turn by rotation of agriculture or levels in regards and 'timed' to everything; I am re-fering to a previous document when I made some remarks that were facts also tested and there is another that concerns my daughter she has a *lobed* bottom right ear, her name being Mary Lou. . . . Much of abstraction has been left unsaid and undone in this product/milk syrup, and others due to economics, differentials, subsidies, bankruptcy, tools, buildings, bonds, national stocks, foundation craps, weather, trades, government in

levels of breakages and fuses in electronic too all formerly 'stated' not necessarily *factuated*. (Underlined words are considered to be neologisms) [p. 395].

The idea that the schizophrenic employs language in order *not* to communicate is an interesting one, but there is a contrary school of thought that also finds considerable support. Ullman and Krasner (1969), for example, argue that in a sense the deficiency is in the listener rather than in the patient. If the listener were able to fill in the gaps, he would "understand" the patient.

This sounds a bit much, perhaps, but the idea is that material which seems unintelligible on the surface may actually make some sort of sense. Of course the patient and the normal listener are not observing the same interactional rules, but according to this view, the desire to communicate in normal terms may actually be present.

Bleuler (1950, cited in Mednick, 1968) considered "disturbances of association" to be a primary difficulty in schizophrenia, and somewhat in the same way, Cameron and Magaret (1951) report that schizophrenic patients themselves frequently complain about the confusion in their speech and thinking. Their thoughts and words all seem jumbled in a way they find it impossible to untangle. The implication is that at some level, at least, such patients would like to be able to communicate normally.

Robertson and Shamsie (1968) have reported a case that casts more doubt on the "secret language" hypothesis, this time from a linguistically more technical standpoint. A native of India, whose mother tongue was Gujarati and who had an excellent spoken and written command of Hindi and English, as well as a smattering of German and Norwegian, was subjected to a variety of tests and tasks, to see whether his neologisms were gibberish or should more properly be considered manifestations of a secret language.

If the latter were the case, the neologisms should have reappeared with some consistency of meaning. Apparently they did not, however. The neologisms appear to have been *ad hoc* productions, which effectively obscured communication, but lacked the sort of consistency that would seem to be necessary for so systematic a phenomenon as an actual language. Thus the communication is "secret," but it is not language. The Indian was playfully prepared to utter unlimited amounts of the gibberish, but he rejected any attempt to investigate it directly. He had no objection to communication as such, yet he maintained the privacy of his own communication.

In brief, then, the utterances of the schizophrenic range from more or less normal speech, in which painful or unacceptable notions are blocked or disguised, to a rather thoroughgoing disruption of normal speech. The term "word salad" is often used to describe the more bizarre verbalizations of schizophrenics, but samples rarely appear in print in any useful form, such as a phonetic transcription. Robertson and Shamsie (1968) apparently felt that a simple interspersing of neologisms among meaningful strings of familiar words is sufficient to warrant the labels "gibberish" or "word salad."

A great deal of literature on schizophrenic speech is devoted to the study of oppositions of the literal-metaphorical, concrete-abstract, and particular-contextual sort. But as Brown has pointed out (1958), the performances of schizophrenics and normals overlap in such a way as to indicate that these characteristics are not reliably diagnostic. Moreover, even when patients insist on dealing with questions very concretely they may have a clear awareness of conceptual categories, as Maria Lorenz (1968, p. 36) concluded on the basis of such examples as this: a patient is asked to define "table," and answers "What kind of table? A wooden table, a porcelain table, a surgical table, or a table you want to have a meal on?"

The questioner expects an abstract, dictionary-type definition to cover the general case, while the subject rejects that expectation. Normal speakers can seem just as perverse, however, if they question the assumptions that underlie everyday interaction, as the following example from Garfinkel (1967, p. 44) shows.

> A naïve subject waves his hand cheerily at the experimenter: How are you?
> Experimenter: How am I in regard to what? My health, my finances, my school work, my peace of mind, my—
> Subject, red in the face and suddenly out of control: Look! I was just trying to be polite. Frankly, I don't give a damn how you are.

As Garfinkel (1967) puts it, in conducting everyday affairs, people refuse to let each other understand "what they are really talking about." If Garfinkel is correct, a good deal of our daily interaction depends on ambiguous or vague communication, which seems designed to bind two parties but actually ensures their separation.

The ethnomethodological studies of Garfinkel and others demonstrate interesting means of comparing the unspoken rules of normal communication with those that guide the verbalizations of the schizophrenic. In some cases the principal difference between the normal subject and the schizophrenic seems to be that the latter makes explicit the vagueness that is left in the background of ordinary interaction.

Thus schizophrenic speech may reflect forbidden thoughts in some cases, or a general antipathy for interaction in other cases, while in yet other cases it appears that the patient wants to communicate in the normal sense, but cannot because of severe cognitive disturbances.

The perversity shown in Maria Lorenz' example, given above, seems to reflect a rejection of the unspoken assumptions of normal interaction. A phenomenon that goes still further in the same direction, perhaps, is what Forrest

(1968) calls the *poiesis* of schizophrenic productions. The simplest example, perhaps, is the kind of cognitive derailment that follows from accidental relationships among words that are independent in meaning, as in clang associations. Thus Forrest cites one of Kraeplelin's (1919) cases, where in response to the word "Bett," a patient replied: *"Bett, Bett, Bett, dett, dett, dett, ditt, dutt. . . ."*

The patient becomes preoccupied with the form of words at the expense of the original thought, in the same way as a poet may lose his argument to the demands of the meter. The poet may then revise his poem, and may even persuade himself that the distorted form was what he had had in mind all along. Forrest (1968, p. 167) argues persuasively for the creativity of schizophrenic productions, and cites Bleuler (1950) on the similarity of schizophrenic productions and artistic productions that incline toward novel, unusual ideas, an indifference to tradition, and a lack of restraint.

The key again seems to be a rejection of ordinary rules, and Forrest seems almost prepared to grant some schizophrenics the status of full-time poets. And perhaps in all cases schizophrenics seek new means of communication—even if through mutism.

References

Bateson, G., D. Jackson, J. Haley, & J. Weakland. 1956. Toward a theory of schizophrenia. *Behavioral Science 1:* 251–264.

Bateson, G., D. Jackson, J. Haley, & J. Weakland. 1963. A note on the double-bind. *Family Process 2:* 154–157.

Bernstein, B. 1962. Linguistic codes, hesitation phenomena and intelligence. *Language and Speech 5:* 31–46

Bleuler, E. 1950. *Dementia Praecox or the Group of Schizophrenias.* New York: International Universities Press, Inc.

Bloodstein, O. 1958. Stuttering as an anticipatory struggle reaction. In Jon Eisenson (Ed.), *Stuttering: A Symposium.* New York: Harper & Row, Publishers.

Bloodstein, O. 1969. *A Handbook on Stuttering.* Chicago: National Society for Crippled Children and Adults.

Bluemel, C. S. 1935. *Stammering and Allied Disorders.* New York: The Macmillan Company.

Bluemel. C. S. 1957. *The Riddle of Stuttering.* Danville, Ill.: Interstate Publishing Company.

Boomer, D. S. 1965. Hesitation and grammatical encoding. *Language and Speech 8:* 148–158.

Brown, R. 1958. *Words and Things.* New York: The Free Press.

Brutten, E. J., & D. J. Shoemaker. 1967. *The Modification of Stuttering.* Englewood Cliffs, N.J.: Prentice-Hall, Inc.

Cameron, N., & A. Magaret. 1951. *Behavior Pathology.* Boston: Houghton Mifflin Company.

Chomsky, N. 1957. *Syntactic Structures.* The Hague: Mouton & Co.

Conner, B. J. 1970. A study of the availability of data on incidence of stuttering among various nations. Unpublished M.S. thesis, Tulane University.

Deese, J. 1961. From the isolated verbal unit to connected discourse. In Charles N. Cofer and Barbara S. Musgrave (Eds.), *Verbal Learning and Verbal Behavior,* pp. 11–31. New York: McGraw-Hill Book Company.

Eisenson, J. 1938. *The Psychology of Speech.* New York: F. S. Crofts.

Ferreira, A. J. 1960. The semantics and the context of the schizophrenic's language. *Archives of General Psychiatry 3:* 128–138.

Flanagan, B., I. Goldiamond, & N. Azrin. 1958. Operant stuttering: The control of stuttering behavior through response contingent consequences. *J. Experimental Analysis of Behavior 1:* 173–177.

Forrest, D. V. 1968. Poiesis and the language of schizophrenia. In Harold J. Vetter (Ed.), *Language Behavior in Schizophrenia,* pp. 153–181. Springfield, Ill.: Charles C. Thomas, Publisher.

Garfinkel, H. 1967. *Studies in Ethnomethodology.* Englewood Cliffs, N.J.: Prentice-Hall, Inc.

Goldiamond, I. 1965. Stuttering and fluency as manipulatable operant response classes. In Leonard Krasner and Leonard P. Ullmann (Eds.), *Research in Behavior Modification: New Developments and Implications,* p. 237–253. New York: Holt, Rinehart & Winston, Inc.

Goldman-Eisler, F. 1958a. Speech production and the predictability of words in context. *Quart. J. Experimental Psychol. 10:* 96–106.

Goldman-Eisler, F. 1958b. Speech analysis and mental processes. *Language and Speech 1:* 59–75.

Goldman-Eisler, F. 1961a. Hesitation and information in speech. *Information Theory, Fourth London Symposium,* pp. 162–174. London: Buttersworth.

Goldman-Eisler, F. 1961b. A comparative study of two hesitation phenomena. *Language and Speech 4:* 18–26.

Goldman-Eisler, F. 1961c. The distribution of pause durations in speech. *Language and Speech 4:* 232–237.

Goldstein, K. 1948. *Language and Language Disturbances.* New York: Grune and Stratton.

Goodglass, H. 1968. Studies on the grammar of aphasics. In S. Rosenberg and J. H. Koplin (Eds.), *Applied Psycholinguistics Research,* pp. 177–208. New York: The Macmillan Company.

Goodglass, H., & J. Berko. 1960. Agrammatism and inflectional morphology in English. *J. Speech and Hearing Res. 3:* 257–267.

Goodglass, H., & J. Hunt. 1958. Grammatical complexity and aphasic speech. *Word 14:* 197–207.

Howell, R. W., & H. J. Vetter. 1968. High and low frequency nouns as sources of hesitation in the production of speech. *Psychonomic Science 12:* 157–158.

Howell, R. W., & H. J. Vetter. 1969. *Hesitation in the Production of Speech 81:* 261–276.

Howes, D. 1967. Some experimental investigations of language in aphasia. In K. Salzinger and S. Salzinger (Eds.), *Research in Verbal Behavior and Some Neurophysiological Implications.* New York: Academic Press Inc.

Jakobson, R. 1955. Aphasia as a linguistic problem. In H. Werner (Ed.), *On Expressive Language,* pp. 69–81. Worchester, Mass.: Clark University Press.

Jakobson, R. 1966. Linguistic types of aphasia. In Edward C. Carterette (Ed.): *Brain Function.* Vol. III. *Speech, Language, and Communications,* pp. 67–91. Berkeley, Cal.: University of California Press.

Johnson, W., & D. Moeller (Eds.). 1967. Speech Handicapped School Children. New York: Harper & Row, Publishers.

Kraepelin, E. 1919. Dementia Praecox and Paraphrenia. Edinburgh, Scotland: E. & S. Livingstone.

Lashley, K. S. 1951. The problem of serial order in behavior. In L. A. Jeffress (Ed.), Cerebral Mechanisms in Behavior. New York: John Wiley & Sons, Inc.

Lenneberg, E. H. 1967. The Biological Foundations of Language. New York: John Wiley & Sons, Inc.

Lorenz, M. 1968. Problems posed by schizophrenic language. In Harold J. Vetter (Ed.), Language Behavior in Schizophrenia, pp. 28–40. Springfield, Ill.: Charles C. Thomas, Publisher.

Luria, A. R. 1959. Disorders of 'simultaneous perception' in a case of bilateral occipito-parietal brain injury. Brain 82: 437–449.

Luria, A. R. 1962. Higher Cortical Functions in Man and Their Disturbances in Local Brain Lesions. (In Russian). Moscow: Moscow University Press.

Maclay, H., & C. E. Osgood. 1959. Hesitation phenomena in spontaneous English speech. Word 15: 19–44.

Maher, B. A. 1966. Principles of Psychopathology. New York: McGraw-Hill Book Company.

Mahl, G. F., & G. Schulze. 1969. Psychological research. In Norman Markel (Ed.), Psycholinguistics: An Introduction to the Study of Speech and Personality, pp. 318–352. Homewood, Ill.: The Dorsey Press.

Martin, R., & G. Siegel. 1966. The effect of response contingent shock on stuttering. J. Speech and Hearing Res. 9: 340–352.

Mednick, S. A. 1968. A learning theory approach to research in schizophrenia. In Harold J. Vetter (Ed.), Language Behavior in Schizophrenia, pp. 75–92. Springfield, Ill.: Charles C. Thomas, Publisher.

Moore, W., G. Soderberg, & D. Powell. 1952. Relations of stuttering in spontaneous speech to speech context and verbal output. J. Speech and Hearing Disorders 17: 371–376.

Penfield, W., & L. Roberts. 1959. Speech and Brain Mechanisms. Princeton, N.J.: Princeton University Press.

Robertson, J. P. S., & S. J. Shamsie. 1968. A systematic examination of gibberish in a multilingual schizophrenic patient. In

Harold J. Vetter (Ed.), *Language Behavior in Schizophrenia,* pp. 139–148. Springfield, Ill.: Charles C. Thomas, Publisher.

Schuell, H. 1946. Sex differences in relation to stuttering: Part I. *J. Speech Disorders 11:* 277–298.

Shames, G., & C. Sherrick. 1963. A discussion of non-fluency and stuttering as operant behavior. *J. Speech and Hearing Disorders 28:* 3–18.

Travis, L. E. 1931. *Speech Pathology: A Dynamic Neurological Treatment of Normal Speech and Speech Disorders.* New York: D. Appleton and Company.

Travis, L. E. 1957. *Handbook of Speech Pathology and Audiology.* New York: Appleton-Century-Crofts.

Ullman, L. P., & L. Krasner. 1969. *A Psychological Approach to Abnormal Behavior.* Englewood Cliffs, N.J.: Prentice-Hall, Inc.

Van Riper, C. 1971. *The Nature of Stuttering.* Englewood Cliffs, N.J.: Prentice-Hall, Inc.

Van Riper, C. 1972. *Speech Correction: Principles and Methods.* Englewood Cliffs, N.J.: Prentice-Hall, Inc.

Van Riper, C. 1973. *The Treatment of Stuttering.* Englewood Cliffs, N.J.: Prentice-Hall, Inc.

Wepman, J. M., & L. V. Jones. 1964. Five aphasias: A commentary on aphasia as a regressive linguistic phenomenon. *Assoc. Res. Nervous and Mental Disease 42:* 190–203.

Wepman, J. M., & L. V. Jones. 1966. Studies in aphasia: A psycholinguistic method and case study. In Edward C. Carterette (Ed.), *Brain Function.* Vol. III. *Speech, Language, and Communication,* pp. 141–172. Berkeley, Cal.: University of California Press.

West, R. W. 1958. An agnostic's speculations about stuttering. In Jon Eisenson (Ed.), *Stuttering: A Symposium.* New York: Harper & Row, Publishers.

12

Multilingualism

Most of us tend to think of a bilingual person as one who has native competence in two languages, and of a polyglot as one who commands several languages. Yet the problem of multilingualism is much more complex than these simple definitions would imply. Individuals vary considerably in the degree to which they have mastered different speech varieties (Diebold, 1961; MacKey, 1962), and languages vary widely in the extent to which they resemble each other. *Languages in contact,* whether from the standpoint of the individual speaker or of the speech community, may differ in their relative dominance or importance; they may interfere with each other; and they may result in linguistic systems that differ markedly from their precontact forms. Mutual influences may be considered at phonological, morphophonemic, morphosyntactic, and semantic levels.

BILINGUAL POPULATIONS

The "practice of alternately using two languages," as Weinreich (1953, p. 1) defined bilingualism, has inter-

Extensive passages reprinted with the permission of © Ziff-Davis Publishing Company, 1973.

related psychological and social aspects, besides its linguistic aspects. As Macnamara (1967a) has pointed out, most American academics are so used to monolingual interaction that we are likely to be surprised at the extent of bilingualism. Yet bilingual populations include:

> The Catalans, Basques and Galicians in Spain; the Bretons and Provencals in France; the Welsh and Scots in the United Kingdom; the Flemings and Waloons in Belgium; the Romansh in Switzerland; the Valoise, Piedmontese, Germans in Italy; the Frisians in Holland; the Laps throughout Scandinavia; the Italians, Hungarians, Slovenes, Croations [sic], Albanians and Macedonians in Yugoslavia; the Germans, Poles and Slovaks in Czechoslavakia; the Germans and Ukrainians in Poland; the Hungarians in Rumania; the Macedonians in Bulgaria; the Turks in Cyprus; the Greeks in Turkey; the Finns, Estonians, Latvians, Lithuanians, White Russians, Ukrainians, Germans, Jews and various peoples of the Caucases [sic] in the Soviet Union. [pp. 1–2]

A similar catalogue could be assembled for Latin America, Africa, and Asia, and bilingualism was probably extremely common among many North American Indian groups, especially in areas such as the Northwest Coast, where many diverse tribal groups were in frequent contact.

There are *lingua francas:* English over a good part of the world, Arabic in much of Southeast Asia, and Japanese throughout much of the Far East and the Pacific. Then there are trade languages, such as Melanesian Pidgin, which have developed independent linguistic status through the merging of two or more languages.

A phenomenon that is sufficiently widespread to merit a separate label is *diglossia* (Ferguson, 1956). Originally, diglossia was defined as the existence in a single speech community of (1) a high variety of speech employed for most written or formal purposes, which is not used as the medium of ordinary conversation by any group, and (2) regional or standard vernaculars that *are* used for ordinary verbal interaction. Classical Arabic, for example, is a high variety, which is superposed over the local Arabic vernaculars. More recently, the term diglossia has been used to describe any situation in which there are high and low speech varieties that are used respectively for formal and informal communication (Fishman, Cooper, Ma *et al.;* 1968, pp. 929 ff.). An educated Puerto Rican in New York, for example, might use a literary-based variety of Spanish in formal situations, a local variety of Spanish in family and neighborhood interaction, and one or more varieties of English in non-Spanish contexts. There is a similar contrast in the use of the local standard English and the Creole in Hawaii.

BORROWING

For the linguist, the central problem of multilingualism is how languages in contact influence each other. Perhaps the most obvious influence is the borrowing of words. Study of an unabridged dictionary of American English will reveal not only the pervasive influence of Latin, Greek, and French, but literally hundreds of terms from Chinese, Japanese, Malayan, Tibetan, and many other "exotic" languages.

Of course words are not borrowed without adulteration. In most American communities the Japanese term *kimono* is familiar enough, but it is pronounced as if it were an American term, with a clear stress on the middle syllable and reduced vowels in the first and third syllables: [kəmównə]. Even in Hawaii, where there has been a powerful Japanese influence, and many common terms such as *sashimi* "raw fish," *zôri* "footwear," and *sake* "rice wine" are pronounced in a way that would not create problems for a native Japanese, family names are often thoroughly Anglicized. In the name Yamashita as pronounced in Japan, for example, the /i/ is so reduced as to be scarcely detectable by most Americans, but in Hawaii the /i/ carries the primary stress, even when pronounced by typical second- or third-generation Japanese.

Convergence

For many years it was assumed in the United States that languages in contact could influence each other lexically and phonologically, but that grammatical features were relatively immune to such influence. The idea that borrowing is nearly always superficial was most persuasively promoted by Edward Sapir, while the idea that language contact could result in structural borrowing was argued less influentially by Franz Boas (Emaneau, 1956). It appears that Boas was passed over too lightly. There is growing evidence that prolonged language contact may indeed lead to linguistic convergence.

Gumperz (1967a) has provided a remarkable example of how two local varieties of genetically unrelated languages can converge structurally to the point of virtual identity, while superficially appearing quite unlike each other and close to their respective standards. The following example is based on the local varieties of a Dravidian and an Indo-Aryan language, in central India:

Kannada:	hog-	i	wand	kudri	turg	maR-	i		aw	tand
Marathi:	ja-	un	ek	ghoRa	cori	kar-	un		tew	anla
	verb	partic.	adj.	noun	noun	verb	partic.	pro-	past	
	stem	suffix				stem	suffix	noun	verb	
Literal										
English:	go	having	one	horse	theft	take	having	he	brought	
Idiomatic										
English:	Having gone and having stolen a horse he brought it back.									

Gumperz (1967a; pp. 52–53) also provides a very similar example from the speech varieties of Hindi-Punjabi bilingual college students in Delhi. In both cases the languages differ only in the rules that determine the phonetic shape of the relevant words and affixes. Perhaps the basic idea of how the same underlying structure can be realized in rather different phonetic forms may be illustrated by comparing the English and Spanish forms of a simple equation:

English:	one	and	one	are	two
Spanish:	uno	y	uno	son	dos
Arithmetic notation:	1	+	1	=	2

Here the arithmetic notation represents the essential structure, which is verbally reflected in the structure of the English and Spanish, even though the precise phonetic shapes of the 1, +, =, and 2 are quite different for the two speech varieties.

In the Kannada-Marathi case the local varieties converged structurally over centuries of interaction, even though the identities of the Kannada and Marathi speakers were kept separate through the retention of the traditional phonetic shapes of the vocabulary items.

Because the phonetic shapes of the equivalent strings differ for the two local varieties, and because the local shapes retain an obvious similarity to the corresponding strings in the standard varieties, historical linguists see relationships between the local varieties and their respective standards, but have usually overlooked the grammatical or structural convergence of the two local varieties. As Gumperz (1967a) put it, "Genetic relationships among languages are established largely through a process of matching at the morphophonemic level. Since this is the area of structure where the two varieties differ most, it is not surprising that historical linguists in the past have failed to make systematic analyses of the underlying similarities [p. 54]."

Bilingualism, then, is extremely widespread, but where bilingual interaction has been characteristic of a speech community for long periods of time, the two languages tend to converge, even if originally they were quite different structurally. The effect of convergence is to reduce the distance of the two languages, presumably so that the task of the individual speaker will be less burdensome than it would be if there were no convergence. The task is reduced to mastering one set of structural rules and the alternate realizations of those rules at the phonemic level.

Compare this with the task of mastering two structurally divergent languages, such as Japanese and English, where the number of rules in common is minimal. Of course the linguist is mainly concerned with the linguistic codes themselves, and with how they interfere with each other and thus induce changes in each other, or how they merge more openly and yield pidgins and Creoles (Weinreich, 1953; Haugen, 1956; Reinecke, 1938). The problems of the bilingual speakers are the concern of the psycholinguist, but obviously both the linguistic and social factors are of the greatest relevance to anyone who wishes to understand what transpires psychologically in the speaker.

One social fact that sometimes obscures the bilingual problem is that often different "languages" are merely reflections of political facts. As Gumperz (1967b) says, "Pairs like Serbian and Croatian, Thai and Laotian, Hindi and Urdu, and many other similar pairs throughout the world are merely stylistic variants of each other [p. 37]." That is, speech communities that border different political entities may be differently named, even though they are virtually the same linguistically. Evidently this is extremely common in Europe, where centuries of interaction have led to linguistic convergences so complete that, for example, border-French and border-German may be essentially indistinguishable, yet the former is called "French" and the latter is called "German."

LANGUAGE DISTANCE

It is very difficult to define "language" in a way that clearly distinguishes it from "dialect." Mutual intelligibility is often cited as the criterion, but it is inconsistently applied. Many Japanese dialects, for example, are not immediately intelligible to the Tokyo speaker, yet, with the exception of the Ryûkyû (Okinawa) dialects, they are never described as constituting different languages. If we were to insist that the speech of Kumamoto, in southwest Japan, is a language separate from the speech of Tokyo, and that each of these is separate again from the speech of Sendai in the northeast, we would still have to concede that the Kumamoto man would find either of the other varieties easier to learn than, for example, French or Russian. He might require years to gain competence in the European tongues, while a few weeks might suffice for the other varieties of Japanese.

Why should some speech varieties be easier to add to one's repertory than others? We cannot seriously suggest that it is due to the intrinsic difficulty of the several speech varieties, even though it might be possible to demonstrate that some varieties are in fact more complex or difficult than others. The reason that the Kumamoto man will find Sendai speech easier to learn than Italian, or that the Roman will find Spanish easier to learn than Japanese, is principally that at some level Kumamoto speech and Sendai speech have more rules in common than either has with the European speech varieties, while Italian and Spanish have more rules in common than either has with any Japanese variety.

Once we have phrased the problem in terms of the rules required to switch from one speech variety to another, we are in a position to appreciate the conceptual differences of switching between a formal and an informal style, between a local dialect and a standard language, between languages that are closely related historically, and between languages that are less closely related or are not related at all. The more distant two speech varieties are historically or genetically, or geographically and typologically, the more rules will have to be constructed in order to convert one into the other, and the more difficult it will be for a speaker of one to learn the other.

Types of Bilingualism

It is customary to distinguish *compound* and *coordinate* bilingualism, and it should be clear by now that it is useful to consider a third variety, *convergent bilingualism.* The coordinate form includes two languages that are maintained as separate systems; this is essentially how the popular definition of bilingualism is understood. It is almost meaningless to speak of coordinate bilingualism so far as speakers of the Indian languages already cited are concerned, since the codes themselves have merged and are separate systems only at the lowest structural level. And even if a speaker operates in two sociolinguistically discrete environments, we may expect to find evidence of some convergence within the speaker himself. At the very least, there will in most cases be some interferences with one or both phonemic systems, and because different languages are typically employed in different social situations, they tend to include somewhat different semantic domains. Robert Lowie, for example, had a superb command of English, but admitted that affairs of the kitchen were for him almost exclusively a matter of German, even though he had consciously attempted to maintain equal proficiency in both languages (Lowie, 1945).

So far as the learning process is concerned, in coordinate bilingualism different labels imply different conceptual entities. For an English-Korean bilingual, a *house* might be a wooden or brick structure, roughly square in shape, with interior plaster or wallboard, painted, with rugs or carpets on the floor, and so forth. A *cip*, on the other hand, might be a reddish, dried-mud affair, L- or U-shaped, with plain oiled paper covering the floors and walls. Similarly, *subway, underground, metro,* and *chikatetsu* all refer to subterranean train systems, but they appear in different cultural contexts, so that the Japanese *chikatetsu* is scrubbed and litter-free, while the American subway tends to be filthy, noisy, and so on. The smells and visual stimuli differ for each; they *are* the different entities that the different labels imply.

Ervin and Osgood (1954) have devised a learning paradigm which suggests in effect that there are independent stimulus-response systems in coordinate bilingualism, in contrast to the case of compound bilingualism, in which the labels of the second language are associated with the labels of the first language. If we see a Korean house and respond directly with the word *cip*, whereas we respond directly with "house" when we see an American house, the action is coordinate; if, instead, we as Americans see a Korean house and think immediately of "house" and then dig for the corresponding Korean word, *cip*, we are associating the words *house/cip*, and the action is compound.

The compound process, which links American words with words from other languages, is what all too often transpires in our language classrooms. Rather than trying to develop associations directly between the labels of the second language and the objects or events to which they refer, the teachers encourage the students to "translate" the labels of the second language into the labels of the first language.

Unfortunately the labels of two languages rarely correspond in a precise way. It is all very well and good to translate Japanese *kome, gohan,* and *raisu* as "rice," but *kome* is uncooked rice, *gohan* is often used as a generic term for food or meals, and when used to refer specifically to rice it designates cooked rice that is served in a bowl and is eaten with chopsticks; *raisu* is also cooked rice, but it is served on a flat plate with Western dishes and is eaten with a fork. *Karê-raisu* (rice curry) is usually served in a bowl, but is eaten with a large spoon. Obviously, if the translation is from English to Japanese, no simple formula of the sort *rice = gohan* is going to be appropriate each time it is applied.

Perhaps compound bilingualism is most highly developed in professional translators, particularly those able to perform the kind of "simultaneous" translations required in the United Nations. Obviously it is critical to have an inventory of verbal equations, but there are a myriad of purely grammatical processes to be taken into account. Components of the second language are related to each other in a way that may not correspond to anything in the first language; idioms may have no ready counterpart in the other language; and ambiguities can only rarely be maintained in translation. Some features of the second language, in short, must be understood in terms of that language, *not* in terms of the original language. Where there is no real equivalence, some sort of convention must be adopted.

In a forum such as the United Nations, of course, the principals will have common types of problems and comparable educations, which may facilitate the formulation of verbal equations. When one language is being translated into another in a coordinate fashion, the problem seems to be more complex. As Ervin and Osgood (1954, p. 143) point out, it involves "true cross-cultural translation," with some theoretical complications, because each system is intact, and thus the verbal labels of each refer primarily to external referents or back to their respective grammatical systems, rather than to each other. And yet translation necessarily involves the expression of one system in terms of the other. For more detailed theoretical considerations, the reader should consult Ervin and Osgood (1954). For a somewhat different but also useful discussion of translation problems, see Nida (1961).

Bilingualism and Context

We should expect the precise nature of one's bilingualism to depend on what may be called the "contexts of acquisition." This takes us into some rather tricky theoretical problems, which are not made easier by the different terminologies used by various research teams. Lambert, Havelka, and Crosby (1958) used various concepts and terms derived from paired-associate learning experiments designed to explore problems of meaning. They distinguished the case of individuals whose language usages and acquisition contexts were quite discrete, from the case in which the same individuals would use more than one language in interacting with each other, or the case in which the first language was used to instruct the student in the second language. It was only in the bicultural case, where the contexts of acquisition and usage were consistently different for the two languages, that there were differences in the meanings of translated equivalents. In other words, if our understanding is correct, this means in effect that different labels mean different entities only where the contexts of acquisition and usage are quite distinct. Macnamara (1967c) seems to argue along the same lines, but both cases are confused, it seems to us, by the failure to distinguish the category of convergent bilingualism. In general, the murky areas seem to involve the so-called compound bilingualism, because compound bilinguals (as described in Macnamara's argument) are those who attribute identical meanings to corresponding words and expressions in their two languages. But this can come about either because one language has been learned in terms of the other or because of convergence.

Semantic Satiation

Thus Lambert *et al.* (1958) have suggested that bilinguals who acquired their languages in different cultural contexts tended to maintain separate semantic domains for the two languages, while Macnamara (1967c) interpreted the distinction between compound and coordinate bilingualism as being largely a semantic problem. Another approach to the semantic relationship between compound and coordinate bilingualism has been taken by Jakobovits and Lambert (1961). They found that one difference between the two types lay in the extent to which *semantic satiation* in one language was transferred to the other.

Semantic satiation involves the repetition of a word until it becomes a meaningless sound. This is something we can all see for ourselves, usually after only a few seconds; in the Jakobovits and Lambert study, 15 seconds seems to have sufficed to extinguish the meaning of a word temporarily. They felt that satiation of a word in one language would result in a weakening of the meaning of the corresponding word in the second language, if the labels in the two languages are used for what is culturally the same referent (that is, if the bilinguals are not of the coordinate type, using the two languages in separate systems). Their hypothesis was supported, in that the repetition of a French word resulted in a decrease in the intensity with which its translation was rated on various semantic differential scales. (The semantic differential is a technique for measuring the evaluation, potency, and activity dimensions of meaning, and was developed by Osgood, Suci, and Tannenbaum, 1957.) According to Macnamara (1967c), the findings of Jakobovits and Lambert (1961) have been replicated by a number of scholars (MacLeod, 1966; Lambert, 1967), but he has reservations about similar attempts by others (Olton, 1960; Kolers, 1963; Lambert and Moore, 1966).

In another, more recent study, Kolers (1968) did not directly study the differences between compound and coordinate bilingualism, but rather whether the information and knowledge that a bilingual has are, in effect, centrally stored and equally accessible to expression in either language—or whether, on the other hand, the matter of storage depends on the linguistic associations of that information.

Kolers found that comprehension was about the same whether English-French bilinguals read a passage silently in English, in French, in a form that had English syntax and a vocabulary drawn from both languages, or in a form that had French syntax and a mixed vocabulary. On the other hand, when the passages were read *aloud*, the mixed versions required much more time than the monolingual versions.

This is rather a complicated situation. Kolers felt that the results of the first experiment suggested that there was no need for code-switching when the reading was silent. It is tempting to conclude that the thematic continuity of the passages sufficed to provide comprehension at a relatively high level in the linguistic sense. This would mean that when reading in silence, the subjects had no need to apply the several rules that are required to transform the meanings into phonological shapes, but reading aloud required not only the application of such rules, but also a certain amount of oscillation between the morphosyntactic and phonological levels, because different rules govern the production of French sound-sequences and English sound-sequences.

This may turn out to account for the different amounts of time required under the two conditions; but there are still further problems. Even when individuals are reading "silently," there is often considerable subvocal motor activity. (In the case of the profoundly deaf the activity is in the hand and wrist, the relevant "speech organs" for those who depend on manual communication.) This implies that some of the lower-order rules are applied under both conditions. Further, reading itself depends on a derived system when it is based on a spoken system, though the implications of this fact for Kolers' conclusion are not by any means clear. Certainly it is possible to read aloud without comprehension, much in the way that a telegraph operator can receive and transmit enciphered messages.

Word Association Studies

In order to explore the meanings of words out of their syntactic and thematic contexts, Kolers (1963, also described in 1968) conducted a word-association experiment with native speakers of German, Spanish, and Thai, who all had English as a second language. Words in several semantic categories were used to elicit associations under the several possible conditions. That is, English words were presented and the subject responded with other English words that came to mind; or words in his native language were used to elicit other associated words in the native language; or English words were used to elicit responses in the native language; or, finally, words in the native language were used to elicit associated English words.

Kolers (1968) found that words that referred to concrete, manipulable objects—such as "tree," "lamb," or "thorn"—were more likely to yield similar associations in the two languages than were more abstract words such as "freedom," "justice," or "materialism"; and affect words, such as "hate," "guilt," and "jealousy," were less likely to elicit similar associations in the bilingual's two languages.

These findings support those of Susan Ervin-Tripp (1964), who provided a particularly clear demonstration of the relationship between a language and its associations.

Japanese women who had married American men and were settled in the San Francisco area were each interviewed twice in the same setting, once in Japanese and once in English. Each interview was conducted by a Japanese. The different ways one woman completed the sentences under the two conditions were fairly typical of the general results:

Stimulus 1. "When my wishes conflict with my family . . ."
In Japanese: ". . . it is a time of great unhappiness."
In English: ". . . I do what I want."

Stimulus 2. "I will probably become . . ."
In Japanese: ". . . a housewife."
In English: ". . . a teacher."

Stimulus 3. "Real friends should . . ."
In Japanese: ". . . help each other."
In English: ". . . be very frank."

There seems to be no doubt that language acquisition is accompanied by a train of associations, and these associations may be reinforced or diluted in accordance with the *maintenance contexts.* The latter seems particularly important in the case of the true coordinate bilingual, for if the systems cannot be maintained separately they will converge. The evidence seems strongly to support Gumperz' (1964) statement that

> Whenever several languages or dialects appear regularly as weapons of language choice, they form a behavioral whole, regardless of grammatical distinctness, and must be considered constituent varieties of the same verbal repertoire. [p. 140]

The notion that the speech varieties that constitute a verbal repertoire form an integrated whole gains support from this observation: the use of English by Koreans in the San Francisco area fits rather neatly into the middle ranges of the levels of verbal respect that are seen in Korean verbal interaction. There were times when the Koreans felt that the use of English would be acceptable, and thus they might say either "no" in English or *ani* or *ani yo* in Korean. But where extreme respect must be shown by the lower-ranking member of a dyad, English would not be acceptable—Korean would have to be employed (Howell, 1968).

LANGUAGE DOMINANCE

We have seen some of the ways in which researchers have tried to understand different types of bilingualism in terms of the learning and maintenance processes. A related problem is that of *language dominance;* this has been approached experimentally in ways similar to those in which the various types of bilingualism were approached.

Measures of dominance, as against bilingual balance, have been developed by Lambert (1955) and Lambert *et al.* (1959). They are centered essentially on the different times it takes to perform a variety of tasks in the two languages (see also Triesdan, 1965). The most elaborate attack on problems of measurement and the description of language dominance in bilinguals is that of Fishman, Cooper, Ma, *et al.* (1968) in their study *Bilingualism in the Barrio.* They employed a wide variety of techniques derived from sociology, psychology, and linguistics in their examination of Spanish-English bilinguals living in Puerto Rican neighborhoods of the New York City area.

It is not quite enough to indicate roughly how the language was acquired in order to show the nature of the resultant bilingualism. We need above all to develop measures of linguistic competence and linguistic performance, and for these the results might differ from one context to the next. Intelligibility, for example, is a function of social factors, as Wolff (1964) and Blanc (1960), both cited in Gumperz (1967b), have shown.

Salience

The question of dominance cannot be divorced from the question of *salience*. For an English speaker who is reasonably competent in Japanese, the Japanese language will be salient in a purely Japanese setting, even though in more general terms the native language must be considered dominant. It is difficult to find a truly neutral setting, in which we might expect the dominant language to emerge consistently. Again, if the English speaker who has a fair knowledge of Japanese is placed in a Swahili setting and tries to put his pathetically limited command of the Swahili language into use, the intrusions may not be from English, the dominant language, but rather from Japanese, the subordinate language. Or so we should imagine, to judge from the very common classroom experience in which intrusions appear from a previously studied second language when students are trying to learn a third language. In cases such as these, it seems that the very *foreignness* of the system to be learned is salient: when the system that is most foreign (in terms of prior experience) is attempted, the interference seems likely to be from the next most foreign system. It is as if all the non-first languages were lumped together in opposition to the language one knows thoroughly.

So far as comprehension is concerned, of course, the problem should be greatly reduced or eliminated, since in this case utterances will either be comprehended directly in the second or the third language, or will be comprehended in terms of the first language. But in any event, there does not seem to be any need for response inhibition.

If two languages have been thoroughly mastered in their own terms, as occurs in coordinate bilingualism, and if the third language is being learned in its own terms rather than through another language, then the question of foreignness need not be relevant, and intrusions may be minimal. But where intrusions do occur, we might expect them to be a function of the social situation. That is, if Language A is appropriate to the home and Language B to the world of commerce, then ordinarily each language will be salient in the two situations; and if Language C is associated with either of those situations, the intrusions can be expected to come from the language that is ordinarily appropriate.

On the other hand, if Language C is being learned in terms of Language B, we might expect intrusions to be from the other noninstructional language, A, by analogy with the "foreignness" hypothesis. Thus the noninstructional codominant and the new language would be lumped together in an *ad hoc* category of "noninstructional language." All these possibilities are subject to experimental investigations, though they have not yet been attempted, so far as we know.

The Intellectual Development of the Multilingual

We will conclude this chapter with a brief examination of the intellectual development of the multilingual, because this is a lively academic issue, with serious implications for educational programs.

Many of the relevant studies are keyed to formal learning situations, and give the impression that bilingualism constitutes an intellectual handicap. One of the most influential reports to this effect is that of John Macnamara (1966), who describes the Irish experience thus:

> Native-speakers of English in Ireland who have spent 42 per cent of their school time learning Irish do not achieve the same standard in written English as British children who have not learned a second language (estimated difference in

standard, 17 months of English age). Neither do they achieve the same standard in written Irish as native-speakers of Irish (estimated difference, 16 months of Irish age). Further the English attainments of native-speakers of Irish fall behind those of native-speakers of English both in Ireland (13 months of English age) and in Britain (30 months of English age). [p. 136]

A more optimistic note has been sounded by Peal and Lambert (1962), who found that in Canada, bilinguals performed significantly better than monolinguals in both verbal and nonverbal tests. They argued that the bilinguals have a language asset, are more adept at concept formation, and have a greater mental flexibility. Macnamara (1964, cited in Lambert and Anisfeld, 1969) has taken exception to the Peal and Lambert findings, largely on the grounds that their subjects were brighter to begin with. The rejoinder by Lambert and Anisfeld (1969) suggests that this was not the case. Very likely the debate will continue, but parts of the argument may be at cross-purposes.

Macnamara has been most directly concerned to assess the efficacy of instruction in the weaker of the bilingual's two languages, rather than to study the consequences of bilingualism as such. The kind of handicap to which he refers appears in verbal arithmetical problems, but not in computational problems. In the former case subjects are required to understand and interpret the second language, so that success depends to a considerable extent on their competence in that language.

But as early as 1922 we already had good evidence that there was no significant difference between the scores of bilinguals and monolinguals in nonverbal performance tests, either in Youngstown, Ohio, or in New York City (Pintner-Keller, 1922; Pintner, 1923; both cited by Haugen, 1956). A number of investigators have subsequently confirmed these findings for various groups: American Chinese (Wang, 1926), Indians (Jamieson-Sandiford, 1928),

Mexicans (Garth, 1928; Altus, 1953), Japanese (Yoshioka, 1929), Jews and Italians (Arsenian, 1937), and Italians and Puerto Ricans (Darcy, 1946, 1952). Haugen (1956) concludes from these and other results that general intelligence is not relevant to the question, and that many factors account for differences in language command, including the age of learning, different motivations, and different levels of opportunity to learn all aspects of the language.

Similarly, Carroll (1962) concluded, from his own and other studies of the possibility of predicting success in intensive language courses, that facility in learning to speak and understand a foreign language is a talent or group of talents that are relatively independent of the traits usually included under the rubric of "intelligence." Moreover, Dunkel and Pillet (1957–58, cited in Carroll, 1963), reported that 10 to 20% of the children who show normal or superior progress in most school subjects seem to lack ability in foreign languages, and do not profit much from extra drill or special attention. Nevertheless, since a great deal of the world is bilingual and much of it is multilingual, and since a characteristic of *Homo sapiens* is the capacity to acquire knowledge of and perform with extremely complex patterns of events, it seems that we can again trace the difficulties encountered in the classroom to questions of motivation and social attitudes, rather than to questions of intellectual processes.

It would take us too far from our present focus to delve into the role of social and ethnic identification in the development of attitudes toward different speech varieties, though a great deal of the sociolinguistic literature is devoted to this problem (see, for example, Fishman, Ferguson, and Das Gupta, 1968). But the problem is so salient in South Asia as to warrant an eight-page treatment even in Myrdal's (1968) study of poverty there. Further, it is not difficult to see how a Puerto Rican youngster in New York might develop a negative attitude not only toward American English, but also toward anything offered in that language at school, if he must contend at home with the attitude evinced by Felícita in Oscar Lewis' *La Vida* (1965):

> What I'd like to do to people who show off talking English! If I could be governor of Puerto Rico or the mayor of New York for five or ten minutes I'd take a pistol and I'd shoot every Puerto Rican who has forgotten Spanish. . . . Latins should speak their native tongue at home. Those who don't, can't love their own father and mother. If they want to give up their language they shouldn't call themselves Puerto Ricans. [p. 322]

Despite Macnamara's (1967b) pessimistic attitude toward teaching conducted in the weaker of a bilingual's two languages, studies of the sort reported by Gaarder (1967) suggest that under a proper program, most of the iniquities can be avoided. At the Coral Way Elementary School in Miami, Florida, for example, after four or five years in a system that gives half of the instruction in English and half in Spanish, students seem to learn equally well in either language.

The Coral Way experiment and others mentioned by Gaarder (1967) also have interesting pedagogical implications for language teaching. That is, instructional attention has not been directed toward the classroom language as such, but rather toward the general subject matter treated in conventional schools. The language was not the end of the instruction, but the means. As Gaarder (1967) notes:

> Unquestionably a young child learns a second language quickly and effectively if it is the unavoidable means to his full-time involvement in all the affairs of his life. Much less than full-time involvement will suffice for him to learn the new language. The minimum time, the optimum kind of involvement, and the affairs most conducive to this learning process *in a school* are still largely unknowns. Water falling drop by drop into a bucket will fill it, unless, of course, the conditions are such that each drop evaporates before the next one strikes. [p. 120]

The French-born American writer Julian Green once commented that he was "more and more inclined to believe that it is almost an impossibility to be absolutely bilingual" (1941, p. 402, cited in Haugen, 1956). In part the feeling was engendered by the different personalities that went with each language, which we might expect for the coordinate bilingual but not for the compound or even the convergent bilingual. Green was unable to translate one of his own books from French into English. He had to write an entirely new book instead. "It was as if, writing in English, I had become another person [p. 402]." There is a strong implication that Green was not only bilingual but also bicultural, in the sense that he was the product of two separate, coordinate cultures.

Robert Lowie (1945) commented in very similar terms. "When I speak German to Germans, I automatically shift my orientation as a social being [p. 258]." Also, Lowie felt that the bilingual suffers in either tongue "when judged by the highest standards [p. 257]." But no one who has been treated to Lowie's incisive English, written or spoken, could conclude that he is in any way deficient in his command of the language. Similarly, Joseph Conrad and Vladimir Nabokov handle English with a competence that many of us native speakers find quite demoralizing.

Of course these are exceptional men, but as Fishman (1964) has pointed out, bilingualism has been a trademark of the political and cultural elite throughout history, and where everyone in a speech community is of the same social standing and enjoys comparable bilingual competence, "*no substantial relationship between bilingualism and intelligence is possible* [p. 236]." That is, a range of intelligence will be displayed that is quite independent of bilingualism.

Finally, Fishman (1964) suggests that there has never been a natural bilingual population that could fit a definition which implied that the two systems were fully coordinate, and were both appropriate to all possible interactions. "Every natural bilingual population makes differential use of its several languages and this differential use both serves to integrate the society as well as to preserve its bilingualism [p. 237]."

Thus the problem of bilingualism involves the interaction of linguistic, psychological, and sociological events, and the differential use of the bilingual's languages carries implications even for the personality of the speaker.

REFERENCES

Altus, G. T. 1953. W.I.S.C. patterns of a selective sample of bilingual school children, *J. Genetic Psychol. 83:* 241–248.

Arsenian, S. 1937. *Bilingualism and mental development.* New York: Bureau of Publications, Teachers College, Columbia University.

Blanc, H. 1964. *Communal Dialects in Baghdad.* Cambridge, Mass.: Harvard University Press.

Carroll, J. B. 1962. The prediction of success in intensive language training. In G. Glaser (Ed.), *Training Research and Education,* pp. 87–156. Pittsburgh, Pa.: University of Pittsburgh Press.

Carroll, J. B. 1963. Research on teaching foreign languages. In Nathaniel Lees Gage (Ed.), *Handbook of Research on Teaching,* pp. 1060–1100. Chicago: Rand-McNally & Co.

Darcy, N. T. 1946. The effect of bilingualism upon the measurement of the intelligence of children of preschool age. *J. Educational Psychol. 37:* 21–44.

Darcy, N. T. 1952. The performance of bilingual Puerto Rican children on verbal and on non-language tests of intelligence. *J. Educational Res. 45:* 499–506.

Diebold, R. 1961. Incipient bilingualism. *Language 37:* 87–112.

Dunkel, H. B., & R. A. Pillet. 1957–58. A second year of French in elementary school. *Elementary School Journal 58:* 143–151.

Emaneau, M. B. 1956. India as a linguistic area. *Language 32:* 3–16. (Reprinted in Hymes, 1964.)

Ervin, S. M., & C. E. Osgood. 1954. Second language learning and bilingualism. In Charles E. Osgood and Thomas A. Sebeok (Eds.), *Psycholinguistics,* pp. 139–146. Bloomington, Ind.: Indiana University Press.

Ervin-Trip, S. M. 1964. An analysis of the interaction of language, topic and listener. *Amer. Anthropologist 66.* (Part 2, no. 6, special publication. John J. Gumperz and Dell Hymes [Eds.], *The Ethnography of Communication,* pp. 86–102.)

Ferguson, C. A. 1956. Diglossia. *Word 15:* 325–340. (Reprinted in Hymes, 1964.)

Fishman, J. A. 1964. Bilingualism, intelligence, and language learning. *Modern Language Journal 49:* 227–237.

Fishman, J. A., R. L. Cooper, R. Ma *et al.* 1968. *Bilingualism in the Barrio.* Washington, D.C.: U.S. Department of Health, Education and Welfare, Office of Education, Bureau of Research. Final report on Contract No. OEC-1-7-062817-0297. 2 vols.

Fishman, J. A., C. A. Ferguson, & J. Das Gupta (Eds.). 1968. *Language Problems of Developing Nations.* New York: John Wiley & Sons, Inc.

Gaarder, A. B. 1967. Organization of the bilingual school. *J. Social Issues 23* (No. 2, April): 110–120.

Garth, T. R. 1928. The intelligence of Mexican school children, *School and Society 27:* 791–794.

Green, J. 1941. An experiment in English. *Harper's Magazine 183:* 397–405.

Gumperz, J. J. 1964. Linguistic and social interaction in two communities. *Amer. Anthropologist 66* (Part 2, no. 6, special publication. John J. Gumperz and Dell Hymes [Eds.], *The Ethnography of Communication,* pp. 137–153.)

Gumperz, J. J. 1967a. On the linguistic markers of bilingual communication. *J. Social Issues 23* (No. 2, April): 48–57.

Gumperz, J. J. 1967b. *The Measurement of Bilingualism in Social Groups.* Mimeographed paper.

Haugen, E. 1956. *Bilingualism in the Americas: A Bibliography and Research Guide.* American Dialect Society, Publication No. 26. Alabama: University of Alabama Press. (Pages 69–86 The Bilingual Individual, reprinted in Saporta, 1961.)

Howell, R. W. 1968. Linguistic choice and levels of social change. *Amer. Anthropologist 70:* 553–559.

Hymes, D. (Ed.). 1964. *Language in Culture and Society.* New York: Harper & Row, Publishers.

Jakobovits, L., & W. E. Lambert. 1961. Semantic satiation among bilinguals. *J. Experimental Psychol. 62:* 576–582.

Jamieson, E., & P. Sandiford. 1928. The mental capacity of Southern Ontario Indians. *J. Educational Psychol. 19:* 313–328.

Kolers, P. A. 1963. Interlingual word association. *J. Verbal Learning and Verbal Behavior 2:* 291–300.

Kolers, P. A. 1968. Bilingualism and information processing. *Scientific American 218* (no. 3, March): 78–86.

Lambert, W. E. 1955. Measurement of the linguistic dominance of bilinguals. *J. Abnormal and Social Psychol. 50:* 197–200.

Lambert, W. E. 1967. *Psychological studies of the interdependencies of the bilingual's two languages.* Mimeographed paper. Cited in Macnamara, 1967.

Lambert, W. E., & E. Anisfeld. A note on the relationship of bilingualism and intelligence. *Canadian J. Behavioral Sciences.* In press.

Lambert, W. E., J. Havelka, & C. Crosby. 1958. The influence of language-acquisition contexts on bilingualism. *J. Abnormal and Social Psychol. 56:* 239–244. Reprinted in Saporta, 1961, pp. 407–414.

Lambert, W. E., J. Havelka, & R. Gardner. 1959. Linguistic manifestations of bilingualism. *J. Personality 72:* 77–82.

Lambert, W. E., & N. Moore. 1966. Word association responses: Comparison of American and French monolinguals with Canadian monolinguals and bilinguals. *J. Personality and Social Psychol. 3:* 313–320.

Lewis, O. 1965. *La Vida.* New York: Random House, Inc.

Lowie, R. 1945. A case of bilingualism. *Word 1:* 249–259.

MacKey, W. F. 1962. The description of bilingualism. *Canadian J. Linguistics 7:* 51–85. Cited in Macnamara, 1967c.

MacLeod, F. 1966. *A study of Gaelic-English bilingualism: The effects of semantic satiation.* Unpublished thesis, Aberdeen University. Cited in Macnamara, 1967c.

Macnamara, J. 1964. The commission on Irish: Psychological aspects. *Studies* (Summer) 164–173. Cited in Lambert and Anisfeld, 1969.

Macnamara, J. 1966. *Bilingualism and Primary Education.* Edinburgh, Scotland: Edinburgh University Press.

Macnamara, J. 1967a. Bilingualism in the modern world. *J. Social Issues 23* (no. 2, April): 1–7.

Macnamara, J. 1967b. The effects of instruction in a weaker language. *J. Social Issues 23* (no. 2, April): 121–135.

Macnamara, J. 1967c. Linguistic performance. *J. Social Issues 23* (no. 2, April); 58–77.

Myrdal, G. 1968. *Asian Drama.* New York: Pantheon Books, Inc. 3 vols.

Nida, E. A. 1961. *Some problems of semantic structure and translation equivalents.* In A William Cameron Townsend en el vigésimoquinto aniversario del Instituto Linguistico de Verano, Mexico, D. F., pp. 313–325.

Olton, R. M. 1960. *Semantic generalization between languages.* Unpublished M. A. thesis, McGill University, Montreal. Cited in Macnamara, 1967c.

Osgood, C. E., J. S. Suci, & P. Tannenbaum. 1957. *The Measurement of Meaning.* Urbana, Ill. University of Illinois Press.

Peal, E., & W. E. Lambert. 1962. The relation of bilingualism to intelligence. *Psychological Monographs 546* (Vol. 76, no. 27).

Pintner, R. 1923. Comparison of American and foreign children on intelligence tests. *J. Educational Res. 14:* 292–295.

Pintner, R., & R. Keller. 1922. Intelligence of foreign children. *J. Educational Res. 13:* 214–222.

Reinecke, J. 1938. Trade jargons and Creole dialects as marginal languages. *Social Forces 17:* 107–118. Reprinted in Hymes, 1964.

Saporta, S. (Ed.). 1961. *Psycholinguistics.* New York: Holt, Rinehart & Winston, Inc.

Triesman, A. M. 1965. The effects of redundancy and familiarity on translating and repeating back a foreign and native language. *Brit. J. Psychol. 56:* 369–379.

Wang, S. L. 1926. A demonstration of the language difficulty involved in comparing racial groups by means of verbal intelligence tests. *J. Applied Psychol. 10:* 102–106.

Weinreich, U. 1953. *Languages in Contact.* New York: Linguistic Circle.

Wolff, H. 1964. Intelligibility and inter-ethnic attitudes. In Dell Hymes (Ed.), *Language in Culture and Society,* pp. 440–448. New York: Harper & Row, Publishers.

Yoshioka, J. G. 1929. A study of bilingualism. *Pediatric Seminars 36:* 473–479.

13

Pidgins
and
Creoles

In our discussion of multilingualism we dealt with some problems of languages in contact, from the standpoint both of the effects on the languages themselves, and of what happens in the head of the individual speaker. Until recently, the relatively limited interest in problems of languages in contact was restricted to long-term situations that involved two or more viable codes. In the case of the individual, this would mean that attention has been focused on the bilingual who has reasonable competence in two speech varieties, rather than on the monolingual who has picked up a smattering of another language. In the case of speech communities, interest has centered on political border areas where, for example, "French" and "German" have coexisted for generations, exercising a mutual influence to such a point that linguistically the two local varieties resemble each other more than either resembles its national standard variety.

Short-term situations, in which the speaker knows one language well and has a short-lived experience of a second language, or in which members of separate speech communities are brought into initial contact, have been largely ignored, or at most, treated as rather amusing curiosities. Yet there are potentially important theoretical questions in this area, important not only in the problem of language change, but also in more general problems of language and thought.

Half a century ago, for example, Otto Jespersen (1922) drew a series of analogies between pidgins and child language; he included "errors of pronunciation, extreme simplification of grammar," and "scantiness of vocabulary [p. 225]." Within recent years, fortunately, we have learned a great deal about first language acquisition, and increasing attention is being devoted to situations of relatively short-term contact. In particular, the process of pidginization, the creation of a makeshift language based on an imperfect approximation to one of the two varieties in contact (Reinecke, 1938) has been drawing scholarly attention, and Creolization, the process whereby a pidgin language develops autonomy and has native speakers, has received even more attention.

PIDGINS

There are two highly predictable features of short-term contact situations, where the "short-term" contact includes the duration necessary to develop a reasonably consistent medium of communication, such as a useful pidgin. The first is that the major accommodation will be made by the socially subordinate speaker or group of speakers. (Various complexities govern the long-term situation, including the possibility that politically dominant foreign groups will be assimilated into the majority culture, as has happened so often in China.) The second highly predictable feature of the short-term situation is that the accommodations on the part of the superordinate will be in the direction of simplification, though there are interesting complexities here too.

The importance of social dominance is reflected both in the speech variety and in the behavior of the individual. Thus we speak of English- or French-based pidgins and Creoles, for example, and these terms seem to reflect the present or past ascendancy of a cultural or political entity. Thus the Master of a British coastal passenger-freighter operating out of Hong Kong advised a Chinese crew member that "Missy want to go up there at two o'clock." In this particular instance, the British captain was both the superordinate on his ship and a representative of the British Crown Colony. The crewman had to accept minimally modified English; the captain used no Chinese in this case, at least, and accommodated only in omitting the third person singular marker and using a conventionalized personal reference term.

The example also illustrates one feature of what Ferguson calls "foreigner talk." Ferguson (1971) suggests that many, if not all, speech communities have a speech variety that is used with people who are assumed not to understand the normal speech of the community: foreigners, babies, the deaf, and so forth. The special speech forms are thought to be simplified versions of the language, and thus to be more easily understood. In the case of babies and foreigners, at least, the special variety may be considered an imitation of the way the person addressed uses the language (Jesperson, 1922, p. 225). Ferguson checked the last point in the obvious and proper way, by asking informants how babies or foreigners talk in his areas of investigation.

"Bamboo English"

A closer look at one case of pidginization, however, suggests that the situation may be rather complex. Interactions between American military personnel and Japanese barmaids (*circa* 1960) shows a considerable linguistic mix of Japanese and English components, depending largely on each party's conception of the other's competence in the non-native language; but both sides seem to learn a common speech variety that shows considerable independence of both the component languages.

When a GI says "Takusan bû-chan jôsan," for example, he obviously is not trying to imitate his idea of how the Japanese speak English. He is generating an approximation to Japanese, and wants to convey "A very fat girl." In the local pidgin, *takusan* "a lot of" is generalized beyond Japanese usage (originally by the Americans, presumably, and subsequently by the Japanese with whom they interact). This fits Ferguson's suggestion nicely. But subsequent "generations" of Americans learn the generalized usage from the barmaids, and the same process probably covers the other expressions in the example. *Bû-chan* seems to be from *debu* "fat" plus the diminutive suffix -*chan,* and is a slang designation, possibly limited to the pidgin, for a fat person. It is not considered by most to be particularly insulting. *Jôsan* is pidgin for any relatively young woman (older women and proprietesses are *mamasan* in pidgin). It derives from *ojôsan,* a young, unmarried woman. The total sequence "Takusan bû-chan jôsan" is not Japanese, even though the lexical items are derived from Japanese, and it is clearly not English, even though it fits English syntactic order ("[A] very fat girl").

While the use of pidgin depends to some extent on the speaker's perception of the other party, the perspectives of the speakers of each basic speech variety differ. In general, the more experienced Americans tend to gain increasingly closer approximations to Japanese (especially in adding to their Japanese vocabularies), and the Japanese women tend to achieve closer approximations to English. That is, each side gains increasing mastery of the other's language, rather than both sides gaining mastery of a third code, pidgin. (It is possible that the same process, skewed in the direction of English, accounts in part for the gradual disappearance of the Hawaiian Creole—"Hawaiian pidgin.")

In the Japanese case, it is predictable that the pidgin lexicon would reflect common interests, and in particular the concerns of the American military. Perhaps the most elegant example of this was produced when a barmaid who had been complaining of a headache later remarked, "Take APC, headache go PCS." The APC is the super-aspirin tablet used, one feels, for every conceivable ailment in the U.S. military; PCS is "Permanent Change of Station," as against a temporary duty assignment in the military.

The pidgin that developed between the U.S. military and the "indigenous personnel" (mostly barmaids) in Japan and Korea has received some casual attention in the literature, but not of the caliber it deserves. Grant Webster (1960), for example, who provides the entertaining example of *Cinderella* in pidgin that is excerpted below, is perhaps typical of such chroniclers in that he lacked relevant background experience. In discussing "Korean bamboo English," he recognizes "honcho" as Japanese, but guesses that it might be derived from Honshû (the main Japanese island). It is *hanchô,* literally a "squad leader." He suggests that the leader of a Korean working party is called a "skivvy honcho" because of the apparel of his men, deriving "skivvy" from the Navy term for underwear. This etymology of skivvy has also been offered in Japan, but it is a minority opinion, and in Japan, at least, the term is clearly from *sukebei,* "lecherous," and *sukebei hanchô* is used (usually jocularly) to designate a particularly "horny" troop. Similar problems arise with terms of Korean origin. Of course the study is not without value; it certainly indicates the remarkable Japanese component in Korean-English pidgin, an artifact of R & R (recreational leave) in Japan for troops stationed in Korea, and of alternate tours of duty done by Americans in Japan and Korea. (Only the older barmaids would have learned any appreciable amount of Japanese under the Annexation, which ended in 1945.)

The following passages from *Cinderella* (anonymous, offered by Webster, 1960, pp. 264–265) reflect the predominance of military vocabulary and Japanese loans:

> Taksan[1] years ago, skoshi[2] Cinderella-san[3] lived[4] in hootchie[5] with sisters, poor little Cinderella-san ketchee[6] no fun, hava-no[7] social life.[8] Always washee-washee,[9] scrubee-scrubee, make chop-chop.[10] One day Cinderella-san sisters[11] ketchee post cardo[12] from Seoul. Post cardo speakie[13] so: one prince-san[14] have big blowout,[15] taksan kimchi,[16] taksan beeru,[17] play 'She Ain't Got No Yo Yo.'[18] Cindy-san sisters taksan excited, make Cinderella-san police up[19] clothes.
>
> Sisters go blackmarket,[20] ketchee fatigues, new combat boots,[21] bring to hootchie and Cinderella-san cut down[22] fatigues, shine-shine boots. Come night of big shindig,[23] sisters speak sayonara,[24] leave Cindy-san by fire.

1. taksan = Japanese *takusan* "a lot of"
2. skoshi = Japanese *sukoshi* "a small quantity of"
3. -san = Japanese polite suffix
4. past tense marker is a little improbable
5. hootchie, "pad," a term popular in Korea (etymology uncertain) but not in Japan
6. ketchee, "catch," i.e., "have, obtain"; also familiar in Japan
7. hava-no, "lack," also familiar in Japan, but more experienced barmaids are likely to use appropriate English or "no have"
8. "social life" is improbable for the pidgin
9. washee-washee, "wash," probably obsolete in Japan
10. chop-chop, "food, meal," not common in Japan
11. sisters, the plural marker tends to be dropped
12. post cardo seems clearly to be an American innovation, since the -r- would not be expected from either Korean or Japanese speakers, and the paragogic -o would fit a Japanese pattern more readily than a Korean pattern
13. speakie probably would not ordinarily be followed by "so"
14. prince is unlikely for pidgin; -san is the Japanese polite suffix, which in the case of a prince would usually be given the more formal shape of -sama
15. blowout, not common in Japan

16. kimchi, pickled vegetables, a Korean staple
17. beeru, "beer," from Japanese *biiru*
18. song title represents a parady of the Japanese favorite, *Shina no Yoru*, "China Nights"
19. police up, a military expression for cleaning up or straightening up, probably known to many non-U.S. pidgin speakers in Korea and Japan
20. at the time, nearly anything available in U.S. military warehouses was available on the Korean black market
21. fatigues and combat boots, standard work clothes of army personnel
22. cut down = modify or tailor
23. shindig, not common in Japan.

Most such accounts of "Bamboo English" deal with lexical items, describing with uncertain accuracy contemporary usages, usually those of the Americans rather than of their companions. While some of the Americans spent several years in the pidgin community, during the period in question the tour in Korea was typically to be measured in months. The barmaids, on the other hand, were "permanent party," and used the pidgin over a period of years (in most cases).

In commenting on the excerpts from "Cinderella-san," we have by implication, at least, indicated a measure of expectation, a sense of what is probable and what is improbable, on the basis of largely informal experience with the pidgin employed between Americans and Japanese near military bases in Japan. The point is not so much whether one reporter is more accurate than another, as that even this pidgin has conventions. Thus "prince" simply is not part of the vocabulary of ordinary interaction between members of the two groups. Similarly, on one occasion (in Japan) a barmaid, when asked if she were "plastered," responded "Who's a bastard?" The conventional term for "drunk" was "stinko," and "plastered" was not part of the joint lexicon. The conventional nature of pidgins may also distinguish them from "broken" varieties of English, Japanese, or other "natural" language.

Hawaiian Pidgins

While the short-term contact pidgin situation has not been fully exploited academically, more stabilized situations have received serious attention in recent years. Hawaii, for example, is a particularly exciting area for contemporary research, because there is a continuum of speech varieties, which begins with the broken English of the new immigrant, a pidgin that in most areas has crystallized into a Creole, and that in many areas has become de-Creolized into the local Standard English.

Carr (1972) divides the speech continuum into five stages as a matter of convenience, while admitting that one could make almost any number of categories (as the term continuum implies, of course). Typical of her Type I speaker is a 70-year-old woman who was born in Korea, and came to Hawaii in her early twenties to marry a plantation worker. The broken quality is revealed in such statements as "only Korean school study" (she only studied in Korean schools) and "school-time, baby name me no like. That's why change" (she did not like her original Korean name, and later changed it to a Western-type name). The woman was being interviewed by her granddaughter, who is a university graduate and a speaker of Standard English, but as the interview progressed she accommodated her speech by pidginizing it, though she probably did not originally intend to. The process is seen in a succession of questions: "When did you come to Hawaii?"; "When you come to Hawaii, what island you live on?"; "When you come to Hawaii, what island you live?"; and "How long you live Kauai?"

The phonetic transcription (and the analysis by Dong Jae Lee) reveals the presence of considerable phonological interference from Korean, and except for a number of extremely common phrases ("I think," "I don't know"), the construction of her utterances tends to be Korean (Carr, 1972, pp. 32–33).

Carr (1972) calls her Type II speech "The early creole remnant," and illustrates the speech variety through an interview with a 69-year-old woman of Hawaiian-Chinese ancestry who grew up in the relatively isolated Waipio Valley on the island of Hawaii. Her speech is more fluent, perhaps less pained, and somehow less foreign-sounding: "I stay with my grandfather, my grandmother. When my grandmother die, my grandfather go back China. He did! He went! But he die already." Although this brief passage contains "did" and "went," her speech represents, according to Carr's analysis, a "preinflectional stage in her handling of English [p. 40]." It is not meaningful to speak of phonological or grammatical interference from any specific language, but Carr does note that the woman applies primary stress in the stress-timed manner of standard English, rather than in the locally more common syllable-timed rhythm (which Carr assumes to be the result of contact with the Japanese, Korean, or Philippine languages). The reason is presumably that those languages exerted no influence in the remote valley in which the informant lived when she was growing up.

Type III is what is thought of as the "typical" contemporary so-called "pidgin." One of the most salient features, perhaps, is the syllable-timed rhythm. A high-school boy, for example, asks ³Wànnà gò shòw tónìght?¹↝ In addition to the comparable stress on most of the syllables, this yes-no question typically bears a falling intonation. Compare the expanded standard form of the question: ²Do you *wànt* to *gò* to the ³*shów* to*nìght*?³↗ (Carr, 1972, pp. 50–51).

Type IV is only a step removed from the standard, and has relatively few departures in either pronunciation or grammar. The post-vocalic /r/ is typically missing, and dental fricatives may still be stops, as in "wit" for "with," or "trow" for "throw." Occasionally forms such as "she like" and "she know" also occur. A characteristic of all the nonstandard forms in Hawaii is the unvoicing of final voiced consonants, and phonetic loss and simplification of final consonant clusters is common. Carr (1972) notes that such phonological considerations can make agreement of the noun and verb impossible; that is, phonology can influence grammar, and it may be particularly obvious in Hawaii.

Carr's (1972) Type V is the standard, and her examples (from the speech of Congresswoman Patsy Mink and history professor Shunzo Sakamaki) are compared with various mainland regional varieties of the standard.

While Carr offers some analysis of the linguistic types she identifies and describes, her discussion seems generally to be in terms of the implied end product: Standard English. (This is not to suggest that she shows a normative or prescriptive attitude—that would be most unjust—but it does influence the presentation and the kinds of questions dealt with.) Nagara (1972) has provided a bilingual description of Japanese "pidgin" English in Hawaii, which involves some interesting technical problems. The possibility of a phonemic description, for example, seems inapplicable to the bilingual case (and Carr, too, deals with only phonetic transcription). The point was raised earlier by Haugen (1954) and Weinreich (1953, 1954), but the general question of "coexistent systems" was discussed even earlier by Fries and Pike (1949). Since phonemes are defined in terms of a single language or code, and since the bilingual case involves two codes, a *diaphonic* description is required; and to include the more general case, when we are providing for morphosyntactic levels we may speak of *diasystems*.

DIASYSTEMS

Whether one is looking at genetically related languages, dialects of a single language, or unrelated languages in bilingual contact, diasystems are to be considered higher abstractions under which the relevant linguistic systems are joined. But, as Nagara (1972, p. 52) notes, the elements that are united in a diasystem need not represent actual occurrences in the speech of a bilingual speaker. To say that English /æ/ corresponds to Japanese /a/ for the Japanese plantation worker in Hawaii does not mean that he will produce either the English sound or the Japanese sound. It is more likely, indeed, that he will utilize a single sound (allowing for some variation, presumably), and that sound will probably be the one found in his native language. This would be the *prime* of the diaphone, a notion which seems at least analogous to that of the phoneme. As Weinreich stated (1954, p. 270; cited by Nagara, 1972, p. 53), "A diasystem is experienced in a very real way by bilingual (including bidialectal) speakers and corresponds to what students of language contact have called 'merged systems'." Or, to refer to the terminology we used earlier, a diasystem describes convergent bilingualism.

The actual diasystemic description involves technical complexities beyond the interest of our discussion, but we may pause a moment to see how Nagara's study relates to that of Carr. First of all, Carr (1972) treats the local speech varieties more or less independently of the ethnic backgrounds of the speakers. To illustrate her Type I, she drew on the speech of an elderly Korean woman who had come to Hawaii as an immigrant nearly half a century ago, and specific features of the woman's speech were discussed in terms of her native language. But Carr could equally easily have drawn on Nagara's (1972) subjects, Japanese plantation workers. If anything, the speech of many of his subjects shows even more obvious influences from their native language. Indeed, Nagara found it necessary to develop an operational measure of whether an utterance was to be regarded as Japanese or Japanese-Hawaiian pidgin English. All utterances were considered to be pidgin unless their predicate words were derived from Japanese, in which case the utterances were classified as Japanese. Thus the utterance "You study *suru ka?*" (Do you study?) is classified as Japanese rather than Pidgin. Nagara honored the dichotomy because none of his informants could produce a sentence without relying upon the morphophonemic rules of Japanese when the sentence included a predicate word derived from that language.

> In Japanese the predicate verbs, adjectives, and copulas are the only elements which are not deletable either in the deep structure or in the surface structure, and also these predicate words are the only elements of the base components which are affected by morphophonemic changes after the tense or negative transformations. In addition, all these Japanese predicate adjectives, verbs, and copulas occur in the final position of a sentence accompanied by inflectional suffixes, and, occasionally, by sentence particles including the question marker. [p. 13]

Further, in the case of Nagara's informants, when a Japanese predicate word occurred, the terminal juncture always conformed to the Japanese norm.

Nagara found it convenient to subgroup his informants into "English-type" and "Japanese-type" pidgin speakers, but it is not evident from the one extended passage used to illustrate the "advanced" type (English) that either group would fit into Carr's Type II. Their speech samples more closely resemble that of the Korean woman (Type I) than that of the Hawaiian-Chinese woman (Type II); and, of course, all of Nagara's informants were immigrants, as were the speakers of Carr's Type I. The Hawaiian-Chinese woman was born and raised in Hawaii.

Hawaiian Creole

The most recent general, detailed treatment of the Hawaiian Creole is that of Perlman (1973), who thinks of his corpus as representing a "post-Creole" continuum, rather than Tsuzaki's (1971) coexistent systems, or various levels (as did Nagara and, more obviously, Carr). Still, to judge from his many examples, most of his informants seem to fit the description that Carr provides for her Types II and III. Perlman does, however, usefully point out, with the other serious students of the so-called pidgin, that it is by no means a uniform and static phenomenon, and unlike most of the others, he adds that the particular speech variety employed by a given speaker is subject to switching, in accordance with rules we can call "social." Perlman includes a chapter on code-switching; his treatment is rather global, but nonetheless welcome, in a work that is more centrally concerned with the grammar of Hawaiian English.

Research into the Hawaiian Creole (or, more accurately, the pidgin-standard continuum) is at present being conducted in depth under the guidance of Derek Bickerton of the University of Hawaii at Manoa. Since Bickerton has done fieldwork in Guiana, and is concerned with Creoles from a general theoretical point of view, the importance of such local studies will no doubt increase sharply in the next few years.

BLACK ENGLISH

The range of speech varieties in Hawaii is not unique. Indeed, there are hundreds, if not thousands, of pidgins and Creoles around the world. The Creole of greatest contemporary interest for many Americans is the one popularly called "black English," though Labov (1972) argues for the term "black English vernacular" (BEV). "Black English," Labov suggests, is better reserved for

> the whole range of language forms used by black people in the United States: a very large range indeed, extending from the Creole grammar of Gullah spoken in the Sea Islands of South Carolina to the most formal and accomplished literary

style. A great deal of misunderstanding has been created by the use of this term, "black English," which replaced our original "Nonstandard Negro English" when the latter became less acceptable to many people. [p. xiii]

The label "black English vernacular" includes the relatively uniform grammar that is typified in the speech of black youth in their teens or late preteens, who participate fully in the street culture of the inner cities. It is found in many urban centers of the United States, but Labov specifically refers to New York, Boston, Detroit, Philadelphia, Washington, Cleveland, Chicago, St. Louis, San Francisco, and Los Angeles.

That the black English vernacular had a Creole origin is not universally accepted, but for most contemporary scholars of the subject the only questions are matters of detail. The most ardent proponents of the Creolist argument are probably Stewart (1969) and Dillard (1972), but at the very least it would be difficult to deny that the old so-called Plantation Creole was considerably influenced by Caribbean Creole English (Bailey, in press).

No matter what the final decision on the origin of BEV, it is now a dialect of English, with its own forms of meaning (Labov, 1972; Spears, 1972). Dillard (1972) feels that the BEV system of verbs best reveals this dialect's differences from white American dialects and thus its closest resemblances to its presumed Creole ancestors.

One of the best-known features of BEV is perhaps the omission of the copula, as in "he sick." But while this may equate to SE "he is sick," it carries the specific implication that the individual is sick at the moment, and it contrasts with "he be sick," which implies that the individual is the victim of a long-term illness. Similar considerations govern the use of the auxiliary "be": "he workin' " (he is working at the moment) contrasts with "he be workin' " (he is always working). Dillard (1972, p. 45) cites several examples of acceptable and unacceptable forms (the latter marked with an asterisk). Thus in the sentence "He be waitin' for me every night when I come home," the "be" agrees with "every night" in specifying duration; and "He waitin' for me right now," without the auxiliary, correlates with the "right now" in indicating "at the moment." Thus it would be semantically anomalous to say "*He waitin' for me every night" or "*He be waiting for me right now."

Similarly, to negate "He waitin' for me right now," the negator "ain' " is appropriate: "He ain' waitin' for me right now." But the negator "don' " is required for the durative marker "be": "He don' be waitin' for me every night." The forms "*He ain' waitin' for me every night" and "*He don' be waitin for me right now" are not grammatically acceptable. To give so few examples of the grammatical differences of BEV from SE is not to slight the number and complexities of the differences; rather, it is a testimony to the intricacy of the problem. A brief appreciation of the difficulties may be obtained from Bailey's (1974) review of Dillard's book; a full appreciation would require a volume of size comparable to this one. Labov (1972) devotes a 65-page chapter just to the "Contraction, Deletion, and Inherent Variability of the English Copula," with specific reference, of course, to BEV.

Whether we look at the varieties of Hawaiian English, BEV, or perhaps those of any area where several speech varieties are employed, there are likely to be serious problems of description. The notion of a universal grammar, of course, implies that there is some way of generating specific alternate realizations ("languages") from an underlying structure. Or, somewhat more concretely, as in the case of several dialects of a single language, there may be hope of describing a core grammar and providing supplementary (presumably low-order) rules to deal with the whole of such a "polylectal" body. This approach has been recently questioned by Bickerton (1973), because some of these varieties differ (in this case from English) at a relatively deep level, and he does not think a "core-and-appendage" grammar could generate them all. He also questions models based on quantified data that express consistent relations between variable elements, essentially because they must be based on the behavior of groups, and group behavior can be misleading with regard to individual rule systems. Thus Loflin (1970) denies that "have" appears in BEV grammar, and attributes the occasional appearance of "have" to interference from SE. Labov, Cohen, Robins, and Lewis (1968, I, p. 223, cited by Bickerton, 1973), on the other hand, argue that BEV does include "have," but that it is usually deleted by phonological rules.

Apparently, Bickerton suggests, BEV is not a homogeneous entity as the argument would imply. More likely, there are both "haves" and "have-nots," because change is taking place in the system. And he cites the sensible and tidy notion of Bailey (1969–70) that "synchronic variation reflects diachronic change." In the present case the change of rule involving "have" has reached some, but not all, BEV speakers.

The point is included here primarily to illustrate the fact that basic problems of language change are increasingly dealt with in the context of languages in contact. Bailey (in press) attributes to Bickerton the assertion that *no change within or across systems occurs without contact with another language variety,* a view that seems compatible with Bailey's own view of language history and language relationships.

REFERENCES

Bailey, C.-J. N. 1969–70. Studies in three-dimensional language theory, Parts 1–4. *Working Papers in Linguistics 1.8, 2.2/4, 2.8.* Honolulu: University of Hawaii.

Bailey, C.-J. N. 1974. Review of J. L. Dillard, *Black English: Its History and Usage in the United States. Foundations of Language 11:* 299–309.

Bailey, C.-J. N. In press. Old and new views on language history and language relationships. *J. East European Social History* (special issue edited by Eric P. Hamp).

Bickerton, D. 1973. The structure of polylectal grammar. In Roger W. Shuy (Ed.), *Report of the Twenty-Third Annual Round Table Meeting on Linguistics and Language Studies,* pp. 17–42. Washington, D.C.: Georgetown University Press.

Carr, E. B. 1972. *Da Kine Talk.* Honolulu: The University Press of Hawaii.

Dillard, J. L. 1972. *Black English, Its History and Usage in the United States.* New York: Random House, Inc.

Ferguson, C. A. 1971. Absence of copula and the notion of simplicity. In Dell Hymes (Ed.), *Pidginization and Creolization of Languages.* London: Cambridge University Press.

Fries, C. C., & K. Pike. 1949. Co-existent phonemic systems. *Language 75:* 25–29.

Haugen, E. 1954. Problems of bilingual description. Report of the Fifth Annual Round Table Meeting on Linguistics and Language Teaching. *Georgetown University Monograph Series on Languages and Linguistics 7:* 9–19. Washington, D.C.: Georgetown University Press.

Jespersen, O. 1922. *Language.* London: George Allen and Unwin, Ltd.

Labov, W. 1972. *Language in the Inner City: Studies in the Black English Vernacular.* Philadelphia: University of Pennsylvania Press.

Labov, W., P. Cohen, C. Robins, & J. Lewis. 1968. *A Study of the Non-Standard English of Negro and Puerto Rican Speakers in New York City.* New York: Columbia University Press.

Loflin, M. 1970. On the structure of the verb in a dialect of American Negro English. *Linguistics 59:* 14–28.

Nagara, S. 1972. *Japanese Pidgin English in Hawaii.* Honolulu: The University Press of Hawaii.

Perlman, A. M. 1973. Grammatical structure and style-shift in Hawaiian pidgin and Creole. Unpublished doctoral dissertation, University of Chicago.

Reinecke, J. 1938. Trade jargons and creole dialects as marginal languages. *Social Forces 17:* 107–118.

Spears, M. K. 1972. You makin' sense. (Review of J. L. Dillard. 1972. *Black English: Its History and Usage in the United States.* New York: Random House, Inc.) *The New York Review of Books XIX,* no. 8 (November 16): 32–35.

Steward, W. A. 1969. Historical and structural bases for the recognition of Negro dialect. Proceedings of the 20th Annual Round Table, Georgetown University.

Webster, G. 1960. Korean bamboo English once more. *Amer. Speech 35:* 261–265.

Weinreich, U. 1953. *Languages in Contact.* New York: Linguistic Circle of New York.

Weinreich, U. 1954. Is a structural dialectology possible? *Word 10:* 265–280.

14

Language
and
Social
Identity

So-called secret languages, of whatever complexity, are employed to ensure that individuals of the social groups for which they were designed will be privy to in-group communications, while all others will be excluded. The Secretary of State may issue a directive in a high-level system to "Chiefs of Missions Only," thus excluding not only those who are ignorant of the system, but also those who lack a "need to know." In a small insurance office two women who were chatting in English immediately switched to Spanish when they were approached by another worker with whom they did not wish to interact (Howell, 1973).

But privacy systems are only the most blatant verbal means of separating in- and out-groups. Routine speech differences reveal different social affiliations. According to Sledd (1969), they are used

> . . . to claim and proclaim his identity, and society uses them
> to keep him under control. The person who talks right, as

we do, is one of us. The person who talks wrong is an
outsider, strange and suspicious, and we must make him feel
inferior if we can. That is one purpose of education. In a
school system run like ours by white businessmen, instruction in the mother tongue includes formal initiation into the
linguistic prejudices of the middle class. [p. 1307]

While some academics, at all levels, perhaps, are able
and even willing to tolerate verbal performances by students that are at the least nonstandard, either to avoid
discouraging the student or because the presentation is not
seen as critical to the substance of the offering, most of us
show greater admiration for the student who can dress
insights and observations in "good" English (or French,
Swahili, and so on). This is not simply because we are part
of a conscious and deliberate plot to suppress a querulous
minority (though such motivation probably cannot be denied in some cases). Among the more innocuous reasons
for such a preference is that in the very process of learning
about history, English, literature, civics, and the like, we
also learn something about the formal language through
which such subjects are taught. Given the tradition of writing in formal English, whether we approve of that tradition
or not, a certain range of styles come to be associated with
formal learning, and we expect the "educated" person to
reflect something of those styles.

To provide a very simple illustration modified from
Gumperz and Herasimchuk, 1972 (pp. 99–100), the following three utterances may be used to describe the same
event:

1. "They are holding a meeting to discuss the issue."
2. "They are getting together to talk it over."
3. "They're sittin' down to rap about it."

But they imply a progression from formal to informal, and
there are restrictions on the use of styles. That is, if the
term "rap" is going to be used, it would seem a bit odd in
this context:

4. "They are holding a meeting to rap on the issue." While two people can sit down and "rap" about something quite informally, the holding of a meeting is more formal, and it implies that there are two or more potentially contesting parties, probably some sort of agenda, and certain understandings about who will talk when. So a verbal expression of the event such as the following would be curious:

5. "They're hav'n a meet'n to discuss the issue."

NONSTANDARD LANGUAGE AND THE SELF-FULFILLING PROPHECY

If a teacher is likely to be made uncomfortable by such relatively subtle stylistic considerations, it is not difficult to understand why even greater discomfort may be created by responses in black English vernacular (BEV), a pidgin, or any forms that are considered to be nonstandard. A dissonance is created which makes it hard to accommodate nonstandard speech varieties with the notion of being "educated"; and very often the evident lack of education implied by the use of nonstandard speech is taken to signify a lack of intelligence. Even if one disregards the imputation of genetic inferiority on the part of nonstandard speakers, the assumption is commonly made that such speakers are culturally and/or verbally deprived. And if a teacher makes such assumptions, lower performances may be expected from such students, who will then, in effect, learn to perform at a lower level than they otherwise might.

Lewis (1970) offers a simple illustration of how a presumably well-intentioned and presumably benevolent teacher put the process into effect. The second-grade teacher of an "integrated" class was a reserved but pleasant woman in her early twenties who, as an immigrant, had had trouble with her English; she had been discriminated

against on the basis of her ethnic origins, and thus felt
sensitive to problems of language learning and to the social
difficulties encountered by minorities. Her class was divided into "fast" and "slow" groups, with perhaps a dozen
in the former group and three in the latter. During Lewis'
periods of observation only two of the slow group were in
attendance (both of them were black). The teacher's way of
teaching the presumably slow students to read was to deal
with the sound values of individual letters, rather than of
larger sequences. Later, when it was time for them to read
aloud, the sentence in question was "I am a man." She
asked one of the "slow" students, "*Can* you read that,
Joe?" The youngster glanced at the picture of the beaming
man to which the sentence referred, and replied "He is a
man." While the child was evidently interpreting the sentence, the teacher assumed that he had been unable to read
it accurately, and proceeded to take him phonetically
through the first part of the sentence. The student was
rather perplexed, since he understood the sentence and
had been conveying its meaning.

When Lewis asked why the two black students were
assigned to a slow category, the teacher said that they came
from "nonliterate backgrounds," but that with special help
they would be able to catch up with the other students. But
her low expectation of their performance was revealed in
the way she posed her question: "*Can* you read that"—not
"will," "would," "please," or any other form that would
have implied the assumption that he had ability to read.
These were beginning students, but Lewis feels that the
chances are good that they will learn to accommodate
themselves to the relatively low expectations held for them
by the teacher. The powerful influence of teacher expectations has been demonstrated even with mice. Lewis cites
Rosenthal and Jacobson (1968), who showed that randomly chosen mice learned mazes more quickly when their
human trainers were made to believe that they were genet-

ically bred for superior maze-learning. On the other hand, mice whose trainers were led to believe they were dealing with animals bred for dullness performed with a corresponding lack of speed, even though there was actually no genetic difference between the two groups. Similar results have been obtained experimentally with students; that is, teachers who feel their students are relatively bright elicit better performances than do teachers who are led to believe their students are relatively slow (Lewis, 1970, pp. 12–14). Lewis cites a number of studies which suggest that the teacher in this case was exacerbating whatever problems may have existed originally by dealing with individual sounds rather than with larger contextual events. (She did use contexts with her "fast" group.)

A study that bears upon Lewis' observations was reported by Blodgett and Cooper (1973). These investigators surveyed the attitudes of 210 elementary school teachers in Tuscaloosa, Alabama, toward the BEV employed by their students. According to their results, one-third of the teachers perceive BEV as an "underdeveloped, undesirable, or uneducated manner of speaking [p. 121]," and more than two-thirds agreed with statements recommending that the school should initiate some kind of remedial program for children who speak BEV.

NONSTANDARD LANGUAGE AND "VERBAL DEPRIVATION" THEORY

Examples such as those given above are practically innocuous when compared with the thoughts of some academics who are able to influence public policy. The most extreme view of this sort maintains that for all practical purposes, lower-class black children have no language at all! Labov (1972) discusses at length the practical program offered by Carl Bereiter, Siegfried Engelmann and their associates (Bereiter *et al.*, 1966; Bereiter and Engelmann, 1966). Working with four-year-old black children from Urbana,

> Bereiter reports that their communication was by gestures, "single words," and "a series of badly connected words or phrases, such as *They mine* and *Me got juice*. He reports that black children could not ask a question, that "without exaggerating . . . these four-year-olds could make no statements of any kind." . . . Thus Bereiter concludes that the children's speech forms are nothing more than a series of emotional cries, and he decides to treat them "as if the children had no language at all." [Labov, 1972, p. 205]

Some of the improbable findings made by people such as Bereiter are attributable to the intimidating nature of the interview situation. Labov notes that he and his associates had to employ special techniques to tap the verbal ability of black ghetto youth under the age of about ten years. Even Clarence Robins, a skilled black associate of Labov, who was familiar with the sociolinguistic problem and with the inner city subculture, could elicit only minimal responses from an eight-year-old when he was interviewing the child. But when Robins brought along potato chips, lending a party air to the situation, and the boy's best friend was present, and taboo words and taboo topics were introduced (thus communicating the permissibility of both) into the interaction, which Robins conducted sitting on the floor of the lad's own room (thus reducing the physical intimidation), the results were quite different. The boys proved, of course, to be highly verbal (Labov, 1972, pp. 205–213).

We know that the BEV is a fully-fledged language (or dialect, if one prefers), and we know (and Labov and associates have been able to demonstrate) that black youth are highly verbal. To back up for a minute, to see what the ruckus is all about, Lewis (1970) suggests that there have been three stages in the academic and popular views of black culture in the past decade or so. First came the view that there was no such thing as a black culture apart from the larger American culture, a notion that was compatible with the assimilation-integration approach of the contemporary civil rights movement. Then various liberal, sympathetic, but culturally biased white middle-class sociologists (and particularly specialists in "abnormal psychology") fostered the idea that blacks did have a subculture, but that it represented a kind of social pathology. And finally, the concept that an identifiable black culture existed which was not pathological, but in fact was laudable, developed in connection with the "Black is Beautiful" movement, which represented a conscious effort to revive a sense of pride in the heritage of Afro-Americans. At the same time (or perhaps lagging somewhat behind) came the championing of BEV as the appropriate and laudable speech variety.

The first stage involved educational policies and techniques that required no accommodation to the black subculture (which was but a minor component of the American Melting Pot). The second stage required "correctional measures" to deal with the social pathology, or the presumed cultural and linguistic deprivation, of the blacks. So programs were designed on the assumption that students who were willing and able would be brought up to snuff. But as Labov (1972) notes:

> The essential fallacy of the verbal deprivation theory lies in tracing the educational failure of the child to his personal deficiencies. At present, these deficiencies are said to be caused by his home environment. It is traditional to explain a child's failure in school by his inadequacy. But when failure reaches such massive proportions, it seems to us necessary to look at the social and cultural obstacles to learning and the inability of the school to adjust to the social situation. Operation Head Start [for example] is designed to repair the child, rather than the school; to the extent that it is based upon this inverted logic, it is bound to fail. [p. 232]

Labov then goes on to note that the people who evaluate such programs are precisely those educational psychologists who designed them. "The fault will be found not in the data, the theory, nor in the methods used, but rather in the children who have failed to respond to the opportunities offered to them [p. 232]." Given that process, it is little wonder that Jensen (1969) produced his now infamous argument on the genetic inferiority of ghetto children. Since Labov (1972) has dealt with Jensen's paper in detail, we need not labor the issue here.

THE LINGUISTICS OF WHITE SUPREMACY

Under the impetus of the "Black is Beautiful" movement, the "legitimacy" of black culture in America and the BEV have been increasingly recognized as important and valued symbols of black identity. Yet this puts the linguist concerned with such problems in something of a bind. As we have indicated explicitly earlier, and implicitly throughout, any speech variety is a legitimate object of study, and as a medium of communication it should not be the subject of value judgments. Yet the realities of American social life are that those individuals who speak Standard English have a powerful advantage over speakers of nonstandard varieties. The solution usually considered appropriate these days is that we should admit the legitimacy of nonstandard varieties while trying to induce speakers of those varieties to acquire competence in SE as a second variety, to be used when socially appropriate.

James Sledd (1969) calls this sort of bidialectism "the linguistics of white supremacy," and castigates its promoters for outright hypocrisy:

> The basic assumption of bi-dialectism is that the prejudices of middle-class whites cannot be changed but must be ac-

cepted and indeed enforced on lesser breeds. Upward mobility, it is assumed, is the end of education, but white power will deny upward mobility to speakers of black English, who must therefore be made to talk white English in their contacts with the white world. [p. 1309]

Sledd questions not only the motives of the bidialectists, but their possibilities for success, and even the desirability of their possible success. Programs that teach SE as if it were a second language, Sledd feels, have failed in part because the linguists concerned in effect lack the materials necessary to do the job properly (such as detailed descriptions of the relevant speech varieties, including SE) and because they probably would not know what to do with those materials if they did have them; and in part the programs fail because black children do not always (if ever) aspire to speak in the fashion of the white middle class.

It is not completely clear just what the better course would be. Sledd (1969) said that we should stop wasting money on finding more expensive ways of polluting the universe, more expensive ways of expanding the arms race, and, of course, we should stop wasting money on bidialectal programs: we should, in short, cure all of our social ills. To this we must all cry "Hear! Hear!" though it is clear that we are unlikely to see any crash programs designed by the government to this end. Sledd admits that it is useful to concern ourselves with more effective means of teaching reading and writing (allowing also for the reading and writing of black English). If we read somewhat between the lines, Sledd also seems to be saying that if we really believe all speech varieties to be equally valid, we should act accordingly and accept the BEV; if we hire and appoint without requiring that the appointees use SE, then the language problems may in effect take care of themselves:

> We should learn from the example of the British: the social cataclysm of the Second World War, and the achievement of political power by labor, did more to give the "disadvan-

taged" English youngster an equal chance than charitable
bi-dialectalism ever did. [p. 1314]

Sledd's diatribe has been presented at length not because it has launched any movement, but because it serves
as a corrective to the occasional (if not frequent) oversell-
ing of the linguistic product, and it illustrates the contradiction in the Orwellian position that all speech varieties are
equal, but some are more equal than others. Among the
less equal of the equal varieties are those employed by
Puerto Ricans, Chicanos, Hawaiians (here this is a geo-
graphical rather than an ethnic label), and probably others
whose voices have been more subdued. The speech variety
symbolizes social identity, and yet it obstructs social mobility within the larger society.

The question of language and social identity, however,
is far more subtle than the foregoing would indicate. For
the most part, it operates below the level of awareness of
the speaker. In Hemnesberget, Norway, for example, vil-
lagers who claim local descent show a powerful sense of
local identification, which is marked by the use of the local
dialect, even though outsiders (such as the land-owning
commercial and administrative elite, who originally are
largely from outside the village) consider the dialect to
mark lack of education and lack of sophistication. Any local
resident who spoke the standard with other locals would be
seen by them as putting on airs (Blom and Gumperz, 1972).
But village youth may go to the universities in Oslo, Ber-
gen, and Trondheim, where they will become familiar with
the pan-Norwegian values that are associated with the standard speech variety. Blom and Gumperz (1972) hypothesized that even though members of a former peer group
from the village, who would return from the universities in
the summer, all claimed to be speakers of the pure local
dialect and to embrace local attitudes about dialect use,
they would switch varieties when topics appropriate to the
local or the broader identities respectively were discussed.

Not only was their hypothesis supported in their experimental situation (a social gathering of the peer group, in which relevant topics were introduced), but when Blom and Gumperz (1972) played the taped conversations to a linguistic informant who had been working with them, he refused at first to believe that they had been recorded locally. After he had recognized the voices of the participants, he showed disapproval of the mixing of speech varieties. Indeed, some of the participants themselves were upset when they heard themselves on the tape. They vowed not to switch away from the local dialect in future sessions, but nonetheless they did. Blom and Gumperz noted that when an argument required that the speaker should validate his status as an intellectual, he would switch to the standard forms that symbolized that status. They thus concluded that code selection rules are similar to grammatical rules, in that both operate below the level of consciousness, and may even be independent of the speaker's overt intentions.

The Norwegian example is more subtle than the matter of a Creole or BEV versus standard, but Labov (1963) provides an example of even greater subtlety from Martha's Vineyard, Massachusetts. Some members of this island community centralize the onset of the diphthongs /ay/ and /aw/, while others retained the standard southeast New England values for the diphthongs. This sort of distinction is not particularly elusive to anyone whose ear has been trained, but the local people on the island had not noticed it. Labov correlated the centralization of the diphthongs with such things as age level, occupation, ethnic group, and geography, but in the end the key to the centralization of the diphthongs was the attitude of the speaker toward the island. Those who identified with the island, who had positive feelings toward it, centralized the diphthongs, and those who had negative feelings about the island did not. The effect was found even in four 15-year-old boys, all of whom planned to go away to college, but only two of whom planned to pursue their careers on the island: the two who saw their futures on the island centralized, and the two who saw their futures off the island did not.

There are other ways in which language and social identity show their relationship. Fred C. C. Peng (personal communication), for example, has noted that nasal prosody is a feature of Japanese singing, but not of Japanese speech; further, it is not a feature of all kinds of singing in Japan, but rather of the singing of traditional Japanese songs, typically while wearing a kimono, and so forth. Japanese rock singers or singers who generally perform in a nontraditional way usually lack the nasal prosody. The reason is not clear, but it is apparent that somehow the nasalization goes with "Japaneseness."

LANGUAGE AND SOCIAL RELATIONSHIPS

All of these examples deal with identity more or less in the sense of ethnic identity, but with this more general framework we can also see shifting styles and levels of politeness in accordance with more specific social identities. In Korean, for example, there are about six more or less clearly marked levels of politeness, and the way in which the speaker perceives himself in relation to the other party governs which level is chosen. That is, the speaker and listener enjoy a specific identity relationship, and if there are several facets to the social relationship, several identity relationships may be involved. Thus, when a Korean graduate student became the lover of his female supervisor on a research project, he was in a contradictory situation. When on the job, he had no choice but to speak to her deferentially; he was in turn addressed familiarly, and because she was his mentor and his elder, he would be required even in private to continue the interaction pattern in Korean. But the personal relationship in private was intimate and equal, and therefore could not be accommodated in Korean (where an age difference of even a couple of years requires deference by the junior), so in private they both used English (Howell, 1967).

A more detailed account of the same phenomenon, in which the verbal interaction pattern must reflect a shifting social relationship, is provided by another Korean couple (in Howell, 1968). The well-heeled son of a manufacturer was staying at a resort hotel not far from Seoul, nursing his disappointment over having failed an entrance examination to the university of his choice. One morning he was awakened by a fetching young woman whom he had noticed on the beach, but had never got around to meeting. She had noticed him, too, and because she was evidently about to leave the hotel for the city, she took the initiative and invited him out for a swim. At this stage both exchanged extremely polite language, and on the way to the water they jockeyed to see where they stood with respect to each other socially (primarily in terms of relative age). The girl was more artful than the young man: when she learned his age, she admitted to the same age, and when she learned of his recent academic disappointment she implied that she, too, had met with a similar reversal. Well, not only were there no traditional obstacles (in the way of an age difference), but they were both licking their wounds, so to speak, and the way was clear for a very personal relationship. In the course of the initial encounter (a matter of some hours, apparently), the couple shifted from very polite forms to very familiar forms. Romance blossomed for a month, until the lad learned from his friends that the girl was actually three years his senior—in age and in school.

The societal norm required deference on his part; the identities that were salient for him now were not those of lovers, but rather those of junior and senior. He had to symbolize that relationship by using language more polite than hers. But she was still motivated by the personal considerations that prompted her deception in the first place, and each time he raised his level of politeness she tried to match him. If she had tried to continue to symbolize the love relationship by using the more familiar forms, she would have been using those familiar forms that were her privilege as a senior. Predictably, the young man matched her politeness with yet greater politeness, which she would try to match, but soon she would simply lapse into the more familiar forms that were her privilege, and of course the romance was dead.

Korean is a particularly convenient language for such studies, because the levels of politeness are clearly marked linguistically, but even in English we have ways of indicating our social relationships verbally: cold politeness toward a former friend indicates that something has happened to change the relationship, for example. Or to take a common developmental case in American universities, if a professor who once addressed a student formally as "Ms. Y." now calls her by her given name, he implies that their relationship is at least somewhat closer than it had been originally. But these considerations will be dealt with in greater detail in the next chapter.

LANGUAGE PLANNING

The question of how to deal officially with nonstandard speech varieties in America is a problem in language planning, but it is trivial by comparison with the problems faced in many other parts of the world. In the so-called developing nations, for example, it frequently happens that no standard language has been agreed upon. In West Africa, some 500–1000 languages, typically divided into many dialects, are spoken in the fourteen nations that have emerged from the Cameroun Republic and Senegal (Armstrong, 1968). Of course English and French are widely known throughout the area, but they are reminders of the old colonialism, and their use favors those already in power. Similar objections exist in most former colonies around the world.

Where a few large factions are competing for the selection of their own languages as the standard, the question can get quite bloody, as it has in India. In West Africa there is not a single country in which a given language is spoken by more than a sizeable minority of the population. As Armstrong (1968) points out, if one minority language is chosen, the native speakers of that language will have a great advantage in the matter of examinations for the schools and for the civil service; hence the speakers of the other minority languages would naturally object. Politically the problem is sticky, and it may be generations before widely accepted and uniform policies are developed. In the meantime some nations continue to rely on the European languages, while others name more than one indigenous language as standard. Ghana selected 9 of its 45 languages for national status, while Guinea granted national status (at least in principle) to all of its languages.

In a simpler situation, where language labels are political more than linguistic (as in Scandinavia), it is still necessary to select a speech variety as standard and to gain its acceptance. On the matter of selection, one school of thought is that the variety should be an existing vernacular, but another school feels that the variety should be eclectic, representing what amounts to a compromise among the several vernaculars. Haugen (1968) calls the first approach the unitary thesis and the second the compositional thesis. Once the choice is made, however this is done, there are problems of standardization of vocabulary, spelling, and implementation (including the preparation of schoolbooks, teachers, and so on); and after a norm has been codified and elaborated by its users, its original base may no longer be identifiable. Haugen feels it will have become "an independent artifact in the culture, one of the devices by means of which a particular group, usually a power elite, manages to maintain or assert its identity and, when possible, its power [p. 268]."

In 1948 Kroeber discussed the problem of how language spells identity in terms of ethnic revivals, or in the case of black English, "ethnic discovery" might be a more apt expression. Kroeber was writing immediately after the war that led directly to the withdrawal of European colonial power around the world, before most of the developing nations achieved that identity and developed the consequent language problem. At that time two cases seemed of particular interest, and both were seen as more or less experimental. The first was Gaelic, a dying language, and the second Hebrew, which probably had not been anyone's vernacular for two thousand years or more. The Irish case seems established, though there is still controversy over problems of bilingualism in the educational process (see Macnamara, 1966). Gaelic was at least spoken in some rural areas when the push to make it a national language began. Hebrew was no one's native tongue, apparently, when efforts were first made in Palestine in the 1880s to revive it as a spoken language. Yet in 1948, according to Kroeber, some tens of thousands of Palestinian Jewish children spoke nothing but Hebrew. By 1961, 75% of Israel's Jewish population indicated that Hebrew was their only language for daily interaction, or at least their main one. According to Blanc's (1968) interesting account, there were still no native speakers of Hebrew in 1900, and the typical speaker of Hebrew was likely to have been East European by birth, and to have had Yiddish as his first language. He had to refer constantly to written sources and authorities for guidance, and freely employed other languages for purposes of communication. In 1930, the typical 45-year-old still was not a native speaker, but his children might be, since they were probably raised in Hebrew-language schools. At this time there were already differences in the speech of the young and of their parents, and a leveling influence appeared in the speech of the young as they interacted together.

By 1960, there was about a 50-50 chance that the middle-aged speaker would have had Hebrew as his first language. Whereas their grandparents had spoken Hebrew as a matter of ideology, by 1960 the native speakers were relatively little concerned with the ideological factor; they spoke it for the same secular reasons that we all speak our native languages. In the case of recent immigrants, Hebrew is spoken largely as a matter of simple convenience. In both cases, of course, this does not mean that religious considerations are completely irrelevant, but simply that other considerations are important enough by now to give the language autonomy. At present there are some million native and near-native speakers; a variety of formal and informal styles have developed; and at the same time, a general standardizing process has been operating to give modern spoken Hebrew its own distinctive form.

REFERENCES

Armstrong, R. G. 1968. Language policies and language practices in West Africa. In Joshua A. Fishman, Charles A. Ferguson, and Jyotirindra Das Gupta (Eds.), *Language Problems of Developing Nations*, pp. 227–236. New York: John Wiley & Sons, Inc.

Bereiter, C., S. Engelmann, J. Osborn, & P. A. Reidford. 1966. An academically oriented pre-school for culturally deprived children. In F. M. Hechinger (Ed.), *Pre-School Education Today.* Garden City, New York: Doubleday & Company, Inc.

Bereiter, C., & S. Engelmann. 1966. *Teaching Disadvantaged Children in the Pre-School.* Englewood Cliffs, N.J.: Prentice-Hall, Inc.

Blanc, H. 1968. The Israeli koine as an emergent national standard. In Joshua A. Fishman, Charles A. Ferguson, and Jyotirindra Das Gupta (Eds.), *Language Problems of Developing Nations,* pp. 237–251. New York: John Wiley & Sons, Inc.

Blodgett, E. G., & E. B. Cooper. 1973. Attitudes of elementary teachers toward black dialect. *J. Communication Disorders 6:* 121–133.

Blom, J. P., & J. J. Gumperz. 1972. Social meaning in linguistic structure: Code-switching in Norway. In John J. Gumperz and Dell Hymes (Eds.), *Directions in Sociolinguistics,* pp. 407–434. New York: Holt, Rinehart & Winston, Inc.

Gumperz, J. J., & E. Herasimchuk. 1972. The conversational analysis of social meaning: A study of classroom interaction. In Roger W. Shuy (Ed.), *Report of the Twenty-Third Annual Round Table Meeting on Linguistics and Language Studies.* Washington, D.C.: Georgetown University Press.

Haugen, E. 1968. The Scandinavian languages as cultural artifacts. In Joshua A. Fishman, Charles A. Ferguson, and Jyotirindra Das Gupta (Eds.), *Language Problems of Developing Nations,* pp. 267–284. New York: John Wiley & Sons, Inc.

Howell, R. W. 1967. Linguistic choice as an index to social change. Unpublished doctoral dissertation. Berkeley, Cal.: University of California.

Howell, R. W. 1968. Linguistic choice and levels of social change. *Amer. Anthropologist 70:* 553–559.

Howell, R. W. 1973. *Teasing Relationships. An Addison-Wesley Module in Anthropology.* Reading, Mass.: Addison-Wesley Publishing Co., Inc.

Kroeber, A. L. 1948. *Anthropology.* New York: Harcourt, Brace & World, Inc.

Labov, W. 1963. The social motivation of a sound change. *Word 19:* 273–309.

Labov, W. 1972. *Language in the Inner City: Studies in the Black English Vernacular.* Philadelphia: University of Pennsylvania Press.

Lewis, L. 1970. Culture and social interaction in the classroom: An ethnographic report. Working Paper No. 38, Language-Behavior Research Laboratory. Berkeley, Cal.: University of California.

Macnamara, J. 1966. *Bilingualism and Primary Education.* Edinburgh, Scotland: Edinburgh University Press.

Rosenthal, R., & L. Jacobson. 1968. *Pygmalion in the Classroom.* New York: Holt, Rinehart & Winston, Inc.

Sledd, J. 1969. Bi-dialectism: The linguistics of white supremacy. *English Journal 58:* 1307–1315, 1329.

15

Language
and
Social
Change

In 1935 J. R. Firth declared sociological linguistics to be "the great field for future research," but until the 1960s the prophesy was largely unfulfilled. Sociolinguistics, the study of how linguistic and social events covary, was represented by isolated articles that more often than not were the by-products of research in linguistics, anthropology, sociology, or psychology. The situation has changed dramatically in the past decade. Many universities now offer courses in sociolinguistics; and a body of literature specifically on sociolinguistics has fully emerged and is growing rapidly.

Just as there are grammatical constraints on speech (rules that permit some sequences and preclude other sequences), there are also social constraints on speech. And much as grammatical relationships are marked in certain ways, for example through the use of the plural *s* or the past tense *-ed,* social relationships are linguistically marked.

They are marked in many ways, as through the choice of pronouns (*tu* versus *vous*), terms of address (first name versus title plus last name), special verb forms (in languages such as Japanese and Korean), the local versus the standard dialect, or through the choice of language in a multilingual community. Changes in social relationships are marked by changes in the patterns of verbal interactions, whether those changes are momentary or enduring; and social change can be considered over a wide range of levels, from the momentary falling-out of intimates to sweeping changes that transform the society and take millennia to be fully realized. Yet at all levels we may expect to see the changes reflected in altered patterns of verbal interaction, and in the options for linguistic choice.

DIMENSIONS OF VERBAL INTERACTION

Social aspects of verbal interaction are conducted along at least two dimensions, which seem to have validity not only for humans, but also for most other animals (see Brown, 1965, and Callan, 1970, for useful discussions). The first dimension is that of relative closeness or familiarity; the second is that of relative power. Familiarity can be thought of as a horizontal dimension, ranging from solid or intimate relationships to relationships of complete nonfamiliarity or extreme social distance. The power dimension is vertical, in that it marks degrees of dominance and submissiveness. In general, if there is no question of relative power or social rank, then the vertical dimension is not immediately relevant, and interaction takes place on the horizontal dimension in accordance with the relative "closeness" of the parties concerned.

The two dimensions are related to each other in that they employ the same verbal markers, but they differ in the patterns by which the markers are used. Perhaps this relationship of the dimensions was first recognized by Garvin and Riesenberg (1952), in their study of respectful behavior in the finely stratified Micronesian society of Ponape. They found it necessary to distinguish between verbal and nonverbal manifestations of attitudes toward superiors in title (power dimension) and respected equals (intimacy dimension) on the one hand, and attitudes toward inferiors in title (power) and intimate equals (intimacy) on the other. That is, with equals one speaks the way one is spoken to: there is reciprocal use of given forms and the pattern of usages is symmetrical. But one addresses superiors differently from the way one is addressed by them: there is a nonreciprocal use of given forms, and the pattern of usages is asymmetrical. Moreover, the way one behaves toward intimates is the way one behaves toward inferiors, and the way one behaves toward non-intimates is the way one generally behaves toward superiors.

The expression of social distance and social rank in terms of symmetrical and asymmetrical patterns of linguistic choice was more broadly discussed eight years later by Brown and Gilman (1960). They argued that the use of the pronouns *tu* and *vous* (or their equivalents) in some 20 languages of Europe and India vary along the dimensions of solidarity and power. The nonreciprocal use of *tu* (T) and *vous* (V) is associated with a disparity in social status, the higher-ranking individual being addressed as V and the lower as T. The reciprocal use of T is associated with relative intimacy, and the reciprocal use of V with relative distance or formality. Brown and Ford (1961) found that the same patterns of usage existed in terms of address in American English. The use of the first name (FN) and of the last name plus title (TLN) correspond respectively to the use of T and V. That is, the reciprocal use of FN implies intimacy, reciprocal use of TLN implies distance, and nonreciprocal use of FN and TLN implies a difference in the social ranks of the speakers.

The evidence, though almost exclusively based on Indo-European languages, led Brown and Ford to formulate a concept of the relationship between the power and solidarity dimensions. They suggested that the abstract link of intimacy/condescension and distance/deference may be a [socio]linguistic universal. They were limiting their formulation to matters of personal address, and apparently did not know about the Garvin and Riesenberg (1952) study, but a series of independent characterizations all support the formulation and its generalization. Clifford Geertz (1960), for example, described levels of polite speech in Java, which fitted their formulation, as did Foster's (1964) study of pronouns of address in a Mexican village and Howell's (1965) study of the utterance endings in Korean translations of Blondie cartoons. Further support for the principle has been found in Japanese pronouns of address (Brown, 1965), the uses of Spanish and Guarani in Paraguay (Rubin, 1962), and Yiddish pronouns of address (Slobin, 1963). Finally, the principle is supported by Howell's (1973) general treatment of familiar and nonfamiliar behavior.

There is considerable evidence, then, that interaction can be usefully described in terms of symmetrical and asymmetrical patterns that involve dimensions of relative closeness and relative power. Now Brown and his associates were dealing with very broad patterns, so it is not surprising that some difficulties have arisen with specific applications. Friedrich (1966), for example, found it impossible to understand pronominal usage in nineteenth-century Russian literature on the basis of the two-dimensional model, and pointed out that *switching* of patterns occurs in accordance with a number of variables, including the topic and the setting. Friedrich underscored how difficult it is to predict linguistic choice when one considers the full range of options generally available with which to show various degrees of familiarity or respect. The problem is not so much in the model offered by Brown and associates as in the fact that terms of address or pronouns tend to be polar, while it is possible through the use of nicknames, diminutives, and the like, to register relationships that fall between the poles of familiarity and respect symbolized by T-V, FN-TLN, and other markers.

DYADIC RELATIONS

The simplest social interaction involves only two parties, a dyad. We can observe how specific people interact together, and learn something about the nature of their relationship from the way they speak to each other, or we can look at the speech that characterizes "identity relationships" (Goodenough, 1965) or role relationships, such as physician-nurse, physician-patient, and so forth. It often happens that two individuals will stand in more than one identity relationship, as with two schoolteachers who are married to each other, and thus are at once colleagues and spouses. In private they may exchange pet names, while in front of students they may use rather formal terms of address.

In considering dyadic interaction, it is helpful to realize that any two parties will have a basic pattern that characterizes their normal interaction, and any departure from that basic pattern signals a shifting in some aspect of the relationship. Multifaceted social relationships and the different interaction patterns associated therewith are not directly included in Brown's model, though he does discuss semantic conflict in dealing with sociolinguistic change (Brown, 1965). To cite an actual example of a shift in linguistic choice in accordance with the changing salience of identity relationships, a Korean sergeant found himself working for a captain who had gone to the same high school some years earlier. In settings where the military aspect of their relationship was salient, the sergeant addressed the captain by his military title, but in the absence of third parties, he used the term for "elder brother," thus marking the more basic and enduring aspect of their relationship. In general, it is likely that the more facets there are in a given dyadic relationship, the greater the likelihood will be of shifting patterns of verbal interaction.

Thus there is a basic pattern of interaction for any dyad, but that pattern shifts in accordance with changes in the salience of different aspects of the total relationship. This is analogous to the way departures from "normal" intonation and stress patterns in English signal differences in meanings.

THE AMBIGUITY OF PATTERNS

It is convenient to think that when the higher-status member of a dyad uses T or FN while receiving V or TLN, he is exercising a unilateral privilege, but the meaning of such an asymmetrical pattern varies with the circumstances under which it is established. When a pattern that was originally TLN-TLN becomes TLN-FN, as so frequently happens with university faculty members and certain students, the implication is that a degree of intimacy has now been attained which was not there originally. When the professor who used to call the young woman Miss Taniguchi now calls her Dolores, it signals a reduction in social distance. But suppose he had from the start called her Dolores? It would not be immediately apparent from the use of the terms alone whether he wanted to be chummy, or whether he was simply flexing his higher-status muscle. Of course, if he also issues an invitation to the student to call him Humbert, he is clarifying the situation. That is, the TLN-FN pattern is ambiguous unless the faculty member has explicitly invited the reciprocal use of the first name.

The reason that the asymmetry which develops from an initially symmetrical TLN-TLN pattern is not ambiguous is that respect for the lower-status individual has been established by the initial use of the TLN. Once the respect has been symbolized, the subsequent use of FN clearly implies friendliness or solidarity on the part of the higher-status member.

Reciprocal use of TLN, then, may symbolize either social distance or mutual respect. A similar ambiguity arises when a higher-status member invites FN but continues to receive TLN. While the subordinate member of the dyad may wish only to signal respect, the higher-ranking individual may interpret the use of TLN as a deliberate attempt to maintain social distance.

Just as the mutual expression of respect may not symbolize extreme distance—diplomatic correspondence aimed at a rapprochement of governments is typically expressed in the most elaborately polite language—so the reciprocal use of familiar markers may not symbolize either solidarity or intimacy. Antagonists may abuse each other in the foulest terms—obviously, each is thereby denying respect to the other.

All three patterns are thus potentially ambiguous. Mutual V-V signifies that neither member of a dyad wishes to presume upon the privilege of familiar expression; mutual T-T means either that both parties grant the privilege of familiar expression, or that both have taken it unilaterally. The asymmetrical V-T means that the higher-status member of a dyad is exercising the privilege of familiarity, with or without the consent of the lower-ranking member.

POWER AND INTIMACY DIMENSIONS

The most detailed account of changes of pattern in verbal interaction over time is by Brown and Gilman

(1960). They found that in Europe, prior to the fourth century, the second-person singular pronoun (T) was used only to address one person, and the second-person plural pronoun (V) was used only to address more than one person. Then people began to use the V when addressing the emperor (of whom there were then two), whence the practice spread to European court circles in general, until around the seventeenth century (and much earlier in certain areas), V was *the* second-person pronoun employed between members of the upper classes of Europe, and T was *the* second-person (singular) pronoun employed among the lower classes. Thus there was symmetrical V for the upper classes, symmetrical T for the lower classes, and asymmetrical V-T between classes. This asymmetrical "power" relationship was followed by the later development of a "solidarity" dimension, in which, for both classes, T was used between intimates and V between persons who were distant but socially equal. European society was then operating on two sociolinguistic dimensions: an asymmetrical status dimension and a symmetrical intimacy dimension. Thus, in the use of the second-person pronoun as a linguistic status marker, there were a status dimension, a simultaneous status and intimacy dimension, and an intimacy dimension. We should bear in mind, however, that there were other status markers, such as terms of address, in which the older pattern was (and is) still to be discerned.

Evidently a unidimensional system based on power obtained in Europe, until for some reason, a second dimension developed to differentiate forms of address among power-equals. The two dimensions coexisted in equilibrium for an unspecified, but certainly long, period of time. But reciprocal and nonreciprocal relationships are mutually exclusive and thus may involve structural incompatibilities, or "semantic conflict," to use Brown and Gilman's term (1960, pp. 258–261). Thus there is a power differential between father and son, and yet they are intimates in the same household. When it somehow became possible that persons separated on the basis of power could be joined on the basis of intimacy, the two-dimensional system became unstable, but it continued to exist well into the nineteenth century. Since then the semantic conflicts have been resolved in favor of reciprocal address patterns, until today there is in effect a unidimensional system based on intimacy or solidarity.

Brown sees the asymmetrical patterns as products of a relatively static, or closed, society, in which status is largely ascribed, and is closely tied to the feudal and manorial systems in Europe. The reciprocal solidarity norm has grown with the open-class society and the egalitarian ideology. The semantic conflict in the norms of address was resolved by the suppression of status in favor of solidarity, presumably because of its congruence with other far-reaching changes in European society (Brown, 1965, pp. 61–62). With the suppression of the status norm in favor of the solidarity norm, Brown notes a decline in shifting use of the pronouns to express transient sentiments—transient shifts between T and V—and an expansion of the areas regarded as appropriate for the use of T. The expanded use of the familiar pronoun is important to the idea that there has been a reduction in the proportion of asymmetrical identity relationships, which corresponds generally with an increase in the possibilities for upward mobility.

While broad treatments such as those of Brown and others are often so abstract that they may lack a direct behavioral validity, they do provide important clues for our understanding of the establishment and expression of social relationships, and may be used as guides in our examination of contemporary interaction among smaller groups. If, for example, steps are taken to establish an equal basis for possible upward mobility, the effect of those steps should subsequently be reflected in changed patterns of verbal behavior.

Thus, in parts of the American South, a generation ago, the social boundaries of the asymmetrical white-black relationship were marked, among other ways, by a general pattern that required Negroes to use respect language (including TLN) toward whites, while receiving familiar language (including FN) in return. There were finer expressions of social relationship within the general pattern, as in the use by blacks of TFN toward a former preadolescent white companion or toward an employer, but we lack the documentation to discuss these distinctions in detail. Brown's logic would suggest that if the recent moves to improve the status of the Negro in the South are proving effective, then there should be a discernible tendency toward the development of symmetrical patterns of white-black verbal interaction. The following account was given by a white participant observer in a federally-sponsored program to train rehabilitation personnel. The informant was identified as a Californian rather than a Yankee, and he was specifically concerned to observe interaction patterns. His background includes previous training and fieldwork in anthropology. The observations were made in Knoxville, Tennessee, in 1964. Unfortunately no information is available on specific interactions in that particular setting a generation ago. The picture given here, then, is an "after" picture, and we have no comparable "before" picture other than what is generally assumed to have been the case for "the South." (From Howell, 1967, pp. 80–83.)

1. About one hour was spent observing white and Negro employees of the city engaged at the same rate of pay for the same unskilled labor on a street-repair project. There was no apparent racial disharmony. The whites addressed their Negro peers by FN. If the blacks had replied with TLN, they would have been acknowledging a status differential, while to use FN would have been to claim overtly that if there was a status differential, it was at least

secondary to a relationship characterized by intimacy or solidarity. During the relatively short period of the observation, no black used *any* address term to a white.

2. A Negro woman was employed as a teacher at an all-white school for the handicapped, and her interaction with her white colleagues was observed over a period of months. In formal situations she would be addressed by TLM, and in informal situations by FN. Again, she seemed to avoid using any terms of address to her co-workers.

3. At a formal reception of the visiting faculty from the Negro school (which was supervised by the director of the local white school for handicapped children), all parties were introduced by TLN and all shook hands. In less than half an hour, however, the Negro contingent took leave of the gathering, evidently to minimize the opportunity for awkward interaction. While the interaction of the two faculties was quite polite and formal, the early departure of the visitors seemed again to be a manifestation of avoidance behavior.

More casual observations, including informal conversations with various local Negroes and whites, suggest that the evident use of avoidance does indicate a departure from the earlier practices, in which Negroes, here as elsewhere, had contributed to the linguistic marking of asymmetrical social relationships by using TLN or TFN toward whites.

Avoidance also probably enters the picture in the contrary case, where Negro and white youngsters have been close companions, exchanging FN or nicknames, but as adulthood approaches they are required to conform to an asymmetrical pattern. There is probably a period in which the Negro adolescent avoids the use of any address term to his former white chum, though he will continue to be addressed by FN.

SOCIOLINGUISTIC CHANGE IN JAPAN

The Knoxville case is particularly interesting as an example of a specific linguistic manifestation of rather sweeping social changes. A somewhat different example is provided by a particularly well-documented case study of a small Japanese agricultural village (Yoshida, 1964).

Until the turn of the present century, Morô included three social strata: an upper class of land-owning gentry, a middle class consisting mainly of independent farmers, and a lower class consisting mainly of tenant farmers. Household heads of the upper class were called *totsan,* and special honorific terms were used to address the wife of the *totsan,* his son, and his daughter. The heads of middle-class households were addressed as *tosan* by their social inferiors, while the term *ishi* was used by social superiors to address lower-class tenants and clients.

The patron-client relationships were independent of class relationships, though most of the upper-class household heads were in fact patrons. But relative class refers to relative social rank, while the patron-client relationship was contractual. A man became a client by receiving land (for faithful service to a wealthy farmer, through marriage to an upper-class girl, or through the establishment of a branch house of the lineage–but only the first of these was a common way of becoming a client; branch houses and client relationships were usually quite distinct). In return for the land and certain rights, such as the right to borrow money or grain without interest, the client was obliged to give a certain amount of annual labor service. The amount of service to be performed was negotiated at the time the land was transferred, but it was binding upon the client's descendants without the right of reduction. Some of the Morô patron-client relationships had been established more than 200 years ago, and at least in one case, some 60 days of service were required each year.

In addition to the negotiated labor service, the clients performed additional labor for debts incurred to their patrons, instead of making repayments in cash. Since most clients were also tenants, their burden of labor service was correspondingly increased. Moreover, the clients were often required to provide not only their own labor, but also that of all members of their families who were old enough to work, particularly at the time of rice planting.

We can appreciate the difficulties encountered by the lower class under these conditions, without entering into a discussion of the general inability of the small farmer in Japan to survive without supplementing his farm income (Fukutake, 1962, pp. 55 ff). In the twentieth century, Morô has been torn by conflict born of the inequities described above. In the late 1920s the lower class managed to win the right to have local headmen elected from their ranks, a privilege formerly held only by the upper class. In 1943 the clients struck successfully for the abrogation of their contracts. Finally, a third conflict resulted in cash rents being charged on irrigated land, rather than rents being paid in kind. This was, of course, just before the postwar agrarian reform.

Today the honorific term *totsan* is still used toward the upper-class household heads, but the corresponding honorifics for their wives and children are practically obsolete. Likewise, the terms *tosan,* as a term of address by inferiors to middle-class household heads, and *ishi,* as a term of address to social inferiors, have virtually disappeared.

Two factors appear to underlie these linguistically marked social changes, both of which are indirectly attributable to industrialization. First, the availability of jobs in the cities, heightened by wartime production, provided young men with outward mobility. Then the availability of jobs outside the community reduced the economic dependence of lower-class families on the largely upper-class patrons. It seems likely that the increase in economic independence made upward mobility possible. At any rate, Yoshida suggests that the relative independence which came with outside jobs enabled the lower class to organize the long-standing protest that finally won them further independence.

The Morô case illustrates concomitant changes in social structure and verbal behavior, which are adequately documented and have taken place over a relatively short period of time. We will conclude this brief treatment of change through time by comparing two divergent speech communities; one of these changed its patterns drastically, while those of the other were virtually crystallized for nearly two centuries.

PRONOMINAL USAGE IN A CANADIAN MENNONITE COMMUNITY

The study of contrasting *du/Sie* patterns in a Canadian Mennonite community (Howell and Klassen, 1971) began as a routine check on symmetrical and asymmetrical patterns of pronominal usage, with a particular focus on the suggestion by Roger Brown (1965) and associates that symmetrical patterns have come to prevail in Western Europe and its extensions, thus linguistically marking the change from a closed, rigidly stratified society to one that is open and egalitarian. Largely on the basis of work done in French Canada, Lambert (1967) showed that Brown's case was overstated, in that broad social changes do not uniformly influence all segments of a society at the same rate (Howell, 1968). We must then look more closely for factors that account for differential rates of change.

The Mennonite study examines two patterns of pronominal usage in a single speech community, one of which supports "the triumph of the solidarity semantic," while the other pattern denies it. The explanation seems to lie in the different histories of the two groups that comprise the congregation of the Mennonite Church in Herschel, Saskatchewan, in the Canadian prairie.

Herschel is an agricultural community with a village population of about 150 persons, most of whom are English-speaking and non-Mennonite. But there are some 55 Mennonite families on farms outside the village, and they comprise about a third of the rural population of Herschel. The Mennonite Church has a congregation of about 300 individuals, drawn not only from the immediate area, but also from other communities 20 miles or more away. English is used for business transactions, while, as Jaquith (1970) reported for Mexican Mennonites and Dawson (1936) reported for other Canadian Mennonites, a variety of Plattdeutsch is typically used for interaction in the home, and Hochdeutsch is the language of the church. Recently, however, there has been increasing pressure to use English, not only at home but also in the church; and Sunday-school classes in Herschel have been conducted in both Hochdeutsch and English for the past several years.

Among the German speakers in the Herschel congregation there are two distinct patterns for the use of second-person pronouns. A symmetrical pattern (except where an adult interacts with a child under the age of 16 years) is characteristic of immigrants from Danzig. Among the larger group of immigrants from the Ukraine, there is a distinct preference for asymmetrical patterns. Six informants from each group (Ukraine and Danzig immigrants) were interviewed extensively regarding their use of pronouns and terms of address, and were subsequently observed interacting with various other members of the community. In addition, personal and business letters were examined in the search for systematic differences between the two groups.

The Danzig Mennonites were unanimous in their insistence that *Sie* (V) is used symmetrically by adults who are not relatives or close friends; *du* (T) is exchanged by relatives, close friends, and individuals under the age of 16 years. Individuals under the age of 16 use *Sie* to their elders, and receive *du*. Between adults, the shift from *Sie* to *du* is made by mutual consent, and is initiated by the senior party. Except in cases that involve individuals under the age of 16, there is no pronominal marking of differential status between father and son, employer and employee, tradesman and customer, or teacher and student. The pattern for such dyads is symmetrical.

There is a close correspondence between the pronoun used and the degree of formality expressed by other terms of address. First names are exchanged by people who exchange *du,* and TLN is used by people who exchange *Sie.* The pattern is modified in the case of relatives who exchange *du:* uncles, aunts, and sometimes cousins are addressed by the kin term plus FN; nieces and nephews are addressed by FN. Father, mother, grandfather, and grandmother are addressed simply by the kin term (without a name), and they use the FN in return. The Danzig Mennonites are relatively informal in correspondence, and never use the Gothic script; only the elderly had even learned the older script in school.

In general, then, the use of pronouns and address terms among the Danzig group agrees with the picture of contemporary usages offered by Brown and associates. The Ukrainian Mennonites, on the other hand, present rather a different picture. Differential social rank is regularly marked by second-person pronouns. *Sie* is used for ascending generations of kin, who use *du* in return. Employers use *du* and receive *Sie.* An age difference of about 10 years seems to require an asymmetrical pattern, with deference being paid to the elder of the two. But while senior kin ordinarily engage in asymmetrical patterns with junior kin, personal friendship and the lack of a clear age differential (to judge from a single instance) can result in a symmetrical usage pattern: a niece and her aunt, who was only two years her senior, exchanged *du.*

As might be expected, individuals who receive *Sie* also receive a title *(Herr, Frau, Fräulein)* plus the last name. Unrelated individuals who are a generation or so senior to the speaker are addressed as *Tante* or *Onkel* plus the last name. Ukrainian Mennonite correspondence is much more formal than that of the Danzig group; it includes such honorific salutations as *Hoch geehrter Herr* and *hochachtungsvill,* and the Gothic script is still commonly used. Even those who have abandoned the Gothic for the Latin script said that they were familiar with it through their early schooling (they were taught it in Canada as well as in Russia, though it is not being taught today in the Mennonite schools used by the Herschel population).

Thus the Ukrainian Mennonites are much more conservative than the Danzig Mennonites in their linguistic interaction patterns. They still pay linguistic homage to differential rank, while the Danzig group has switched to patterns governed by relative solidarity.

There are more general differences between the two groups. The Ukrainian Mennonites, for example, show greater adherence to older forms of German and to traditional Mennonite precepts: they remain opposed to drinking, dancing, swearing, and military service. On the other hand, they are more receptive to loanwords. They have incorporated many Russian terms for foods and plants, and have adopted the English terms for common products of modern technology: car, radio, phone, and so forth. Where the Danzig group uses *anrufen* for "to make a telephone call," for example, the Ukrainian group uses *phonen,* and reserves *anrufen* to mean "shout at." Given the traditional German predilection for coining new words out of native elements, in this regard the Ukrainian group appears less conservative than the Danzig group.

As was indicated earlier, the rather different sociolinguistic patterns just described seem to arise from the different histories of the two groups. The Mennonites initially migrated from the Netherlands, in the sixteenth century, to the swampy Vistula Delta near Danzig, where they were left pretty much alone for some two centuries. Dutch continued to be the principle language of the group for a considerable period, but by around 1750 *Hochdeutsch* had become the language of the pulpit and *Plattdeutsch* the language of the home (Krahn, 1949; Francis, 1948). The split of relevance here came in response to a pair of manifestos issued by Catherine II in 1762 and 1763, inviting non-Jewish Europeans to immigrate to Russia (Francis, 1955). According to the Ukrainian group in Herschel, they migrated to the southern part of the Ukraine in the last two decades of the eighteenth century. In the Ukraine, the Mennonites settled in closed communities. Russian and Ukrainian were studied as foreign languages in the higher schools, but the lower schools relied on German, and German was the language of everyday interaction. Moreover, their textbooks, the models for formal language instruction, were the ones they had brought with them at the close of the eighteenth century. Since communication with Prussia was not maintained for long, the Ukrainian group was effectively cut off from the language changes that were taking place there. In the Ukraine the Mennonites were not only a religious minority, they were also a linguistic enclave. The use of German reinforced their Mennonite identity, and thus it may have taken on something of a religious aspect.

As their population increased, the Ukrainian Mennonites simply opened up new tracts of the abundant land. The principal occupation continued to be agriculture, and the settlements remained rural. The Mennonite families seem to have prospered; a great deal of their interaction with the indigenous peoples took the form of employer–employee relationships in the fields and the mills, and it seems likely that this further encouraged the use of asymmetrical patterns of interaction.

The Herschel group of Ukrainian Mennonites (some 40 families) left Russia after the Revolution, between 1924 and 1926, because they were in danger of losing their exemption from military service, and their use of German in the schools and churches was also threatened. Their relatively conservative sociolinguistic patterns are probably due to their isolation, which also led to the perpetuation of eighteenth-century asymmetries in pronominal usage. By contrast, the Danzig group that had remained in Prussia had to accept local restrictions on the acquisition of land, and so the surplus population moved into the cities to take up nonagricultural occupations. This gave them increased contact with non-Mennonites, especially since the children were educated in the regular schools; this ensured that they would use the local standard German. The Danzig group remained a religious minority, but they were not a linguistic enclave. They were subject to those forces of urbanization and industrialization that induce wider ranges of social interaction and tend to weaken traditional boundaries. At the same time, the Danzig Mennonites were subject to the general egalitarian shift away from verbal marking of class and status differences, evidently pretty much in the way described by Brown and his associates.

The Danzig group remained in East Prussia until after World War II, when their homeland became part of Poland; they either resettled in West Germany or migrated to other countries. Thus in 1949, some 25 years after the arrival of the Ukrainian group, 10 families from the Danzig area acquired farms around Herschel.

In the Herschel community today, both groups are subject to each other's influence and to the influence of the English speakers with whom they necessarily have contact. While the Danzig group is more egalitarian in its verbal interaction patterns, informants from the group reported that they had felt great discomfort when they were first confronted with the extreme informality of English speakers. In particular, they were disturbed when FN was used without any prior formal agreement. Finding it difficult to reciprocate, they often avoided the use of any terms of address to English speakers. Now the members of both groups seem quite able to accept the use of FN in their interaction with English speakers, but they still show reticence over the use of FN in German. Similarly, the Ukrainian Mennonites preserve a preponderance of asymmetrical patterns within their own group, but are aware of the greater degree of symmetrical interaction among the Danzig Mennonites, and they accommodate themselves to this greater informality when interacting with them.

That Brown's equation of egalitarian developments and symmetrical patterns is not peculiar to Europe (where it accounts for the Danzig case) is shown by the appearance of the equation in such non-European areas as Japan (Yoshida, 1964) and Indonesia (Wittermans, 1967). We have not accounted for Lambert's contradictory findings in French Canada, but the case of the Ukrainian Mennonites suggests that there may at least be some influences in common. It is abundantly clear, for example, that the French Canadians cherish their language as a critical symbol of their identity, perhaps in the same way as the Mennonites have identified with the German language; and this may constitute a conservative influence in the preservation of asymmetrical patterns. There are other parallels, also, such as the bi- or multilingualism of the two groups; since the second language is the language of the larger society, it is seen as posing a threat to the maintenance of group identity. This line of inquiry may prove productive wherever Brown's equation does not appear to balance.

SOCIOLINGUISTIC CHANGE IN CHINA

To conclude this chapter, we are most fortunate in having some pertinent observations on how language usages have changed in China during the past 25 years, under a political philosophy that actively deplores social class differences. Fincher (1973) noted the predictable popularity of *tóng zhi* "comrade," the radical abandonment of social titles, and the strong aversion to professional and governmental titles. There is great emphasis on the role of the individual as a contributor to collectivity, and Fincher states that "circumlocutions for leadership positions abound. The society systematically deprives 'responsible authorities' of their personal titles in an effort to make them more responsive authorities [p. 167.]"

Fincher (1973) suggests that various lexical changes can be grouped according to their relationship with various societal changes, such as nationalization, political socialization, and the spread of technology. One of the most interesting lexical developments is the popularization of the term *aì-rén,* "lover," as the usual way of denoting one's own or another's spouse or fiancé. It is a particularly liberated expression, and has implications for family structure. The original connotations of courtship or extramarital sex are retained outside of the Peoples Republic, which makes it a little embarrassing for outsiders to use the term, but those connotations have been lost in popular mainland usage.

Aì-rén is one of several localisms that reflect historical landmarks. It is identified with the Long March to Yenan in 1935, and was used by the Yenan community, which provided so many of the leaders of the Peoples Republic. Since Yenan has the image of a Spartan, egalitarian, but puritanical society, Fincher thinks it somehow fitting that the term lost its sexual connotations there.

Not only lexical changes, but also certain changes in grammatical constructions, were in accord with the new political philosophy. One that sounded "foreign" to Fincher (1972) appeared when she heard a Travel Service official in Shanghai talking on the telephone to a colleague in Nanking. Fincher had been reporting a sudden decision to stop there *en route* to Peking. The agent said, "I'm sorry to have made you passive" to his colleague; this was by way of an apology, because circumstances had forced him to take the initiative away from the colleague. Instead of indulging in "commandism," he should have been soliciting the suggestions of his colleague.

The actively promoted increase in bilingualism has been much less subtle, but it has had an enormous practical impact. This has been achieved by using Mandarin as the language of instruction in the schools throughout the country. At the same time, regional speech varieties are maintained with official blessings. As Fincher (1972) reports:

> At group sessions in Peking—for example, banquets—it was always a great asset to be able to pass as a native speaker of Cantonese and Amoy as well as of Mandarin. And while touring, speakers of Mandarin as a second language were still happy to find out I could understand and use their home dialects. But what we enjoyed with each other was our common similarity in being able to communicate with each other in *both* dialects or languages. The spread of Mandarin in a bilingual setting liberates people to enjoy their own dialects with no trace of uneasiness or inferiority. [pp. 338–339]

REFERENCES

Brown, R. 1965. *Social Psychology.* New York: The Free Press.
Brown, R., & M. Ford. 1961. Address in American English. *J. Abnormal and Social Psychol. 62:* 375–385.

Brown, R., & A. Gilman. 1960. The pronouns of power and solidarity. In Thomas A. Sebeok (Ed.), *Style in Language,* pp. 253–276. New York: John Wiley & Sons, Inc.

Callan, H. 1970. *Ethology and Society.* London: Clarendon Press.

Dawson, C. A. 1936. *Group Settlement: Ethnic Communities in Western Canada.* Toronto: The Macmillan Company.

Fincher, B. H. 1972. Impressions of language in China. *China Quarterly 50:* 333–340.

Fincher, B. H. 1973. The Chinese language in its new social context. *J. Chinese Linguistics 1:* 163–169.

Firth, J. R. 1935. The technique of semantics. *Transactions of the Philological Society (London):* 36–72. Also in *Papers in Linguistics 1934–1951.* London: Oxford University Press; and in Dell Hymes (Ed.), *Language in Culture and Society,* pp. 66–70. New York: Harper & Row, Publishers.

Foster, G. M. 1964. Speech forms and perception of social distance in a Spanish-speaking Mexican village. *Southwestern J. Anthropol. 20:* 107–122.

Francis, E. K. 1955. *In Search of Utopia.* Altona, Manitoba: Friesen & Sons.

Francis, E. K. 1948. The Russian Mennonites: From religious to ethnic group. *Amer. J. Sociol. 54:* 101–107.

Friedrich, P. 1966. Structural implications of Russian pronominal usage. Condensed from a contribution to William Bright (Ed.), *Proceedings of the Los Angeles Conference on Sociolinguistics.* The Hague: Mouton & Co.

Fukutake, T. 1962. *Man and Society in Japan.* Tokyo: University of Tokyo Press.

Garvin, P. L., & S. H. Riesenberg. 1952. Respect behavior on Ponape: an ethnolinguistic study. *Amer. Anthropologist 54:* 201–220.

Geertz, C. 1960. *The Religion of Java.* New York: The Free Press.

Goodenough, W. H. 1965. Rethinking "status" and "role": Toward a general model of the cultural organization of social relationships. In *The Relevance of Models for Social Anthropology.* A. S. A. Monographs 1. New York: Frederick A. Praeger.

Howell, R. W. 1973. *Teasing Relationships. An Addison-Wesley Module in Anthropology.* Reading, Mass.: Addison-Wesley Publishing Co., Inc.

Howell, R. W. 1968. Linguistic choice and levels of social change. *Amer. Anthropologist 70:* 553–559.

Howell, R. W. 1967. Linguistic choice as an index to social change. Unpublished doctoral dissertation. Berkeley, Cal.: University of California.

Howell, R. W. 1965. Linguistic status markers in Korean. *The Kroeber Anthropological Society Papers 55:* 91–97.

Howell, R. W., & J. Klassen. 1971. Contrasting du/Sie patterns in a Mennonite community. *Anthropological Linguistics 13 (no. 2):* 68–74.

Jaquith, J. R. 1970. Language use of Mexican Mennonites. Research report. *Newsletter Amer. Anthropol. Assoc. 11 (no. 6):* 9.

Krahn, C. 1949. *From the Steppes to the Prairies (1874–1949).* Newton, Kansas: Mennonite Publications Office.

Lambert, W. E. 1967. The use of *tu* and *vous* as forms of address in French Canada: A pilot study. *J. Verbal Learning and Verbal Behavior 6:* 614–617.

Rubin, J. 1962. Bilingualism in Paraguay. *Anthropological Linguistics 4 (no. 1):* 52–58.

Slobin, D. I. 1963. Some aspects of the use of pronouns of address in Yiddish. *Word 19 (no. 2):* 193–202.

Wittermans, E. P. 1967. Indonesian terms of address in a situation of rapid social change. *Social Forces 46:* 48–51.

Yoshida, T. 1964. Social conflict and cohesion in a Japanese rural community. *Ethnology 3:* 219–231.

16

Language
and
Culture*

Because language is the keystone of the cultural edifice that more than anything else distinguishes man from the rest of the animal kingdom, the ethnographer, more than most other social scientists, requires at least a modicum of linguistic sophistication. There are both pragmatic and theoretical reasons for this.

As a practical matter, when the ethnographer goes into the field he must have *some* means of communicating with the subjects of his study, and unless he already has considerable competence in the relevant language, he will have to prepare himself for that indispensable part of his fieldwork. Thomas Rhys Williams (1967), for example, found it desirable to seek the minimum competence in Dusun (a language of Borneo) necessary to deal with the daily routine,

*We wish to thank CRM Books of Del Mar, California for giving us their permission to draw heavily in this chapter from material prepared originally for the revised edition of *Anthropology Today*.
Reprinted with the permission of © Ziff-Davis Publishing Company, 1973.

and he seems to have drawn on his linguistic training to transcribe and analyze Dusun utterances. In the meanwhile, of course, he was dependent on an interpreter and also, apparently, on the use of Malay as a contact language. Even after he had gained some proficiency in Dusun, he frequently had to rely on his interpreters. Some possibilities for misunderstanding may be avoided that way; the interpreter is likely to know which topics require tact, and how one should apply that tact. If the investigator has a sufficient command of the language in question, he can monitor his interpreters and at least ensure that his questions are indeed being asked, and that the answers are not being edited for him.

Earlier generations of ethnographers, especially those under the influence of Franz Boas, were strongly encouraged to gather textual materials in the native language in order to develop what were in effect archives analogous, if not quite comparable, to the documentary sources for the classical civilizations (Lowie, 1937, p. 132). Today the texts are more likely to be on microfilms and tape recordings. The loss of interest in written texts, except when used for linguistic purposes, stems from a number of considerations besides the development of other media. There is less interest in "salvage" anthropology today than there was in the past, when it seemed important to chronicle preliterate cultures before they disappeared. Virtually without exception, they have disappeared, through the processes of assimilation, acculturation, and sheer extinction, and so there is less to salvage in the older sense. Further, while the earlier ethnographers tried to record everything imaginable about the cultures they were describing, the tendency these days is to enter the field with one's interests directed toward a particular problem, and thus to forego the encyclopedic inventories that were popular in the past.

Languages as the Key to a Culture

Among the arguments most frequently used to gain support for foreign language programs is the argument that foreign languages provide the key to the understanding of other cultures. There is certainly a great deal of truth in this belief, but the case is overstated if it is taken to imply that study of a foreign language *automatically* plugs the student into another culture in any very useful or economical way. We can learn more about Japanese history, traditions, and world view from a few hours of intensive reading in English than we can from many weeks of intensive study of the Japanese language. Of course, our English texts would be filled with Japanese names (Tôkyô, Tokugawa, Meiji) and labels for cultural items and ideas that have no ready English equivalent (*kimono, Zen, harakiri*), so it is also obvious that the language question enters in at some point.

Just where the language question enters in, and how crucial it is, is hard to assess. We would certainly look askance at a foreign anthropologist who called himself an expert on Americans and yet did not know English. But at the other extreme, being a native speaker does not automatically enable one to describe the rules of the language, and being the product of a culture does little more than assure us of the presence of the intuitive base on which an explicit descriptive statement must ultimately rest. What is critical is that we should know what questions to ask and how to ask them, and that is more a matter of professional training than of the language as such. For the moment, we can concede that the *kinds* of information readily available will depend to a considerable extent on the language competence of the investigator.

CULTURAL LABELS

As was previously indicated, one who is reading competent accounts of another culture in English will encounter foreign words for which there is no very convenient equivalent in English. But this is just the most superficial indication that the foreign words are labels for cultural objects and events, and even these words are a distillation of the much larger word-pool that the writer could have drawn upon if he had sought greater accuracy. For, as will be discussed later, there is such a close correspondence between linguistic and cultural events that relatively few labels can be translated precisely.

We learn our labels in a cultural context. To take an obvious example, to one who has never travelled on an underground train, and knows of it only through written or verbal references to the "subway," the label will have the same limited meaning whether it is applied to the corresponding mode of transportation in New York, London, Paris, Toronto, or Tôkyô. But if the New York commuter visits Tôkyô, he will find the underground experience there quite different from what he is used to. Instead of riding in noisy, filthy, unreliable trains, he will be riding in clean, quiet, and highly reliable trains. The crowding during the rush hour may cause him to think nostalgically about what he used to consider an impossible situation in New York, while the sights and smells will also be different. The full meaning of *chikatetsu* cannot simply be rendered by the term "subway," and similar differences in meaning will also be found for the Paris *metro*, the London "underground," and so forth.

To take a somewhat different example, we might assume that loanwords, at least, would have a comparable range of meaning to that of the original. But the Japanese *kimono* is essentially a formal garment, while the American use of the label (particularly popular in the 1930s) described a wrap-around woman's housecoat that corresponded more closely to the Japanese *nemaki*. To take an example in the other direction, Americans and Japanese may both regale themselves *in* a bar, but the Japanese cannot sit *at* the bar. He sits at the *counter,* which the Americans usually do only in eating establishments.

Clearly the ethnographer will do well to learn the range of meanings of the labels used in the culture he is studying, even though he will have to edit his findings in order to present an economical account in his own language.

Briefly, then, language is used in anthropology first as a medium of communication, and next as a primary source of information about culture and society. In addition to a concern with the facts of language as such, and with the way language and society influence each other, there are at least two other areas of major anthropological interest here. The first, the study of the way language influences our perceptions, follows without difficulty from the idea of cultural labelling. The other is the question of how techniques of linguistic analysis can be utilized to reveal the structure of cultural entities. The way in which language influences perception has been most famously discussed by Benjamin Lee Whorf.

THE WHORFIAN HYPOTHESIS

When a Conference on the Interrelations of Language and Other Aspects of Culture was held in Chicago in March, 1953, virtually the whole conference was taken up, according to Hoijer (1954, p. vii), with a consideration of "the hypothesis suggested in Benjamin L. Whorf's *Collected Papers on Metalinguistics* (Washington, D.C., 1952)." The *Collected Papers* appeared some 11 years after Whorf's death in 1941, at the age of 44, though the principal papers on "the hypothesis" had appeared during the two years or so before his death, and the essential idea had been voiced a century earlier.

In 1940 Whorf described "a new principle of relativity, which holds that all observers are not led by the same physical evidence to the same picture of the universe, unless their linguistic backgrounds are similar, or can in some way be calibrated" (Carroll, 1956, p. 214). Thus the idea is known also as the theory of *linguistic relativity*. Our grammars are not simply systems for reproducing ideas; they actually shape our ideas, guiding our mental activity and our analyses of our impressions. Whorf puts it thus:

> The world is presented in a kaleidoscopic flux of impressions which has to be organized in our minds—and this means largely by the linguistic systems in our minds. We cut nature up, organize it into concepts, and ascribe significances as we do, largely because we are parties to an agreement to organize it in this way—an agreement that holds throughout our speech community and is codified in the patterns of our languages [Carroll, p. 213].

In 1929, more than a decade before Whorf offered his formulation, Edward Sapir, with whom Whorf was later to become closely associated, elaborated the idea that "We see and hear and otherwise experience very largely as we do because the language habits of our community predispose certain choices of interpretation" (Mandelbaum, 1949 p. 162). Appropriately enough, the concept is known as the Whorf-Sapir (or the Sapir-Whorf) hypothesis. Indeed, the idea is usually traced even further back, to Wilhelm von Humboldt, who is credited with stating in 1848 that man lives with the world around him principally as language presents it (Trager, 1959). The most detailed discussion (in English) of von Humboldt's view of linguistic relativity is that of Brown (1967), who shows not only that even von Humboldt had predecessors, but that his views must be culled laboriously from his works.

Before describing linguistic relativity more specifically, we may speculate briefly on why the idea was so slow to catch fire. Since von Humboldt has been translated into English only very recently and since he had a tiresome style in German, it is not surprising that his influence has only been belated and indirect in America. Sapir, of course, was wonderfully articulate, and Whorf was very persuasive, yet both were long dead before the concept of linguistic relativity became fashionable. Dell Hymes (1961) is probably correct in attributing the lag to the studied indifference (extending to active hostility) shown by descriptive linguists toward problems of meaning. During much of the 1930s and 1940s, it was an accepted doctrine that linguistic analysis should rely on form to the exclusion of semantic considerations (aside from the necessary minimum to establish contrasts).

It is not clear why interest should have been so dramatically revived. Perhaps it happened in part because the idea caught the fancy of anthropologists who were not primarily linguists. Also, it fitted an atmosphere primed by a generation of culture and personality studies, which culminated perhaps, in Benedict's (1946) brilliant analysis of Japanese character. This drew heavily on the linguistic labelling of culturally important behavioral categories (especially the complex system of obligations).

Perhaps part of the answer lies also in the character of Whorf himself. A chemical engineering graduate of M.I.T., who became a fire prevention engineer with the Hartford Fire Insurance Company, and was eventually an executive with the firm, Whorf never received an advanced degree in anything. Yet he developed his linguistic abilities (essentially on his own) to a point of considerable professional respectability, and he served for a while as a lecturer in anthropology at Yale—never, in the meanwhile, severing his connections with his insurance firm (Carroll, 1956).

At any event, Whorf's argument has in one way or another been a source of fascination and debate for a generation, and nothing has really been settled. Fishman (1960) has written a "systematization" of the Whorfian hypothesis that has proved particularly useful. The first of four levels that Fishman discerns deals with the way in which language codifies experience. Thus we may expect to find that vocabularies will reflect culturally important categories. Since snow, for example, is very important to the Eskimos, they have many terms to describe it, and this means that in their language it is easy to *refer* to the different kinds of snow. On the other hand, the Aztecs have little need to concern themselves with cold-weather phenomena; consequently they have few terms to describe distinctions that would be critical in a different environment.

That languages codify phenomena in this way is the most widely accepted part of the hypothesis. To give a less concrete, and therefore less obvious, example at this level, Gastil (1959) has noted that the French use one term for both "conscience" and "consciousness," which means that the distinction between the two is not as readily available to the French as it is to the English speaker. On the other hand, the French do see a partial identity in our two terms that it would be hard for us to appreciate. Lindeman (1938), for example, argued that this linguistic difference has led to a greater conceptual fusion between the two usages by French philosophers than has been made by English or German philosophers.

Thus the first level discerned by Fishman (1960) concerns a language-language correspondence. The second level relates linguistic codification to its behavioral concomitants. In order to support the idea that native speakers of different languages have different mental experiences, which is the essence of the hypothesis, we must show that there is some correspondence between the presence or absence of a particular linguistic phenomenon and the presence or absence of a particular nonlinguistic response (Carroll and Casagrande, 1958).

There has been some experimental support for the hypothesis at this level. As early as 1889, Lehmann showed that to identify each of nine different shades of gray with a different number was a considerable help in discriminating among those shades of gray (Fishman, 1960). Much more recently, Brown and Lenneberg (1954) demonstrated that when a range of colors is presented to a subject, he can name those that fit into the range of a single word, such as "red," more quickly than he can label colors for which there is no single term, such as "reddish brown." These and similar experiments indicate clearly that verbal labelling facilitates the perceptual handling of events, but sometimes their implications are carried further, to suggest that people actually *see* colors in accordance with those labels. Thus we have two words, "blue" and "green," but the Japanese word *aoi* is sometimes used where we would use one of our terms, but not either of them at random. Thus *aoi* describes the "blue" sky, "green" edible seaweed, and the "green" of inexperience (our "greenhorn").

It appeared, then, that the continuum of the color spectrum was arbitrarily segmented according to various cultural conventions, and labels were assigned to those segments in ways that need not correspond from one culture to another. The members of the various cultures were assumed to perceive colors in accordance with these cultural and linguistic labels. Then, in 1970, Berlin and Kay (Berlin, 1970) announced the results of a cross-cultural study in which they had found substantial agreement among the cultures on the perception of color loci. Members of different cultures essentially agreed on the area of the bluest blue, the reddest red, and so forth, even though the *boundaries* of the color terms still showed the lack of concord that had been noted previously.

Fishman's first two levels are basically lexical. The first

level concerns the fact that the number of coded categories related to a given range of events will vary from culture to culture; the second level deals with the actual behavioral consequences of those coded categories. The third level relates linguistic *structure* to its cultural concomitants. If cultural behavior has been conditioned by language, then since language has structure, we should be able to find a relationship between the structure of a language and the structure of the behavior of its speakers (Trager, 1959; McQuown, 1954). Whorf (1940) argued that we polarize nature in our English language, dividing most of our words into noun and verb categories that have different grammatical and logical properties. Nootka, a language of Vancouver Island, on the other hand, seems to us to contain only verbs; this implies that the speakers have a monistic view of nature, utilizing a single class of words to treat all kinds of events. In Nootka, "a house occurs" or "it houses" corresponds to our noun "house." The reason the Nootka terms seem like verbs to us is that they are inflected for durational and temporal nuances. A house can thus be an enduring house, a temporary house, a house that used to exist, a house that will exist in the future, or many other kinds of house.

Inspired by Whorf, Hoijer (1954) tried in a similar vein to show that Navaho religious views were closely congruent with the implications of Navaho grammar. He stated that to the Navaho, "the way to the good life lies not in modifying nature to man's needs or in changing man's nature but rather in discovering the proper relation of nature to man and in maintaining that relationship intact [p. 101]." The universe is given, and the Navaho must adjust to it. Similarly, Hoijer argues, the actors in a Navaho utterance are not divided into the active and passive categories—performers of action or the ones on whom actions are performed—as in English. Rather, the actors are entities that are linked to actions which have already been defined in part as pertaining to classes of beings.

Without laboring the point, the argument is intriguing, but we can easily see that it is susceptible to endless debate. Experiments may not end debate, but they may elevate the quality of the debate. It is fortunate, then, that Fishman's fourth level, which deals with linguistic structure and its behavioral concomitants, has been examined experimentally. Carroll and Casagrande (1958) explored the differences between Navaho and English verbs, and looked for evidence of behavioral reflections of the differences.

Navaho verb forms vary in accordance with the shapes of the objects to which they refer, while English verbs have the same form no matter what the object looks like. That is, we "carry" balls, sticks, squares, and so on, without requiring that the morphological nature of the object be given expression. Carroll and Casagrande worked with two groups of Navaho children; one group had Navaho as its primary language, and the other had English as its primary language. The children were presented with two objects that differed in both color and form, and then were asked to associate one of these with a third object, which was the same shape as one of the first two and the same color as the other. (Given a white ball and a black cube, for example, a black ball could be associated with the cube on the basis of their common color, or with the other ball on the basis of their common shape.) If the children's responses were guided by the requirements of the Navaho verb forms, we should expect that objects of the same shape would be placed together, rather than objects of the same color but different shapes.

As a control group, middle-class white children of comparable age in the Boston area were also given the test. The results were in the direction we would expect from the Whorfian hypothesis, but the question did not rest there. The children who mainly speak Navaho *did* choose on the basis of the Navaho verb system significantly more often than the Navaho children who mainly speak English, but the young Bostonians were *more Navaho* in their responses than the dominant speakers of Navaho! The most likely explanation seemed to be that the Boston children were raised with toys that capitalize on a variety of shapes; this explanation seemed to gain support from a subsequent finding that Black Harlem children in New York responded more in the fashion of the Navaho children who had English as their dominant language.

While the Harlem children may not have had the variety of commercial toys that were said to account for the Boston choices, it is far from clear that they lacked exposure to a wide variety of shapes. Even the grimmest picture of a slum does not present a uniform surface: peeling paint, rats, cockroaches, and garbage all provide a diversity of shapes. It may not be the existence of shapes as such, but rather the extent to which children are encouraged to manipulate them, that is significant. Fishman (1960) suggested that the Boston findings raise the question of *degrees* of linguistic relativity. After all, we can learn to see things in unaccustomed ways, and we can usually find a way to describe events that are alien to our customary experiences. As Fishman suggested, profit lies less in efforts to "prove" or "disprove" the Whorfian hypothesis than in future efforts to delimit more sharply the kinds of language structures and nonlinguistic behaviors that do or do not show the Whorfian effect, to establish the degree to which it is effective, and to determine to what extent it can be modified.

THE MEANING OF KINSHIP TERMS

The anthropological study of kinship systems predated Whorf's work by many decades, but the topic is admirably suited to Whorfian notions. We may illustrate this by examining, with Lee (1950), two Ontong Javanese kin terms.

If we ask an Ontong Javanese man what he calls his sister, he will supply the label *ave*, while the corresponding label for "brother" is *kainga*. To this point it seems clear enough that *ave* = "sister" and *kainga* = "brother." As a matter of routine, perhaps, we will double-check by asking the sister what she calls her brother, and we will learn that he is her *ave*, while her sister is *kainga*. The terms are now reversed, with *ave* = "brother" and *kainga* = "sister."

We need not assume that our informants are indulging themselves at our expense. Evidently, whereas we place a premium on absolute sex in kinship labels, the Ontong Javanese label according to relative sex, so that siblings of the same sex are covered by one label, while opposite-sexed siblings are covered by another label. A male's brother and a female's sister are both *kainga*, while the male's sister and the female's brother are both *ave*. There is nothing remarkable about this; indeed, Koreans have two separate sets of sibling terms, one used by males and one used by females, which yields four different terms for "elder sibling."

But the Ontong Javanese have not finished with us yet. Now we are told that the man's *kainga* includes not only his brother, but his wife's sister and his brother's wife! And, of course, a woman's *kainga* includes not only her sister, but also her sister's husband and her husband's brother. This distressing bit of news means that sex as such has nothing to do with the terminology at issue. We have been deluded by our own terms for kinship, which are largely descriptive and tend to emphasize the actual biological relationships. Apparently the terms *ave* and *kainga* are governed by different underlying principles from those that govern our sibling terms. They are part of a different kind of semantic network.

While the Ontong Javanese system is different from our own, we should recall that our own system is not strictly biological. After all, we often call friends of the family who belong to the generation above ours "auntie," or "uncle," where no biological relationship exists, and affines of that same generation are typically given the same kinship terms. Further, the social aspect of kinship in our own system is even stronger than has just been implied. A few years ago, when David Schneider remarked to a gathering of the Kroeber Anthropological Society in Berkeley that we call someone "uncle" because he acts like an uncle, this seemed improbable enough to send us scurrying out to find a suitable local informant. We located a male adolescent, determined who his uncles were, and learned that his mother's brothers were uncles no matter what; one of his mother's sister's husbands, however, would not be an uncle any longer in the event of a divorce, but the other member of the category would remain an uncle even if there were a divorce. The difference, it seemed, was that he did not know the first affine at all well, but he was quite close to the second. This second uncle acted like an uncle.

Given this reminder that our kinship system does not depend exclusively on biological relationships, we are better prepared to understand the Ontong Javanese system. It seems that the Ontong man shares the ordinary details of his living routine with his brothers and their wives for a large part of the year. He sleeps in the same large room, he eats with them, and he jokes and works around the house with them. The rest of the year is spent with his wife's sisters and their husbands, in the same free, easygoing atmosphere. So *kainga* relax in each other's company.

The *ave* present a different picture. Inter-*ave* relationships involve great strain and propriety. *Ave* can never spend their adult lives together, though they may on rare occasions be thrown together temporarily. They can never be alone together under the same roof; they cannot chat together easily, and one cannot refer even remotely to sex in the presence of an *ave*. When the *ave* of one member of a group is present, the others must be circumspect. A male *ave* has special obligations toward his female *ave* and her children (though we are not told the nature of these obligations). *Kainga,* in short, means a relationship of ease, cheerful and informal, and filled with shared living. *Ave* means a relationship characterized by formality, prohibitions, and strain.

Even from this brief characterization, it is clear that the social reality of kinship is differently formulated and differently labelled by the Ontong Javanese and by ourselves.

SEMANTIC DOMAINS

It is not difficult to see how researchers can move from problems of labels and their meanings to problems of taxonomies, and thence to the question of semantic domains. Semantic domains seem to constitute the main interest of ethnolinguists, probably because systems of belief have proved vulnerable to the techniques of componential analysis (which are borrowed from structural linguistics).

An early classic in the analysis of semantic domains or cognitive structures is Conklin's (1955) study of color categories among the Hanunóo of Mindoro Island in the Philippines. While working on the ethnobotany of the Hanunóo, Conklin found himself puzzled by some of the ways in which items were classified with respect to color. He had been operating in terms of hue, saturation, and brightness, the dimensions of our Western color concepts, but these constituted a poor guide to the Hanunóo scheme. What did matter was relative blackness, whiteness, redness, and greenness. The largest of the four categories is *mabĩru,* which includes what we generally call black, violet, indigo, blue, dark green, dark gray, and deep shades of other colors and mixtures. *Malagti*ʔ includes white and very light tints of other colors and mixtures. *Marara*ʔ includes maroon, red, orange, yellow, and mixtures in which these colors seem to predominante. The smallest of the categories, *malatuy,* includes light green and mixtures of green, yellow, and light brown. All color terms can be reduced to these four categories, which Conklin calls Level I terms, and on which there is general terminological agreement among the Hanunóo. There is a great deal of overlapping on a second, more specific level, which contains an indefinite number of categories on which it is difficult to get agreement. (Of course we have the same trouble in our own system when trying to agree on whether a particular item is oyster-white, off-white or perhaps a kind of pale beige, and so forth.)

The four main categories are set up according to factors that we would not ordinarily think of as relevant for color, but these factors do have reference to important external environmental considerations. First, a distinction between dark and light is obvious in the contrasted meanings of the first two terms, but there is also an opposition between "dryness" and "wetness" in the last two terms (the "red" and "green," respectively). This latter is important in dealing with plant life: most types of living plant have some fresh, succulent, and often "green" parts. Thus a shiny, wet *brown*-colored part of freshly-cut bamboo is *malatuy* rather than *marara*ʔ .

Besides the opposition of light and dark, and of wet and dry, there is also an opposition between deep, unfading, and thus often more desirable material, and pale, faded, or "colorless" substances. This places the "black" and "red" terms in contrast to the "white" and "green" terms. The contrasts hold not only for natural products, but also for manufactured and trade goods: red beads are more valuable than white beads, for example. Moreover, while objects tend to be regarded as aesthetically pleasing as they approach the focal points of each category, the green of natural vegetation is not prized, and green beads are considered to be unattractive and thus worthless.

What Conklin did, in short, was to isolate the principal ingredients, or components, of this scheme by seeing when different color labels were applied to substances that were being compared. That is, if the same color term were applied to a pair of substances, those substances would not contrast; they would be considered the same color. Conklin continued the search by finding out which substances elicited different labels and thus were considered to have different colors. The members of the categories thus defined by contrasts may then be examined to see what they have in common. In the present case qualities such as blackness, whiteness, redness and greenness appear, though the range of meaning of these terms must be specified. Conklin did not invent contractive analysis, of course, since it was well established in linguistics, and various other linguistically oriented anthropologists were developing similar approaches.

In 1956, Goodenough and Lounsbury each published componential analyses of kinship (Trukese and Pawnee kinship respectively). The idea can be conveyed if we look at the analysis of our own consanguineal (through "blood" rather than through marriage) kin terms, following Wallace and Atkins (1960). Wallace and Atkins first took the common terms spelled out in Figure 16.1, excluding "ego," of course, and reduced them to primitive kin-types. This expands the original 15 terms considerably, since "grandfather" includes both the mother's father and the father's father, "uncle" includes both the mother's brother and father's brother, and can also include the father's father's brother, the mother's father's brother, and so on. The task of listing cousins is truly formidable: the father's brother's son, father's brother's daughter, mother's brother's son, mother's brother's daughter, father's sister's son, father's sister's daughter, mother's sister's son, and so on. But all of these terms except "cousin" specify the sex of the relative; some of the terms specify whether the relative is lin-

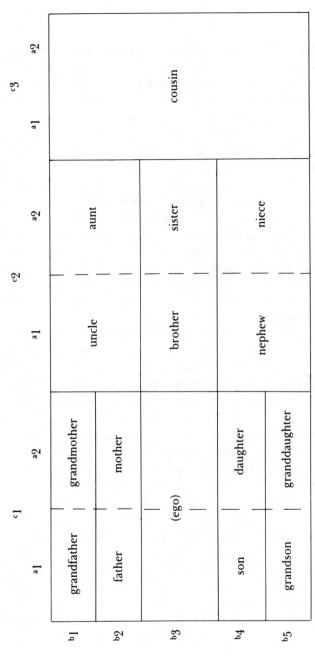

Figure 16.1. A Componential Paradigm of American English Consanguineal Core Terms. (Reprinted by permission from A. Wallace and J. Atkins, The Meaning of Kinship Terms, *American Anthropologist*, 62, 1960.)

eally or nonlineally related to the ego ("father" versus "uncle," for instance); and all of the nonlineal terms indicate whether the ancestors of the relative are also ancestors of the ego, and *vice versa* (as with brothers and sisters) or not (as with cousins).

From these observations it appears that three dimensions are sufficient to define all of the terms. First is the sex of the relative, which can be designated as (a); a_1 indicates a male, and a_2 a female. Second is the generation of the relative (b), which is here indicated by b_1 for two generations above the ego, b_2 for one generation above the ego, and so on, down to b_5 for two generations below the ego. Finally, lineality (c) is marked; c_1 indicates lineals, c_2 colineals, and c_3 ablineals (those who are neither lineals nor colineals).

There are complications that are not duplicated here, and Wallace and Atkins (1960) used the example as strictly illustrative, and made no pretense that it was an exhaustive study of American kinship. Clearly, however, the approach can be applied to virtually any semantic domain, and in addition to kinship, notable treatment has been accorded ethnobotany (Berlin, Breedlove, and Raven, 1973) and disease categories (Frake, 1961). But not all anthropologists have been carried along on the bandwagon of structural semantics.

Burling (1964), for example, has issued a useful, if harsh, criticism of the largely implicit claims for componential analysis, suggesting that it might be more appropriately regarded as "hocus pocus" than "God's truth." The point that seems to have bothered Burling, as it has bothered many others, is the idea that the analysis actually reflects the psychological reality of the members of the culture in question. It is a hard thing to be sure about, since we cannot actually see through the eyes of a member of another culture (somewhat, perhaps, as we cannot be sure that the experience of pain as felt by one individual is precisely the same as that felt by another individual). Perhaps we can gain some appreciation of the question by looking at some aspects of the semantic domain of Japanese surface anatomy.

The label *kubi* includes the head and neck, or to put it more graphically, what is lopped off when one is decapitated. This *kubi* we may designate $kubi_1$; it includes the *atama* "head" and the $kubi_2$ "neck." That is, the simple term *kubi* may refer either to the head plus the neck, or just to the neck. This kind of dual representation recurs time and again in the discussion of Japanese surface anatomy.

The more inclusive, higher order, $kubi_1$, is found not only on (or off!) humans, but on most animals, including insects and birds—but not on fish. It is productive, with a number of extensions: *kamakubi* "sickle-*kubi*" describes a snake poised to strike or a "goose-neck," while $kubi_1$ by itself describes the neck on a bottle, the zone to which the hairs on a writing brush are attached, and the nob and stem on an alarm clock (but not on a wristwatch, because there is no appreciable gap between the body of the watch and the part of the stem that is turned—the head, so to speak); $kubi_1$ also describes the part of the floor lamp below the bulb(s), when the shade is removed. (The shade is a *kasa* or umbrella, so that a floor lamp with a shade and a mushroom fall into the same morphological category.)

Evidently it is the relative horizontal discrepancy of the stem and the part that appears over it which determines whether a form will be a $kubi_1$ or a (nonanatomical) *kasa*. An important feature of $kubi_2$ is its frailty, when compared to that of the *atama* "head." There are times when *atama* is used in place of $kubi_1$, as to describe the nob on either an alarm clock or a wristwatch, but this seems to derive from a lower-order $atama_2$, which designates the crown of the $atama_1$. The $kubi_1$ also appears in *chichi-kubi* "nipple," since the apparatus of the breast plus the nipple bears a resemblance to a decapitated head (though there is no evidence that any informant would spontaneously associate it with the *kubi*₁ of the dead human).

The lower-order *kubi*₂ appears in *te-kubi* and *ashi-kubi* (the place where the hand joins the wrist and the foot joins the ankle respectively). It may be worth noting that while the *kubisuji* is the term for the nape of the neck of either sex, the female nape is also called *erikubi,* and the corresponding anatomical zone is sexually provocative to men. (There are other terms for the nape, but here we are considering *kubi* terms.)

Theoretical Implications

We are trying to make two points here. One is that we can take something as universal as body parts, which we might assume would be divided up in pretty much the same way, no matter where we went, and we find that actually there are some interesting differences from one culture to another. We only see *kubi*₂ as a unit ("neck"), and we have some of the same extensions. We can refer to the neck of a bottle, for example, but the shape of the head plus neck (*kubi*₁) provided other possibilities for extensions in Japanese. The whole network of concepts built up from *kubi* constitute a rather different entity from the network based on "neck." This also holds for many of the labels of surface anatomy in Japanese and English. Since the same differences could be found in many semantic domains, such as things to eat, coins, or just about anything, the implication is that the Japanese have a wholly different way of looking at things than the Americans. Many of the differences are subtle, no doubt, but whether they are subtle or gross, it would probably be difficult to gain a real understanding, a visceral understanding, of a different cultural view of the world. We know that bilinguals, whose two languages are essentially maintained in two cultural settings, respond to stimulus words and phrases with different associations. It

is likely that only really coordinate bilingual, bicultural individuals can provide the answer to the way perceptions
differ, and so far we have not posed the right questions to
reach an answer. There may be a difference between learning to understand events in terms of another culture and
perceiving them more spontaneously in those terms. When
the American, for example, sees the bus coming from a
distance, he says "the bus is coming," while when the Japanese sees the same event he says "the bus has come." It is
not too difficult to learn to translate the present, progressive action of the English expression into the completed
action implied by the Japanese expression, but is this also
to learn to perceive the action of the bus as having been
completed? Perhaps the point will be made more clear if we
cite the case of obscenities. Those of us who have led sheltered lives may wince upon hearing one of our earthy An-
glo-Saxonisms, but no matter how clear the foreigner's
understanding of the term may be, can he be induced to
wince?

The second point to be made on the basis of the Japanese example of the *kubi* is the notion of a dual representation. Is there a perceptual difference between a system that
lacks dual representation and one that draws on it heavily?
The Japanese term *te* can mean "hand," but it can also
include the whole appendage from the shoulder to the
fingertip; the *ashi* may describe the whole leg or more
specifically the foot, and so forth. Is there a perceptual
difference between the Japanese and the Americans? Or is
the concept really so different? Is there anything in English
that is similar? As a matter of fact, there is at least one
analogous example: "hair." This term may refer to a single
strand, "a hair," or to all of the hairs at issue: "Your hair
is turning gray." Grass is physically similar, but we cannot
say "*a grass," when meaning "a blade of grass," or even
"a joint of grass." (The latter, facetious example is not

appropriate, because the shape of the commercial pot is too unlike hair.)

At any rate, we find it difficult to perceive the difference between hair and grass in Whorfian terms, and yet we feel that we should be able to if the Whorfian hypothesis were correct.

We can get into the same trouble if we worry about the fact that Japanese does not ordinarily distinguish between singular and plural, while English does. At first blush we would think that this should be important, since we are obliged by our grammar to indicate the distinction, and at times we may even feel uncomfortable if we do not know whether an object is singular or plural (as when we are obliged to translate from a language such as Japanese). We cannot point to our own zero-marked plurals, such as "deer" and "sheep," because we usually have other markers to tell us whether they are one or many. But if we examine the "many," we can see that we are not much concerned that we cannot know, when a plural form alone is used, just how many are involved. In other languages, on the other hand, the person may be singular, dual, trial, or plural. How would a speaker of such a language analyze English? Would he count our plural as a neutralization of dual, trial, and plural?

While Frake's (1962) componential analysis of our category of "something to eat" and Conklin's (1962) analysis of the terms we use to designate our everyday units of monetary exchange (nickel, quarter, and so on) seem intuitively valid, the question of psychological reality has not really been answered. In other words, to skip back to *ashi* as "leg" and *ashi* as "foot," is the dual representation different from our lumping together of trial and plural? We have no comfortable answer, but the hypothesis would seem to require one.

The Grammar of Culture

Somewhat in the way grammar consists of rules for the generation of utterances, a grammar of culture consists of rules for the generation of patterns of behavior. It is necessary, of course, to determine the components of cultural patterns, just as it is necessary to determine phonemes, morphemes, and the like. But a mere inventory of components does not constitute a language, any more than a listing of culture traits constitutes a culture.

Goodenough (1971) has recently mentioned forms, beliefs, and values as the points of reference for behavior. The behavior itself, whether obvious or not, is purposive: purposes and goals give coherence to action, and we interpret the actions of others in terms of the purposes and goals that we impute to them. Goodenough puts it thus:

> All meaningful behavior is in this respect like speech behavior. The communicational intent of an utterance provides the focus around which words and grammatical constructions are selected and arranged syntactically into coherent sentences. Similarly, the intended consequences or purposes of other kinds of behavior provide the foci around which people, things and acts become organized syntactically into coherent activities. [p. 30]

Goodenough suggests that for most recurring purposes, people develop recipes or formulas. Thus there are recipes for ways to dress, for conducting parties, for seeking favors, for wooing members of the opposite sex, or, less overtly perhaps, members of the same sex.

Goodenough distinguishes recipes from routines and customs. Recipes refer to ideas and understandings about ways to do things, while in his terminology, routines and customs refer to the execution of the behavior. We may develop highly personal routines. We have recipes for setting a table for dinner, but except perhaps for the requirement that the tablecloth (if one is used) be placed first, there is no special order for performing the individual steps in the routine. That is, we tend to develop our own routines for setting out dishes, chopsticks, and other paraphernalia. Where people bring their individual routines into group activity, one routine may become the standard and thus part of the recipe itself, in that there will now be a "right way" to perform the routine. This is how Goodenough sees customs:

> Unlike routines, which arise from habits of executing particular recipes, customs have to do with habits of choice among alternative recipes and alternative developed routines. . . . A custom, then, is a recipe or a routine for executing a recipe that is regularly resorted to, . . . in preference to alternative recipes or alternative routines for executing them. Customs arise when the choice of recipes or routines for given occasions has itself been routinized. [p. 32]

Goodenough carries his discussion to successively higher levels of behavior, but to follow him further would be to depart too far from our language orientation.

METHODS OF ANALYZING CULTURAL PATTERNS

If we can speak meaningfully about "a grammar of culture," we should be able to apply methods of grammatical analysis to the analysis of culture patterns; this has been done to get at the cognitive structures, as already discussed, though we have not actually gone through the analytical processes whereby we arrived at the structures. We have also noted that we need rules for the sequencing of events. Goodenough has commented on some of the kinds of sequences, but has not actually tried to write the grammar. (See also Berne, 1964).

Here we would like to offer a hint as to how the problem of sequencing might be approached; we are using some of the concepts developed by Sidney M. Lamb (especially as described in 1964).

One of the basic notions in Lamb's system is that an event on one level or stratum is realized on the stratum immediately below. Thus the plural morpheme (on the morphemic level) will be realized in various ways on the phonemic level, depending in part on the phonetic context. After the unvoiced stop at the end of "dock," the plural is realized as /-s/, but after the voiced stop at the end of "dog," it is realized as /-z/. In baseball, a "ball" can be realized in several ways: outside a fairly clearly defined space, determined by the location and width of the plate, or by passing inside that space in the direction of the batter, or by passing within the space, but either above or below a height that is fixed by the dimensions of the batter. The extent to which the ball misses the target area is not relevant; what is relevant (emic) is whether the unpire decides that the ball did or did not pass through the space in question. The actual realizations of the "ball" correspond to the so-called free variations in the realization of a phoneme.

The "strike" is a little more complicated. It may be realized by the passage of the ball through the area that the "ball" did *not* pass through. In this case, and in the case of the "ball," the realization depends on the batter's not making any attempt to contact the ball with his bat. If the batter swings at the ball and misses, that is a "strike," no matter where the ball passed. A "strike" may be realized if the batter contacts the ball with the bat and it subsequently passes somewhere other than into that part of the field which is designated "fair" territory, so long as no opposing player catches it before it touches the ground. In each case there is permissible variation, such as catching the inside corner, the outside corner, right down the middle, and so forth; or the ball may be fouled either to the right or left of the playing field or directly behind the place. For the execution of the "ball" and the "strike," it does not matter whether the batter stands to the right or left of the plate, but he is obliged to remain in the appropriate "box."

These low-level examples of realization show another important feature of Lamb's model, *diversification.* Diversification refers to the existence of alternate realizations, on a given stratum, of the events of a higher stratum. Thus the "strike" is a higher-order event than either the swing-and-miss or the alternate realization "called strike."

Another important feature of realization is *neutralization,* which is in some ways the opposite of diversification. It involves the common realization of events that are different at a higher stratum. For example, /ˊɔ ə dágz/ is ambiguous, because it may mean either dog-plural, dog-possessive, or even dog-plural-possessive. At the morphemic level the plural and the possessive are separate, but they sometimes show up in the identical form on the phonemic level. Similarly, the intentional and the unintentional walk are the results of different decisions at a higher level; in the latter case the decision was to "pitch to" the batter, while in the former case the decision was to "put the man on" base, usually for tactical reasons, such as to facilitate the execution of a double play, or to be able to force him out later. Both decisions, though, are realizations of a still higher-order decision, to "retire the side" by getting three men out.

A *composite realization* is one in which an event is realized by a combination of events at the stratum immediately below. Thus the "intentional walk" is realized by a sequence of four balls. The opposite of composite realization is *portmanteau realization;* the most famous linguistic example of this may be the French /o/ as a realization of *á + le.* A good example from baseball would seem to be the "home run," which is simultaneously a "hit," "a run scored," and "a run batted in."

In the last example, incidentally, it should be noted that the "home run" is on a lower stratum than each of the events for which it constitutes a portmanteau realization. The home run is only one of several realizations of "hit," of "a run scored," and of "a run batted in," though it is the only portmanteau realization of all three higher-level events.

Zero realization may be illustrated linguistically by the absence of a plural marker for "sheep"; in baseball it occurs as the third out when the home team breaks a tie in the ninth inning, since the game ends without a final out having been made, though the higher-order rules call for three outs to retire a side.

The opposite of zero realization is *empty realization.* A linguistic example would be the "it" in "it's raining," since the "it" lacks any referent. In baseball, every uncaught foul after the batter has made two strikes would appear to be an empty realization of the "strike," since it does not advance the game. That is, it seems to represent nothing at a higher stratum.

Anataxis is the last feature of realization that Lamb deals with. This means that the order of units of one stratum differs from the order of their corresponding realizations on the lower stratum. In ordinary linguistic parlance, anataxis is called metathesis, and refers to the interchange of two phonemes. Some English speakers, for example, pronounce "ask" as if it were "ax" (aks). An example of this in baseball might be the case in which a pitcher is removed from a game with a man on base, when that man later scores. The run in this case is charged not to the current pitcher, but to the man who has already left the game.

Lamb's concepts provide various ways of getting from higher- to lower-order events, though one must also spell out the tactics in order to describe the sequencing of events. In a way these are spelled out in considerable detail for most games, and, as Goodenough (1971) has indicated, they are also spelled out by individuals such as Dale Carnegie and Emily Post for certain kinds of social behavior. But for the most part, anthropologists have described sequenced patterns without showing sufficient explicit concern for what is emic and what is etic in their descriptions.

Finally, a very brief illustration from Ervin-Tripp (1969) can give us an idea of how sequenced behavior might be approached from the generative viewpoint. The ritual is that of "leave-taking." Leave-taking (LT) has two parts for two actors. Thus:

Leave-taking————[is rewritten] ⟶ LT 1 + LT 2

This means that leave-taking consists of two parts. The LT 1 can then be expanded to

LT 1 ⟶ Goodbye + CP

Here the second component is a courtesy phrase of some sort, which can be represented in various ways:

CP ⟶ $\begin{cases} \text{I am glad to have met you.} \\ \text{I hope to see you again (soon).} \end{cases}$

The brace includes alternate expressions, and the parentheses indicate optional elements. Then

LT 2 ⟶   Thank you (+ yes, we'll have to get together again).

Obviously the ritual has descriptive possibilities that are only hinted at here. A much more detailed study, of sequencing in telephone conversations, has been produced by Schegloff (1972). In the nonverbal area, Goodenough (1971) has made a first step in this direction; he shows a similar point of view, though he has not reduced the analysis to the linguistic-type notion.

It is far too soon to proclaim this the wave of the future in ethnographic description, but the devising of more formal approaches to description and analysis will undoubtedly continue.

REFERENCES

Benedict, R. 1946. *The Chrysanthemum and the Sword.* Boston: Houghton Mifflin Company.

Berlin, B. 1970. A universalistic-evolutionary approach in ethnographic semantics. *Current Directions in Anthropology 3 (no. 3, Part 2):* 3–18.

Berlin, B., D. Breedlove, & P. Raven. 1973. *Principles of Tzeltal Plant Classification.* New York: Seminar Press, Inc.

Berne, E. 1964. *Games People Play.* New York: Grove Press, Inc.

Brown, R. 1967. *Wilhelm von Humboldt's Conception of Linguistic Relativity.* The Hague: Mouton & Co.

Brown, R., & E. Lenneberg. 1954. A study in language and cognition. *J. Abnormal and Social Psychol. 49:* 454–462.

Burling, R. 1964. Cognition and componential analysis: God's truth or hocus-pocus? *Amer. Anthropologist 66:* 20–28.

Carroll, J. B. (Ed.). 1956. *Language, Thought, and Reality: Selected Writings of Benjamin Lee Whorf.* Cambridge, Mass.: The M.I.T. Press.

Carroll, J. B., & J. B. Casagrande. 1958. The function of language classifications in behavior. In Eleanor Maccoby, T. H. Newcomb, and E. L. Hartley (Eds.), *Readings in Social Psychology.* (3d ed.) New York: Holt, Rinehart & Winston, Inc.

Conklin, H. C. 1955. Hanunóo color categories. *Southwestern J. Anthropology 11:* 339–344.

Conklin, H. C. 1962. Comment [on Frake, 1962.]. In Thomas Gladwin and William G. Sturtevant (Eds.), *Anthropology and Human Behavior.* Washington, D.C.: The Anthropological Society of Washington.

Ervin-Tripp, S. M. 1964. An analysis of the interaction of language, topic and listener. *Amer. Anthropologist 66 (Part 2, no. 6):* 72–85.

Ervin-Tripp, S. M. 1969. Sociolinguistics. In Leonard Berkowitz, (Ed.), *Advances in Experimental Social Psychology.* Vol. 4, pp. 91–165. New York: Academic Press, Inc.

Fishman, J. A. 1960. A systematization of the Whorfian hypothesis. *Behavioral Science 5:* 323–339.

Frake, C. O. 1961. The diagnosis of disease among the Subanum of Mindanao. *Amer. Anthropologist 63:* 113–132.

Frake, C. O. 1962. The ethnographic study of cognitive systems. In Thomas Gladwin and William C. Sturtevant (Eds.), *Anthropology and Human Behavior,* pp. 72–75. Washington, D.C.: The Anthropological Society of Washington.

Gastil, R. D. 1959. Relative linguistic determinism. *Anthropological Linguistics 1 (no. 9):* 24–38.

Goodenough, W. H. 1956. Componential analysis and the study of meaning. *Language 32:* 195–216.

Goodenough, W. E. 1971. *Culture, Language and Society. An Addison-Wesley Module in Anthropology.* Reading, Mass.: Addison-Wesley Publishing Co.

Hoijer, H. (Ed.). 1954. *Language in Culture.* Chicago: University of Chicago Press.

Hymes, D. H. 1961. On typology of cognitive styles in language (with examples from Chinookan). *Anthropological Linguistics 3 (no. 1):* 22–54.

Lamb, S. M. 1964. The sememic approach to structural semantics. *Amer. Anthropologist 66 (Part 2, no. 3):* 57–76.

Lee, D. 1950. Lineal and nonlineal codifications of reality. *Psychosomatic Medicine 12:* 89–97.

Lindeman, R. 1938. Der Begriff der Conscience im Französichen Denken. Jena, East Germany: Leipsiz.

Lounsbury, F. G. 1956. A semantic analysis of the Pawnee kinship usage. *Language 32:* 158–194.

Lowie, R. H. 1937. *The History of Ethnological Theory.* New York: Rinehart and Company, Inc.

McQuown, N. A. 1954. Analysis of the cultural content of language materials. In Harry Hoijer (Ed.), *Language in Culture.* Chicago: University of Chicago Press.

Mandelbaum, D. G. (Ed.). 1949. *Selected Writings of Edward Sapir.* Berkeley, Cal.: University of California Press.

Schegloff, E. 1972. Sequencing in conversational openings. In John J. Gumperz and Dell Hymes (Eds.), *Directions in Sociolinguistics.* New York: Holt, Rinehart & Winston, Inc.

Trager, G. L. 1959. The systematization of the Whorfian hypothesis. *Anthropological Linguistics 1 (no. 1):* 31–35.

Wallace, A. F. C., & J. Atkins. 1960. The meaning of kinship terms. *Amer. Anthropologist 62:* 58–80.

Whorf, B. L. 1940. Science and linguistics. *Technology Review 42:* 229–231, 247–248.

Williams, T. R. 1967. *Field Methods in the Study of Culture.* New York: Holt, Rinehart & Winston, Inc.

INDEX

389

Locke, John, 22
Loflin, M., 307
Logographic script, 182
Lorenz, Maria, 259
Loudness, emotion and, 106-8
Lounsbury, F. G., 369
Lowie, Robert, 272, 287, 354
Luba drum language, 195
Luo, 232
Luria, A. R., 256

Ma, R., 281
McCawley, James, 172
Maccoby, Eleanor, 217
MacKey, W. F., 266
Maclay, H., 239, 241
MacLeod, F., 277
Macnamara, J., 267, 276, 277-78, 283-84
McQuown, N. A., 362
Magaret, A., 258
Magoun, H. W., 31
Maher, B. A., 257-58
Mahl, G. F., 244-45
Maintenance contexts, 280
Maltzmann, I., 122, 123, 125
Manchu writing, 183-86
Mandarin Chinese, 36, 159
Mandelbaum, D. G., 358
Manual communication, 32-33
Marathi, 269, 270
Markel, N., 114-15
Martin, R., 248
Martin, Samuel, 115
Mather, V. G., 94, 95
Maurer, David, 191-92
May, L. C., 206
Mazateco whistle language, 197
Mehrabian, A. S., 58
Meinecke, F. K., 26
Melanesian, 27, 28, 267
Melanesian Pidgin, 267
Meltzer, 66
Memory studies, 22
Mennonites, pronominal usage of, 342-48
Metacommunications, 82

Middleton, W. C., 103
Miller, G. A., 214
Miller, George, 22
Miller, W., 215, 217, 220, 221
Modifiers, 225
Moeller, D., 245, 247
Monitoring, hesitation and, 240-43
Mood, body movement and, 65-66
Moore, N., 278
Moore, R., 129, 130, 131, 132
Moore, W., 248
Morisett, L., 122, 123
Morphemes, 154, 160-61, 224
Morphology, acquisition of, 229-32
Morphophonemic rules, 165
Morse, Samuel, 205
Multilingualism, *see* Bilingualism
Multiple alphabets, 202-4
Murray, E. J., 89
Mutual intelligibility, 34
Myrdal, G., 285

Nabokov, Vladimir, 287
Nagara, S., 301, 302, 303
National Romanization System, 187-88
Navaho, 362-64
Neanderthals, 134
Needles, W., 61
Neurophysiological aspects of speech, 139-46
Newman, S., 94, 95
Newman, S. S., 117-19
Nhole drum language, 192
Nida, E. A., 276
Nonverbal communication, 32-33, 44, 58-88
  codification of, 59-62
  contextual analysis, 63-64, 76-86
  traditionally-oriented studies, 63-76, 84-85
Nootka, 362
Norinaga, Motoori, 20
Normative grammars, development of, 14-16
Norwegian, 34
Nucleus, 157-58
Nuttall, R., 123, 124